COGNITIVE COPING THERAPY

Good luck

COGNITIVE COPING THERAPY

Kenneth Sharoff

Brunner-Routledge
New York • London

Published in 2002 by
Brunner-Routledge
29 West 35th Street
New York, NY 10001

Published in Great Britain by
Brunner-Routledge
27 Church Road
Hove, East Sussex BN3 2FA

Brunner-Routledge is an imprint of the Taylor & Francis Group.

Printed in the United States of America on acid-free paper.

10 9 8 7 6 5 4 3 2 1

Library of Congress Cataloging-in-Publication Data

Sharoff, Kenneth.
Cognitive coping therapy / Kenneth Sharoff.
p. ; cm.
Includes bibliographical references and index.
ISBN 1–58391–317–3 (pbk.)
1. Cognitive therapy. 2. Adaptability (Psychology) I. Title.
[DNLM: 1.Personality Disorders—therapy. 2. Adaptation, Psychological. 3. Anxiety Disorders—therapy. 4. Cognitive Therapy—methods. 5. Depressive Disorder—therapy. WM 190 S531c 2002]
RC489.C63 S53 2002
616.89′142—dc21

2001052500

CONTENTS

1

CHAPTER

The Coping Response

Cognitive-behavioral therapy (CBT) has become one of the most popular and widely used treatment approaches of the past generation. There has been a mushrooming of interest in cognition, its role in mental disorders, and its influence on behavioral change. Over a generation ago Mahoney (1977) noted that psychotherapy has undergone a "cognitive revolution," and today it is still going strong.

CBT consists of three approaches: cognitive restructuring, problem-solving therapy, and coping skills therapy (Mahoney and Arnkoff, 1978). Yet in Dobson's two overviews (1988, 2001) of the approaches and innovative developments within the field of CBT, coping skills therapy did not even merit a chapter of its own. Cognitive restructuring has become the "senior partner" in CBT. It has developed a cohesive practice theory and a varied set of techniques that complements and extends the theory. By and large, therapists who use CBT first turn to cognitive restructuring to treat the presenting problem and then pull from coping skills therapy specific skills to fill out the treatment plan. Hence the latter operates as an adjunct treatment utilized on an as-needed basis.

Today, coping skills therapy remains a loose, heterogeneous collection of skills, a grab bag or patchwork of techniques. It has not developed beyond a handful of dominant skills, such as relaxation, communication, assertiveness, and social skills training. Yet there are many more skills that can be employed to resolve various disorders. There is a need for a much fuller understanding and elucidation of those skills. Coping skills therapy has not developed a practice theory of its own or a general methodology. Its theory of pathology is quite narrow, viewing patient disorders mostly as a coping skills deficit. Its methodology is simple: fill the holes in functioning. While there are other ways to understand mental disorder from a skills perspective, this has not been fully enumerated in the literature. Its theory of change and health are rudimentary. In summary, coping skills therapy remains stunted and unfulfilled as a treatment model, a "junior partner" to cognitive restructuring.

Cognitive coping therapy (CCT) is an attempt to rectify this problem. *My hope in writing this book is to move coping skills therapy from a subordinate method into a mainstream model of care.* CCT wants to develop coping skills therapy into a comprehensive, independent model of care and an alternative to cognitive restructuring. CCT is a highly active, directive, didactic, structured approach capable of treating patients in a short period of time. The book presents a practice theory and underlying philosophy for the approach, along with a methodology and guidelines for implementing it. The book refines and further extends cognitive-behavioral practice theory, offering a theory of pathology, health, and change. The chapters on case studies illustrate how to use the model with a variety of disorders. They present numerous coping skills that have not been presented or properly elucidated in other works. The name for this approach, cognitive coping therapy, gives credit to the central role of cognition in forming the skills necessary for managing life problems.

☐ What Are Coping Skills?

First, though, we need to present how this book defines coping skills. Quite simply, a coping skill is an organized response to a situation with the purpose of attaining a goal or resolving a problem. The goal-directed nature of a skill is what differentiates it from a spontaneous emotional expression or physical reaction. Snyder and Dinoff (1999) define coping skills as "a response aimed at diminishing the physical, emotional, and psychological burden that is linked to stressful life events and daily hassles" (p. 5). The dictionary defines *coping* as a way to maintain a contest or combat on even terms. The word *skill* means there is an ability to do something, a response that can accomplish something, a tool or a means to an end. It may be a natural talent or acquired proficiency. Coping skills deal with the issue of execution and carrying out of a plan or policy. Generally, they are maneuvers that are known and have been used in the past, so there is experience in employing them. The word *skill* does not necessarily mean someone is outstanding in that endeavor or is a master of that response. It merely means s/he can satisfactorily perform that response to obtain an end goal. In essence, the response allows someone to enter a problem situation and contend with whatever forces are allied against him/her.

A warning, though: when the term *coping skill* is used in this book, it is not meant to infer that a skill is always rational, realistic, adaptive, productive, good for the individual, or the best choice for resolving a problem. It is used in a value-neutral way. In actuality, someone's characteristic way of responding to a problem may be counterproductive, dysfunctional, irrational, unrealistic, or maladaptive, considering his/her long-term best interests. The term is used only to make the point that people have achieved a level of proficiency in something that they believe allows them to cope. For instance, Michael, age twelve, nags, throws fits of temper, is an obstructionist, and acts oppositional. That is his way of coping, his way to get what he wants. In the process of living, he calls upon specialized, idiosyncratic responses that he believes have utility and value. He has proficiency in being that way, but that is hardly the best way for him to act.

When coping skills are viewed from a treatment standpoint, though, each person's responses have to be judged pragmatically to determine if they are counterproductive or lead to the desired end result. Intricately concerned with the issue of health, rationality, and utility, CCT wants to know how successful or viable a given skill is. Can it be modified to become viable? Is the coping skill rational or adaptive? Does it contribute to or alleviate the presenting problem? In essence, is it good for that person?

☐ Origin of Coping Skills

How do coping responses originate? What transforms spontaneous emotional expressions or behaviors into a skill? So many skills are employed and developed due to genetic tendencies. In that case the skill is dispositionally driven. Personality traits influence the selection and the development of a coping response. Coping skills occur naturally as part of ego functioning. The psychodynamnic perspective maintains that coping skills are built-in defense mechanisms to manage unconscious sexual and aggressive conflicts. They are a way to protect the self against internal instinctual forces (Freud, 1964) or external, environmental threats (Adler, 1929).

Coping skills also develop as a consequence of learning. As young children show their feelings, they soon realize that certain feelings expressed in a certain way are efficacious while others are not. They learn, through trial and error and subsequent reinforcement, which behaviors have instrumental capability. CCT assumes that the nature of people is pragmatic: to search out and select responses that can attain a desired goal. Once a coping skill has been deployed and is successful (in varying degrees), it rewards a person while avoiding a painful circumstance. Reinforcement has a powerful, immediate shaping effect on spontaneous response. There is no such thing as a purely spontaneous emotion or behavior once it recurs repeatedly, because reinforcement will influence the future expression of it. Once an expression of self is reinforced positively, it will then be incorporated into the coping skill armamentarium.

Coping skills develop through social learning (Bandura, 1969; Dollard et al., 1939). Observing the distribution of rewards, the observer gains information that certain actions are beneficial. People learn vicariously that a response has coping skill potential. If the skill appears useful to a role model, it is enlisted as a means to handle situations (Bandura, 1969a). Successfully imitating the response of a model demonstrates a skill can yield reinforcement that strengthens the use of that response in the future. Furthermore, a coping skill is more salient if used by a highly regarded role model. People want to be like their role models, which means copying their solutions or skills.

Coping skills can result from explicit knowledge given to a person by others (i.e., teachers, parents, peers, supervisor). In this regard skill development is taught as part of a didactic format. Rules and procedures are dispensed and incorporated into a knowledge bank.

Finally, coping skills can be developed by the creative mind of the individual. As autonomous beings, people are assumed to be capable of acting independently of operant conditioning and can generate their own responses, based on what they believe will lead to success. Human beings cannot *not* reflect on themselves, augmenting and modifying their emotional expression in turn. Any natural response will be appraised and potentially utilized for its instrumental capacity. A coping response is originated to deal with an event that has been appraised as threatening, potentially harmful, or challenging, or is believed to be exceeding the resources of the person (R. Lazarus and Folkman, 1985). Agreeing with the constructivist perspective (Guidano, 1988), CCT assumes that people are autopoietic systems, meaning they have self-productive or self-renewing capacity. They have "self-organizing abilities . . . to assimilate incoming information and to cope with perturbations arising from its exchanges with the environment" (Guidano, 1988, p. 309). Coping skill development is part of a cerebral process. Problem solving is used to calculate which responses are instrumental.

☐ Formation of Coping Skills

Coping skills are not formed by a single pathway, however. They are formed from a complex interplay between genetic predisposition, self-creation, reinforcement, instruction, and social learning. At some point in a person's development, a spontaneous expression becomes a skill, an adaptation and capacity to attain an end result. To make this point, consider the following vignettes:

- Jill is mad about how her husband is treating her. Her eyebrows rise and her jaw tightens; she looks sad and is about to cry. She pleads for him to change.
- Joe becomes irritated when his sons engage in sibling squabbles. He breathes deeply as his mouth opens and he bares his teeth. He explodes with rage and yells at them.
- Christie, age six, feels lonely and bored. She wants her parents to play with her. Her lips puff out and her forehead wrinkles. She looks sullen, dejected, and sad as she breaks off eye contact with her parents and stares at the floor intently.

In each vignette, the emotional expression can simply be viewed as a discharge of instinctual energy. There is expressive motor behavior, especially spontaneous facial expressions to an activating event that transcends culture and time (Izard, 1977). Emotion occurs as a sensorimotor experience with its unique subjective state. Each specific emotional state has a distinctive pattern. Contained in the central nervous system is a blueprint for expressive motor behavior (Leventhal, 1984). The reader may wonder whether any of these responses are a coping skill and why they would be one.

To answer these questions, the reader must consider the intimate, intricate link between skills and goals. Are the above behaviors linked to a goal? If so, then they are a coping skill because they are a maneuver, calculated and calibrated for a particular effect. The chosen response is that person's characteristic way of confronting the problem at hand and reducing the immediate distress. What may begin as a natural, spontaneous emotional expression in time becomes a coping response. Over the years, Jill has learned how to cope with her anger by unknowingly transforming it into sadness, so it is easier and less threatening for her and others to manage. She uses sadness as a maneuver to meet her needs. She is skilled at showing different facial expressions and voice tones that arouse pity in order to influence her husband's conduct. Joe naturally feels irritated, but he unconsciously escalates his anger into rage to intimidate others, a practice that has been reinforced since childhood. He is skilled in raging and knows how to look fierce upon demand. Christie copes with her boredom by executing a coordinated presentation to influence her parents to give her what she wants. She is skilled in looking forlorn. In each case, each of the above people immediately turns to habitual coping skills not only to manage and regulate his/her emotions but also to secure an end result. Consciously or unconsciously, coping skills are arranged to meet a goal.

What may begin as an innate, "hardwired" response quite rapidly becomes part of a synthetic process where cognition modifies, elaborates upon, and extends spontaneous reaction to become part of an orchestrated response pattern. While CCT agrees with Zajonc (1980) that some affective responses and experiences can be precognitive (prior to higher-level, cognitive processing of information), they do not stay independent for very long. Cognition interplays with emotional schematic processing and cannot be separated from it. Emotion cannot be separated from thought, and thought will inevitably take a position upon and modify emotional responsivity. As Candland (1977) states, there is a continuous feedback loop between perception, bodily and emotional reaction, and cognition. *The normal activation of emotion instantly joins with thought to provide a template for how to meet needs by integrating emotion, thinking, physiological reaction, and behavior.* Thought makes sense of visceral somatic excitation and presents a plan about what to do about the experience.

☐ Skill Selection

Skill selection occurs in the following way. As the person perceives the situation, some information is filtered out while other information becomes salient and is foregrounded. The situation is described (e.g., "I feel stressed") and the meaning about the situation is formulated ("This is a dangerous situation"). A goal is selected ("I've got to relax"). Prototypical features of the present situation are matched with past situations. Old coping responses are coded in memory for their response potential. Memories are retrieved about what has or has not worked in the past for that given situation ("Being left alone to unwind has worked, while talking to the family now, while upset, has not"). The list or bank of coping skills for that situation is reviewed. A prediction is made if the coping skills on that list will help the person attain the goal. Then the brain acts and mediates between responses. A coping skill is selected and activated to respond to the activating event. The choice of coping skill reflects the appraisal and meaning given to the situation.

The appraisal of the situation and the choice of skill can be influenced more by emotion, more by cognition, or more or less equally by both. If emotions are more influential in selecting a coping response, that can occur only with the mind's latent consent to allow or even encourage that response.

The cognitive activity regarding response development and selection can occur on an unconscious level and operate in an automatic, implicit fashion. In that case, the coping skill exists as tacit knowledge about how to manage an event. Or a coping skill can be formulated on a conscious level and is part of a reflective process. In that case, the coping skill is part of a person's explicit knowledge.

Some people have a very short list of skills to be deployed for a given situation and rigidly, habitually, mindlessly select a single skill, while other people are more reflective and flexible and will try out various ways of coping. Once formed, however, a coping response is self-generating and is freely and effortlessly activated, with or without forethought. It allows people to interact with the world in a somewhat consistent, stable fashion. When coping responses are used repeatedly they become similar to a trait: stable over time and across situations. People tend to rely on the same coping responses when responding to similar stimuli.

Once selected, one's coping skills armamentarium is intimately connected to the individual, is part of his/her self-image, and characterizes him/her as a person. One's coping skills are the individual's portrayal of self and a behavioral signature. They form identity and other's image of that person. Hence, they are synonymous with a person and inseparable from his/her personality. Basically, we are our coping skills.

☐ Intent of This Book

This author has several intentions in writing this book. One mission is to encourage the field of psychotherapy to focus on the "how"—how goals are reached. CCT addresses one of the most common, basic problems in mental health practice: a lack of specificity in giving treatment recommendations. So often the many facets of a skill that therapists recommend are not detailed enough. Advice is given without dispensing exact knowledge about how to carry out the advice. For instance, patients are urged to *detach* from a spouse's addiction, but how does one actually detach? Providers identify a *general coping skill* for the patient but often do not detail the links in the coping skills chain, the many *subskills* of the general coping skill. Further, they do not identify the subskills of the subskills, which this book calls *microskills,* or the *support skills* that are not part of the general coping skill but are needed in order to perform that skill effectively. When therapists do not specify the parts of the whole, the methodology for change is vague and incomplete. The pieces of the puzzle have to be clearly defined.

This book impresses upon therapists how complex coping is. Our basic mission is to illustrate the network of skills that are needed to attain a goal. To illustrate the web of interconnecting skills, let us dissect what is involved in following the therapeutic advice: "back off when you get mad." This involves the general coping skill of anger management.

A coping skills therapist has to be able to combine these skills, subskills, microskills, and support skills to form a chain. Some of the above abilities are interpersonal, while other skills are intrapersonal. The coping skills therapist must be adept in intermixing both and then needs to know how to link them together in the proper sequence. If one link in the chain is absent or put in the wrong order, the skill may not be performed adequately. Any general coping skill can be co-opted to facilitate or support other skills. Abilities are like parts of an Erector set, put together and used for any number of purposes. Any one subskill may become a general

TABLE 1.1. Layers of Anger Management

1. Subskill—*self-monitoring:* the ability to determine a present feeling and the magnitude of that feeling
   Microskills:
   a. *discrimination:* the ability to differentiate between levels of anger
   b. *the continuum of awareness:* the ability to remain aware of oneself over time and across situations
2. Subskill—*psychological distancing:* the ability to remove oneself mentally from an irritating, activating event;
   Microskills:
   a. *sensory diversion:* the ability to distract oneself when angry
   b. *self-instruction:* the ability to self-direct to stay distant
3. Subskill—*relaxation:* the ability to lower physical arousal and muscular tightness caused by anger
   Microskills:
   a. *deep muscle relaxation*
   b. *deep breathing*
4. Subskill—*cognitive restructuring:* the ability to change beliefs promoting anger
   Microskill: *anti-imperative thinking*
   Support skill: *psychological distancing* needed to remain cognitively aloof from a situation, allowing the person to objectively examine beliefs and test their validity
5. Subskill—*limit-setting:* the ability to stop others' actions that stimulate anger
   Microskills:
   a. *assertiveness training*
   b. *conflict resolution*
   Support skill: *relaxation* to remain calm while correcting others

coping skill, or any general coping skill, may become a subskill for other skills. This is all part of the ability to *chain skills,* which CCT refers to as a *master skill.* A coping skills therapist must know how to put together and take apart skills for a particular effect. There are skills to promote emotions, such as appreciation training, and skills to diminish an emotion, such as forgiveness training. Thus, another basic mission in writing this book is to develop the therapist's own master skill.

In summary, therapists need to know *how to construct response capacities.* This book provides a method for building this range of behaviors. Procedures are given for training and building a response and for self-regulation. Further, a coping skills therapist tailors skills to the individual and "packages" them so they are attractive to the patient. These tasks too are discussed in these pages.

Another basic mission is to help patients know exactly how they attain their goals and what allows them to be successful. People generate solutions without knowing how they succeeded. For instance, what allows someone to endure punishing situations for so long? How does someone become confident in certain situations? What makes someone stay optimistic in the face of adversity? In each case, there are productive activities that need to be recognized—consciously and explicitly—in order to reproduce a response when it is chosen. This book guides therapists in how to work with the skills patients have traditionally used to solve their problem or attain their goals. CCT wants to use patients' natural and inveterate skills to resolve the presenting problem. So often therapists ignore responses because they are part of the pathology, without dissecting the pathology to find its beneficial components. This book will encourage therapists to delve into pathology to discover the good in the bad, health amidst disease.

A final mission in writing this book is to outline the skills necessary for treating the various mental disorders. There is a lack of knowledge about how a coping skills approach would work with the many *DSM-IV* Axis I and Axis II disorders. This book is the first step in cataloging the skills necessary for treating those disorders. The list of coping skills that have been detailed in the literature to date are only a short list of possible responses. The book broadens the list of skills significantly so therapists are aware of numerous other ways to resolve the presenting problem, using a skills model.

☐ Summary

The definition of a coping skill is organized behavior that secures an end goal. It is usually unconsciously deployed and may or may not be the best choice for an individual, but it is his/her way of satisfying a need. Coping skills originate from genetic predisposition, reinforcement, social learning, other people's teachings, and self-creation. They are formed by a complex interaction of each of these pathways. Spontaneous emotional responses do not operate independently from cognition, which underwrites, elaborates upon, and solidifies emotional tendencies. CCT wants to enumerate the component parts of coping skills, referred to as subskills, microskills, and support skills.

2

CHAPTER

Cognitive Influence in CBT

Cognition is the bread and butter of cognitive-behavioral therapy (CBT). It is constantly, routinely, consistently worked with in treatment. This is true for cognitive restructuring and cognitive coping therapy. Hence, it is vital to understand the nature and functioning of cognition, which is the focus of this chapter. Different types of cognition are detailed, including ones that lead to mental disturbance. The chapter reviews how problematic thinking is treated in cognitive restructuring, to provide the reader with an overview of this approach. Finally, the role of cognition in coping skills formation is presented.

Cognition provides the individual's structure for his world, determining how s/he feels and acts (Beck et al., 1979). Cognition can be a verbal thought or pictorial event that resides in the person's mind but nevertheless influences behavior. People cannot *not* think. Encountering an event, they do something to it. They describe it, evaluate it, make rules for it, or make prediction based on those descriptions or evaluations. When they do this, they simultaneously alter reality to some degree. This is done unconsciously because reality is simply too big, too complex, too confusing to be understood all at once. In order to deal with it, people must form meanings, conceptions, and categorizations. Their personal view of reality is subjective, and each person has a separate reality from one another. From the perspective of CBT, the major question is how close the subjective world is to objective reality. The latter exists uninfluenced by emotion, assumptions, and personal prejudice, is based on observable phenomena, and is factual. It has to be distinguished from a thought someone has about the objective world.

Let us now turn our attention to a list of general types of beliefs. We will return to this list throughout the book. Being able to identify and differentiate between beliefs is important for functioning as a cognitive-behavioral therapist.

☐ Types of Beliefs

Descriptive Judgments

Sensory-based descriptions report experiences using empirically verifiable data. A concrete, verbal image is created derived from that sensory information. Knowledge of an event is objective to a large degree because it is based on observable phenomena. This allows people to remain as close to objective reality as possible.

Meanings are a type of description that judges the meaning of an event. It declares what something signifies or represents to the individual, based to some degree on empirical data. It is a verbal report of the inner experience. When forming a meaning, the perceptual field with all of its complexity and competing meaning is distilled into a conclusion about what is occurring. In actuality, *all statements of meaning are probability judgments or approximations of reality*. While to the individual meaning is isomorphic with reality, this certainly may not be the case. Hence, meanings are to some degree inference, assumption, or interpretation about a situation. Meaning is the link between the subjective and objective worlds. To be realistic, though, conclusions about meanings have to be grounded in sensory-based judgments.

Evaluative Judgments

Evaluative judgments ascertain or fix the worth of a person or thing by estimating its value. Value is set on a continuum from low to high (wonderful to awful, good to bad, great to terrible). While evaluative judgments give little information about the phenomenon, they do give information about the value an individual places on the phenomenon. Evaluations are a rating and contain a hidden comparative judgment, where a person or event is compared to a standard. The standard is based on a criterion of what constitutes goodness. Depending on how close the person or event is to the criterion, the value is established. When the evaluative judgment is exaggerated negatively and becomes severe and extreme, people or events are rated as awful or terrible. Ellis (Dryden and Ellis, 1988) refers to this as *awfulizing*.

Predictive Judgments

Predictive judgments foretell what will happen. Forecasting the future is a probability judgment, where the judgment has a low to high probability that the prediction is accurate. To be a realistic prediction, it needs to be grounded on empirical knowledge.

Normative Beliefs

Normative beliefs set standards for a person, place, or group. They are a rule about how things should be. Norms make a demand on the individual and to some degree insist on something happening. Ellis labels strong insistence that something occur *demandingness* (Dryden & Ellis, 1988). Contained in a norm is a policy for the individual or others. A norm is detected by words such as *should, ought, must,* or *have to*. A norm can be rigid, firm, or flexible (in the last case it operates more as a guideline). Part of a normative belief is the rule for exceptions to the rule—whether they are allowed or even tolerated. For instance, someone sets a norm of perfection and works to achieve it. If the norm is flexible, a person will not become unduly distressed if mistakes occur, because they are then an allowable exception to the rule for becoming perfect.

Instructions

Similar to a normative belief, an instruction is a directive or order. It guides execution of a task. It commands a sequence, arranging successive responses (e.g., "Relax, take it easy, don't push it"). It can operate on a conscious, semiconscious, or unconscious level. It educates and guides a person in how to act, think, manage emotion or bodily responses, or about how to achieve something (e.g., "Don't get angry. Divert myself elsewhere").

Utilitarian Beliefs

Utilitarian beliefs are type of thought that has benefit or utility because it increases the chance that something worthwhile will happen by thinking a particular way. The thought aids adaptation or goal attainment.

Aspects of Beliefs

When working with any of the above beliefs, the therapist must consider the following:

1. *How much conviction* does someone have that a belief is accurate or realistic? Quantify connection from 0 to 100, with 100 equaling total conviction or certainty that a belief is realistic)?

2. In what situation is a belief not applicable? Does someone always follow a belief? For example, is someone a perfectionist everywhere or only in specific situations? Does someone seek approval from everyone or only certain people? These questions measure the *generalizability or breadth of a belief:* how wide an influence a belief has on a person. Regarding treatment, the therapist may work to preserve a belief but limit it to a given context (e.g., work).

3. If someone believes that a belief is applicable for a given situation, *how much does s/he comply with it?* How motivated is someone to follow a rule or instruction? If someone is highly motivated to follow an irrational belief, the therapist has to decide what can defuse motivation: a change in thinking or new coping skills. By changing the coping skill set, an irrational belief may be preserved, but there is less motivation to comply with that belief.

4. How consistent is a belief set, or how changeable is someone's thinking about themselves or other people in a given situation? These questions ask about *the frequency of following a given belief.*

5. *When a belief in something does not occur as expected, how disturbed or distressed does someone become* (from 0 to 100)? In regard to normative beliefs, how long does someone stay distressed and how deeply is s/he distressed when a norm is violated? For treatment, what new beliefs or skills have to be developed so the patient is not so distressed when a belief is not realized or when a norm is violated?

6. Thinking a particular way, *how much distress or disturbance does a belief cause?* What are the ramifications of an irrational, unrealistic belief? This is a measure of the negative effect of thinking a particular way. In regard to treatment, the therapist needs to determine whether a belief will cause as much disturbance if the coping skill set is changed, or whether a change in thinking is required. Does a belief have to be restructured, or can it remain in effect without being injurious, providing new skill sequences are installed? How much does a belief aid or hinder adaptation?

Irrational, Unrealistic, Maladaptive Beliefs

These different aspects of a belief can change the nature of a thought. Below is a list of beliefs that contribute to pathology and have a pejorative overall effect.

Certaintistic thinking is a belief that one's thinking is certainly correct. The term *certaintistic thinking* was coined by this author to describe thinking that has near 100 percent conviction or complete faith in a prediction or meaning about a situation, that it is totally valid and accurate. Certaintistic thinking may be accurate but most of the time it is not. There are two other types of certaintistic thoughts: *pessimistic thinking*, a prediction that is quite negative, that one's future will be bleak and turn out poorly, and *catastrophic thinking*, a prediction that maintains that one's situation will lead to another bad situation, only to be followed by more and more negative consequences. This type of thinking declares that a domino effect will occur, leading to ultimate catastrophe.

Absolutistic thinking is a belief that there must be total compliance to a norm, and that it must be followed unconditionally, with no restrictions or exceptions. This type of belief has near or total certainty that it is a correct way of thinking. The belief is a demand for total, complete loyalty to a given way of thinking and requires that the self be fully motivated to comply with that norm. Moreover, the belief maintains that following the rule is vital, imperative, and of absolute importance. The norm is rigid and unbending (in opposition to a guideline, which is somewhat more flexible).

Extreme negative evaluations rate something as almost totally bad, awful, or terrible. Absolutistic thinking has a derivative effect on the evaluation of the situation if the rule is violated. Because compliance to the rule is deemed to be crucial, noncompliance or rule violations are rated as awful or terrible. For Ellis (Dryden & Ellis, 1988), both absolutistic thinking and extreme negative evaluations (awfulizing) are major causes of pathology.

Reductionistic thinking is a belief that a complex whole is actually much simpler. The many facets of a situation are reduced down to a few qualities. Those few parts of the whole are then thought to be equal to the complex whole. This occurs when a salient quality in someone or an action by that person is believed to represent or personify the total person. For example, someone cheats, so s/he is solely related to as a cheater. This one action stands for the total person.

Attribution errors occur when someone incorrectly attributes the cause of an event to the wrong party. Generally, the cause is incorrectly attributed to external rather than internal factors (Schacter & Singer, 1962).

Salient thinking can cause an attribution error, in that a salient attribute receives most of the attention and because of that is attributed as the cause for whatever occurs in a situation. The less salient factors are then ignored and receive less credit. Attribution errors deal with incorrect assignment of blame and responsibility.

Magical thinking is a belief that a specific outcome will occur even though there is insufficient means to achieve it. This makes the belief implausible and improbable. There is a lack of use or disregard for objective data or lack of inspection of past events that argues against the conclusion.

Nonutilitarian thinking is a type of belief that leads to less beneficial results or a negative outcome.

Maladaptive thinking hinders or harms adaptation or adjustment to a situation.

In general, cognitive-behavioral therapists work with all of the above beliefs. However, if generalizations can be made, cognitive therapy is much more focused on descriptive and predictive thinking. Its approach emphasizes the correction of certaintistic thinking. Rational emotive therapy (RET) emphasizes absolutistic thinking and extreme, negative ratings. In the main, though, there is extensive overlap between these two approaches.

Schemas, Basic Assumptions, and Automatic Thoughts

Beck and colleagues (1979) have proposed other types of irrational, unrealistic, and erroneous beliefs. They theorize that there are deep level structures (unconscious thoughts) called *schemas* that attend to the activating event or stimuli. The schema is an attitude or assumption. It interprets or infers ideas about those events. They mold data into cognition, by "screening out, differentiating, and coding the stimuli" (Beck et al., 1979, p. 13). Then experiences are categorized, evaluated, and interpreted. The schema shapes the meaning given to the data. This results in a consistent, stable response pattern. Everyone has a set of schemas. Some are more active than others, while some are inactive but can become dominant in certain situations or times.

Schemas have a vital impact on information processing. Young (1999) states that schemas become elaborated over time into deeply entrenched, rigid patterns. They distort situations, highlighting some facts and ignoring other facts. Information is processed with a bias to justify the existence of the schema. Data are construed to be consistent with the schema and not objective reality. With no facts to dispute the schema, it is self-perpetuating and remains resistant to change. A schema provides "tacit knowledge"—a priori truths that are taken for granted and guide the individual in how to respond (Guidano, 1988). The judgments that guide responses are often unrealistic because they are based on preconception and not objective reality. This means that self-image or self-concept is also unrealistic. Young (1999) has identified eighteen early maladaptive schemas that lead to pathology, and readers are encouraged to become familiar with them. This book proposes other ones as well.

As a consequence of schemas, *basic assumptions* about oneself, others, and the future are formed. These basic assumptions then lead to *secondary assumptions*. In turn, basic and secondary assumption lead to *automatic thoughts*, which are closest to consciousness. They help to provide the content of thinking (Beck et al., 1979). Kelly (1955) has referred to these underlying assumptions as personal constructs. Hence, one irrational, unrealistic belief generates another. Once in place, there is a hierarchy of dysfunctional thoughts that result in a high level of disruption, intense, negative affect, and self-defeating, self-destructive behavior. They compromise autonomy, intimacy, self-expression, and self-actualization.

☐ Cognitive Restructuring

Having reviewed different types of irrational and unrealistic beliefs, let us now discuss how cognitive restructuring attempts to correct these types of thoughts. CBT postulates that pathology occurs because of a closed feedback system, where cognition is not examined, challenged, tested, and updated when new data are received. Assumptions, inferences, interpretations, and hypotheses are taken as fact, or what life should be. Facts and opinions of others that are contrary to them are distorted, disqualified, or impugned. Thus, the prevailing belief set is sustained and justified.

Cognitive restructuring seeks to create an open feedback system, whereby patients habitually use data to clarify and challenge their thinking. They are trained in how to conduct a scientific investigation. They develop a habit to slow down the process of thinking to give sufficient time to examine cognition. Private meanings and the subjective world are brought to consciousness. Awareness is expanded to learn about recurring, stereotypic thinking. By doing so, patients learn how to use knowledge to discover the nature and limits of a belief set. They learn to inspect their criteria for judging the rationality of a norm. Subjectivity and objectivity become more congruent.

Cognitive restructuring is basically done in the same way in both rational emotive therapy (Wessler & Wessler, 1980) and cognitive therapy (Beck et al., 1979), with some minor differences. However, the list of steps below follows the plan proposed by cognitive therapy:

1. Identify a situation (an activating event) and the emotions, physiological reaction, and behavior in that situation (the response to the activating event).
2. Identify the belief about the event and the belief about the responses to the event. Ask the patient how much conviction s/he has that the belief is correct (from 0 to 100). This measures the degree of certaintistic thinking present. At this point the therapist detects if there are any irrational, unrealistic, or maladaptive beliefs.
3. Help the patient recognize the connection between the event, the belief, and the response to it. This broadens understanding about the central role of cognition in human functioning, regarding its effect on emotions and behavior.
4. Convert the belief into a hypothesis so that it is not taken for granted as correct, realistic, or rational when this may not be the case.
5. Collect evidence to determine whether the hypothesis is correct.
6. Question the data and the beliefs about them.
7. When enough data are collected, ask the patient to confirm whether the hypothesis is correct or incorrect. If the hypothesis is rejected, this means the patient declares that the belief is irrational or unrealistic.
8. New thoughts about the data are substituted for old beliefs. These thoughts reflect reality and are a rational way to view it.
9. The patient uses his/her new beliefs in various situations and then assesses whether they lead to a better consequence. Rehearsal tasks are used to practice new thinking before entering a situation.

To learn about old beliefs and to judge the efficacy of new thinking, performance assignments are given throughout therapy. Patients continue to monitor and change thinking as part of homework that is assigned each session. In time, patients discover for themselves the implicit credo of cognitive restructuring: *think well—feel well!*

RET refers to the step where beliefs are questioned (step 6) as disputation. The rational emotive therapist acts in a more straightforward, confrontive, or persuasive manner. S/he assumes a didactic role to indoctrinate the patient into thinking differently. The rational emotive therapist actively debates with the patient about what is rational and realistic. This is because RET often focuses on absolutistic thoughts that are really philosophical assertions. To change them, RET maintains a debate is necessary about philosophy where the patient is *taught* what is a correct way to think (Ellis & MacLaren, 1998).

This style is compared to that of the cognitive therapist, who structures the discussion to be less confrontive and to help the patient discover for him/herself the inaccuracy of his/her thinking. A Socratic dialogue is used for this purpose, where the therapist uses questioning to learn the facts about beliefs. Beck and colleagues (1979) call this collaborative empiricism.

Ellis (1970; Ellis & Harper, 1975) insists that there are common core cognition at the root of mental disturbance (e.g., life should be fair, mistakes are not allowed, approval is vital). The presenting problem is generally reconceptualized to reflect one of those core cognition. Oppositely, cognitive therapy (Beck et al., 1979) does not focus on core cognition because it believes that patient thinking is more variable and idiosyncratic.

In addition to content, cognitive restructuring studies the process of thinking. This involves how information is processed. Beck and colleagues (1979) have identified systematic errors in thinking, which lead to incorrect, faulty information processing (e.g., arbitrary inference, overgeneralization, magnification, and minimization). Burns (1980) refers to them as cognitive distortions. Both Burns and Ellis (Dryden & Ellis, 1988) have their own respective lists of distortions. When distortions appear during therapy, the therapist makes the patient aware of them.

In summary, the content and process of thinking form the "personal paradigm" of the patient. The paradigm influences personal response and limits factual input, so cognition is not modified and continues to reflect the archaic, faulty ideas of the schemas and basic assumptions. Having presented the cognitive influence on cognitive restructuring, we will now turn our attention to the cognitive influence on Cognitive Coping Therapy (CCT), and in particular how coping skills operate on a cognitive level.

☐ Policy, Executive, and Operational Beliefs

CCT emphasizes that cognition plays a central, crucial role in the development and maintenance of coping responses, by detailing how, when, and what to do when performing a given skill.

Metacognition

To understand coping skills, it is necessay to understand metacognition and how it is involved in the formation of a coping response. Metacognition involves the acquisition of knowledge and the provision of guidelines about how and what to think, or how a person's thinking influences the cognitive machinery and its operations (Meichenbaum, 1971). The object of metacognition is the person's own thought process and his/her operating beliefs; it is the person's cognition about cognition. It operates as self-communication, where one set of beliefs, which can be called the executive process (Belmont & Butterfield, 1977), influences and shapes how the person responds cognitively, emotionally, physically, and behaviorally. Gagne and Briggs (1974) refer to this as a "cognitive strategy," which is a "skill that selects and guides the internal processes involved in defining and solving novel problems . . . it is a skill by means of which the learner manages his own thinking behavior" (p. 29).

Similar to a cognitive strategy, as described by Gagne and Briggs, is another metacognitive ability that CCT calls the *master skill.* The master skill is the person's thinking about how to think to attain a goal, or how to use thinking as a skill. This is an executive skill that has the task of organizing, managing, and overseeing the internal process regarding the use of coping skills. It identifies the skills required to attain a goal, along with the components of those skills (subskills and microskills). Everyone possesses the master skill. The only issue is how well it functions in a given individual: does s/he select skills that are rational and adaptive, and put the skills together in a useful sequence?

Executive Beliefs

When the master skill details how and what to do to attain a goal, it does this by a particular set of beliefs that CCT labels *executive beliefs*. These are *self-instructions that mostly operate out of consciousness and personal awareness.* In that case they are implicit and tacit. They can also be explicit, conscious self-directions, similar to what is used in self-instruction training (Meichenbaum, 1977). Executive beliefs are a *metacognition that is a template or mental program for how to respond.* They have the major responsibility for *orchestrating and conducting the multiple levels of the response, mediating between the activating event and the response to it.* As a cognitive strategy, they chart the internal and external process for solving problems, attaining goals, and satisfying needs. They provide the rules for how to experience the situation. They detail how to conceptualize the event and what to do about it (e.g., "He will overwhelm me if angry, so I must not antagonize him"), thus shaping the definition of the situation and the conviction about the appraisal of the event. By influencing what will be perceived, they shape the degree of trust or confidence that a perspective is accurate. This influences data collection and in so doing affects the confirmation of personal hypotheses (which may objectively be irrational or unrealistic). They have a direct influence on motivation and can cause demotivation.

Essentially, *executive beliefs form the foundation and structure for coping skills*. Specifically, they state how, when, and where to express emotion, what emotion can be experienced, what will be perceived or given attention (or what will be selectively ignored), how to act, and, most important, how, when, where, and what to think in a given context in order to attain a goal. They contain permissions and prohibitions. Executive beliefs underwrite, revise, extend, or elaborate upon an individual's innate or hardwired responses, providing a fuller, broader expression for the emotional experience. They approve of or reject innate or learned coping skills. They detail how to respond on multiple levels of being: verbally and nonverbally, intrapersonally and interpersonally. They tell the individual what to do with the information secured by the senses. They make sense out of that information and predict how the situation will proceed ("Make her scared of me or she will gain the upper hand"). They influence the neural, expressive, and subjective components of an emotional experience. They give information about emotion and its utility ("Look sad, that will make her give in"). They influence the limbic system, bodily organ functioning, and the neuromuscular-cardiovascular systems regarding how to express emotion ("Sag in the chair and look downcast"). They help organize the neural message for facial expression (e.g., grimacing, contracting the jaw to communicate anger).

While CCT concedes that there are distinctive, characteristic facial and expressive motor behavior for the various emotions, it postulates that self-instructions elaborate upon and help orchestrate those emotional expressions. They provides immediate and specific information about what is being felt ("I'm getting uptight") and the effect of that expression upon others, which in turn extends or inhibits further expression ("I'm starting to scare her, so press harder, look meaner, snarl, and she will back off"). CCT is not saying that all emotional process involves self-instruction, because the former can operate independent of the latter. However, there is an intimate connection between the two. It is difficult to know where spontaneous emotional expression leaves off and where self-instruction begins to guide, channel, and shape reflexive responses.

Executive beliefs are coded in memory as instructions for how to handle a specific situation. When an activating event occurs, the individual accesses memory to find similar situations along with the instructions for how that past situation was handled and the consequences of using that strategy. In milliseconds, a strategy is promulgated with minute detail about how to proceed. This is framed as an inherent set of propositions about what will and will not attain an end goal. They provide self-guidance before, while, and after a coping response is performed. In operation, they are accompanied by and can be activated by emotion. Hence, they can be conceived of as a cognitive-affective structure, where each influences the other and where each is reciprocally determinant of the other. As metacognitions, they arrange the cognitive content (termed the operating beliefs).

Operating Beliefs

As stated above, executive beliefs guide how and what someone will think. CCT terms the content of thinking the *operating belief.* It is similar to cognitive therapy's automatic thoughts (Beck et al., 1979) in three regards: (1) both automatically occur by reflex, without reasoning, (2) both seem plausible and are uncritically accepted as valid, and (3) both are involuntary and cannot be tuned out without difficulty. Each is what is communicated to other people. Each is formed by schemas, basic assumptions, and executive beliefs. The primary difference between them is that an operating belief has a function in building coping skills. Operating beliefs are part of the cognitive content of a skill. As a way to carry out a skill, they have instrumental capacity to reach an end goal.

Policy Beliefs

The executive belief is an outgrowth of what CCT calls a *policy belief,* which is a person's *basic life principles, fundamental plans, or proposed course of action.* A policy belief is someone's personal "truth," so it too has a motivating capacity. It is generally an unconscious rule of conduct upon which other thoughts and behaviors are based. It stipulates how people should lead their life, how others should treat them, or how the world should be. *Based on the policy belief, people form their executive beliefs, which have the function of carrying out the policy. In essence, they shape someone's intention.*

What RET (Ellis and Harper, 1975) refers to as core, irrational beliefs, CCT would call a policy belief. For example:

1. One must be thoroughly competent and not make mistakes.
2. Certain actions are awful or wicked, and people who perform such acts should be severely punished.
3. One must get approval from the significant people in one's life.
4. The world should be fair and just.

Notice how the beliefs provide a general plan or guiding principle for the individual, others, or the world at large. They are implanted to influence present and future decisions about conduct and emotional expression. Policy beliefs normally appear as a standard, so they are often formulated as absolutistic beliefs. However, they do not have to be an absolutistic thought and can be structured as a desire or preference. *Policy beliefs do not specify exact instructions about how to feel and act. That is the function of the executive beliefs,* which detail how to enact the life principle.

In summary, an activating event occurs that stimulates an emotional response. At the same time, cognition appraises what is occurring, encodes the experience, and provides a meaning proposition for the event. A policy belief for that occasion is formulated, or past policy beliefs for managing similar events are recalled and reviewed. That influences the formation of executive beliefs that detail how to specifically cope with and manage the event in question. In turn, the executive beliefs help form the operating beliefs, the content of thinking.

Cognitive restructuring is mostly involved with meaning propositions and policy beliefs, although it can also become involved in correcting erroneous executive and operating beliefs. CCT is mostly involved in influencing the executive and operating beliefs, because they are the key components of coping skill formation. However, depending on the patient problem, CCT is not averse to restructuring the policy belief or providing a new one (such as in chapter 9). Many times this needs to occur before work can be done on modifying the executive beliefs (but this is not always the case, because *patients can accept a change in executive belief and still preserve their policy belief*).

Policy beliefs share some resemblance to schemas and basic assumptions, constructs from cognitive therapy (Beck et al., 1979). However, CCT believes that a schema is too general a concept to serve as a template (the guide to ensure that something will turn out as desired and the gauge for measuring whether it has). The concept of an executive belief is better suited to be a template because it offers specific instructions regarding emotional expression, perception, physiology, and behavior. CCT agrees that *a schema influences the nature of the executive beliefs, but it is the latter that provide the exact responses of the individual.* Executive beliefs in part contain basic and secondary assumptions, as discussed by Beck and colleagues (1979). However, the former exists to form the coping response. While basic assumptions certainly do influence multiple levels of being, they do not operate as self-instructions. To illustrate how policy, executive, and operating beliefs actually function, a case study is presented.

Case Study: Deborah

Deborah is having a very difficult time letting go of her relationship with her estranged husband. She knows intellectually that he is destructive for her, which is why she decided to leave him originally. Yet she has become depressed since they separated, and cannot stop thinking about him. She is dependent upon him, misses him dearly, and is in pain. She often makes decisions based on what will lessen her pain the quickest, although this causes her more pain in the long run. This leads her to want reconciliation.

She has a task: how to cope with the pain of leaving someone she desperately wants. She forms a policy belief: "I must have him back in my life because I cannot live without him." It is a preservation policy to not let go of the relationship. She must now find a way to accomplish her plan of returning to the marriage. Her situation is complicated because deep down she knows that reconciliation is not wise and that others will be opposed to it. To overcome her own and others' resistance to reconciliation, Deborah utilizes a coping skill that she has used many times in the past to keep her in the marriage—*impression management*. It is used to persuade herself and others that reunion is advisable. In this effort she creates images of herself, her husband, and their marriage that justifies her decision making.

Table 2.1 lists the executive beliefs that form the impression management skill. These are metacognitions, operating as self-instructions about how and what to think. They direct her in how to perceive events and behave. Impression management only satisfies a short-term need (pain relief), and in this regard it is self-destructive. Nevertheless, it is still a coping skill because it is her way to attain her goal of preserving the relationship. To repeat a point made previously, a coping skill does not have to be rational, realistic, or

TABLE 2.1. Deborah's Impression Management Skill

Executive belief	Operating belief
Disparage life without him.	I am lonely. I hate being alone. Things are not fun since he left. He satisfied my needs.
Rehabilitate his image and past life together.	He's a fun guy, good to be with.
Create a positive expectation that life with him will be good.	Last week he really looked happy. I think he is finally getting it together.
Create negative expectation that life without him will be bad.	I feel if I leave him it will be a mistake. He will become what I want and someone else will get him.
Resume behaviors associated with past relationship.	I think I will go to our favorite restaurant tonight.
Ignore benefits from separation.	I only notice how life is difficult since we separated.

adaptive. It just has to be instrumental—at least in the person's mind—for goal attainment.

The executive beliefs cause her to feel anxious about separating. Her impression management creates a view (which is a distortion of reality) that separation and being single again are bad, and a view of her husband as good. She disparages separation as part of her plan to overcome her own and others' skepticism about reconciliation. She creates data that are bogus and self-serving: that reunion is advisable. By doing this she justifies her policy belief as valid.

In treatment, CCT will not junk the skill of impression management but instead will try to utilize it. New executive beliefs are formed with the patient (see table 2.2) that change her impression of her husband, her marriage, separation, and single's life.

The self-instructions direct her to focus on the benefits from separating and how it can help her. It directs her perception so that she will focus on issues that will support separation. It directs her to engage in actions that do not spur the need for him. As a consequence of her new impression management skill, Deborah gradually adjusts to life as a single person. Thus, her basic tendency to form facts and impressions was used but this time on her behalf.

TABLE 2.2. Deborah's New Impression Management Skill

Executive belief	Operating belief
Praise life without husband.	I am much calmer now. No more fights. I control what I do now. He's not my "big boss" anymore.
Create positive expectation about single life.	I can start over. I can adjust. My single friends enjoy their life, and I can too. Give it a chance.
Be objective about husband. Remember his negatives when weakening and wanting him back.	He took advantage of me so often. He was abusive. I had no self-esteem with him.
Be realistic about reconciliation.	I will fall back into my old rut if we reconcile.
Engage in behaviors that will sustain separation.	Don't call him. Don't drive by the old neighborhood. Don't call his friends to see what he's doing.
Notice benefits from separation.	I dont' feel put down like I did. I don't come to work crying after one of our fights.

Summary

There are several types of judgments, including descriptive, evaluative, predictive, and normative. There are several types of irrational, unrealistic beliefs, including certaintistic thinking, absolutistic thinking, and reductionistic thinking. Schemas, basic assumptions, and automatic beliefs play a major role in mental disturbance. Cognitive restructuring works to change them by having patients challenge their thinking.

Cognition also plays a major role in coping skill development. Executive beliefs detail how and what to think, what to perceive, and how to express emotion. They instruct a person in how to perform a skill. They are developed to satisfy the person's overall life strategy or plan, which is termed the policy belief. The executive belief details the content of thinking, and this is termed the operating belief.

3

CHAPTER

Catalogue of Coping Skills

At the present time, psychotherapy has only identified a small portion of the possible skills patients can use and do use regularly. One of the missions of this book is to list new coping skills and provide detailed information about their component parts to resolve various mental disorders. The book wants to identify the coping responses of various disorders. This is the beginning of a much-needed effort in mental health. The case studies section (chapters 7–10) will present numerous skills that have not been presented yet in the literature.

This chapter catalogues those skills that have already been described. Coping skills involve one of the following: cognition, emotion as action tendency, perception, physiological response, and behavior. This chapter is not designed to provide a review of the literature on these skills. It will not review outcome studies regarding the techniques and skills discussed below. That is beyond the scope of this book.

☐ Cognitive Skills

Cognitive restructuring theorists have developed various techniques to alter a patient's belief set. These techniques can also become a cognitive skill, depending on how they are presented to the patient and whether the patient receives training in their use. They include (1) self-instruction training, (2) objectivity training, (3) meaning change, (4) anti-awfulizing training, (5) blame training, (6) anti-imperative thinking, (7) problem solving, and (8) self-management strategies.

Self-Instruction Training

As stated previously, executive beliefs are *self-instructions*. Self-instructions are the material for a cognitive approach developed by Meichenbaum (1977). Self-instructions are a person's inner speech or self-talk. Luria (1961) and Vygotsky (1962) initially discussed the concept of inner or covert speech in children, but Meichenbaum (1977) developed it into a treatment approach called self-instruction training. He conceived of self-instructions as metacognition that directs how the individual responds. There are several uses for them:

- A directive to check the level of arousal or degree of emotion present (e.g., "How upset am I from 0 to 5?")
- A directive to cue a coping skill (e.g., "Tighten and relax the muscles")
- A directive to cease automatic responding (e.g., "Don't get upset when he does not listen to me," "Don't retreat when he presses me")
- A directive to initiate and guide problem solving, such as defining the problem, selecting options, or making a plan
- A behavioral directive (e.g., "Ask him what he thinks but don't get pushy," "Don't accuse him of anything")
- A directive to stimulate motivation and offer encouragement ("I can control my anger")

Meichenbaum has shown how these self-instructions can be interwoven into a self-dialogue to guide responses on multiple levels (1977, 1985). First, the therapist speaks the self-instructions out loud and then to him/herself, and then asks the patient to copy that format.

Self-instruction training is a fundamental component of CCT technique. It is used repeatedly to develop new skills, guide behavior and perception, and manage emotion. It is the building block for creating new executive beliefs, which form the structure for new or adapted skills. Patients are given preselected, written self-dialogues constructed in the therapy session. They are written in joint collaboration between therapist and patient. Patients are assigned the task to read them at a given frequency throughout the week, and then told to evaluate their efficacy.

Objectivity Training

By teaching the scientific method, cognitive restructurists teach patients *objectivity*, which is an ability to identify and review data in a realistic, objective unbiased manner. Attempts are made to examine facts without distortion or prejudice. CCT seeks to develop an objective ability through the three steps below:

1. *Emotional restraint.* The patient is first taught how to achieve a dispassionate response when first examining cognition. Emotion needs to be quelled or pacified, by using relaxation or by focusing on other images in the perceptual field. Then self-instructions are used to not act on a feeling and remain calm.
2. *Spectator training.* With emotion quelled, the patient moves on to view the data and the situation without judgment or personal bias. The intent at this point is to *convert the patient into being a scientist* who simply examines the data. *Observation without preconception* is promoted. One way to do this is by viewing the situation from someone else's vantage point. Or, the situation can be viewed as if it is occurring on stage or on a screen. This is the subskill of *psychological distancing.* A third method is to train the patient in how to act as a phenomenologist, by using sensory-based judgments to describe the process without evaluating it (Zinker, 1977).
3. *Conducting an evidence search.* The patient seeks facts to support an allegation or assumption. Training is required about what is a fact as opposed to an assumption. Training is required in how to compile sensory-based information and to forestall quick conclusions about that data.

Meaning Change

Statements about meaning involve making sense out of sensory-based data from past, present, or future situations. The meaning-change technique judges and challenges the accuracy of the belief about the meaning or definition of the situation. Essentially, it teaches patients how to engage in cognitive restructuring with themselves. First, the patient identifies the belief about the situation. S/he converts the belief into a hypothesis and collects data on the situation. S/he then compares his/her definition of the situation to the data to see if the facts support the conclusion.

To perform the skill adroitly, the patient needs to be adept at *self-questioning*. The handout below is regularly given to patients to develop self-questioning. Before and after self-questioning, the patient rates the degree of conviction or certainty that a belief is accurate.

Handout 3.1: Self-questioning Meaning Propositions

1. What do I think is the meaning of this situation?
2. How certain am I that my conclusion about the memory of the situation is accurate, from 0 to 100?
3. Where is my evidence for that conclusion? What is my belief based on? What facts?
4. Based on the facts as I see them, are there other ways to think about this situation? Are there alternative meaning for the event?
5. Are there facts to support alternative meanings for the situation?
6. Do the facts warrant my conclusion about the meaning? How do I know that my conclusion is accurate?
7. Do the facts warrant my conclusion about how this situation will affect me in the future?
8. After weighing the data, how certain am I now that my conclusion about the meaning of the situation is correct, from 0 to 100?

Anti-awfulizing Training

The name for this skill comes from the work of Ellis (1971, 1979; Ellis & MacLaren, 1998), who has discussed the pernicious effect of irrational, unrealistic evaluations of a person or event. The anti-awfulizing skill can be performed in two ways. One, language used to rate a person or event can be changed, and then the results from doing this are compared to the previous statement.

RET trains patients in how to manipulate word choice and ratings to create a new affect. They are taught how to evaluate language and substitute new words to alter their response. This is called a *semantic intervention*. The first step is to identify the patient's word choice used to rate a situation. Next, the patient assumes an objective stance and receives other word choices containing milder, less extreme ratings: "This is not preferable" or "This is not desirable." Third, the therapist feeds the patient two statements, one with a severe, extreme rating and another with a milder rating. The patient is then asked to compare how upset s/he feels with each statement. Obviously, the milder rating statement creates less distress. Finally, the patient is asked to change his/her rating for accuracy.

RET discusses how the choice of words for understanding events influences the level of emotional distress. Extreme word choice (e.g., *awful, terrible*) creates a dire meaning for the situation and makes the event appear far more threatening, challenging, and intolerable than it actually is. In essence, language formation precedes emotional and physical response. In turn, language choice intensifies any negative feelings that are already present (e.g., anger turns to rage, sadness turns into depression). Oppositely, more mild or moderate ratings will cause tolerable negative feelings. *While the perceived meaning of the situation affects the language chosen to describe it, the language people select also determine their meaning for the situation.*

A second method of anti-awfulizing training is to teach *self-questioning*. Patients are trained to question their own ratings for accuracy. Handout 3.2 prepares patients to do this. The intent is to create a tendency to identify evaluative thinking.

Handout 3.2: Self-questioning the Rating for a Situation

1. Am I upset with myself or another person? How much am I upset, from 0 to 100, with 100 being extreme distress?
2. How am I evaluating myself or another person? What is the evaluation I give myself or another person? How bad do I think I, another person, or the situation actually is, from 0 to 100, with 100 the absolute worst?
3. How certain am I that the rating or evaluation is accurate, from 0 to 100, with 100 being total certainty the evaluation is correct?
4. What makes myself, another person, or the situation that bad or awful? What am I basing this evaluation on? What data or reasoning am I using?
5. Is there another way to view myself, another person, or the situation besides the way I presently think? Could I have used another rating in its place? What is that rating?
6. Is the behavior I dislike really awful or just not preferable?
7. Why am I not changing my thinking to label an action as "not preferable"? What makes me stick to the rating I have given?
8. What action could I or the other person have taken that would be even more awful than the present action?
9. Rank deeds by degree of awfulness. Compare the action rated as awful to other actions rated awful. Which is worse and by how much?
10. Now rate how certain am I that my rating for the situation is accurate, from 0 to 100.

Blame Training

People routinely cast blame or decide what is responsible for an action or event. The issue is how skilled is someone at doing this? Beck and colleagues (1979) discuss how patients inaccurately ascribe responsibility to someone or something, and that results in a negative emotional state. This can occur in three different ways:

1. *Inaccurate causal belief.* A person blames the existence of a negative condition on someone without considering alternative causal factors.
2. *Attribution error.* The person maintains that internal factors in an individual are responsible for a negative state of affairs when external factors are not considered or given much weight. Conversely, a person contends that factors external to someone are responsible for a misdeed without considering internal factors in that person.
3. *Inaccurate consequential belief.* A person is blamed for causing a negative consequence, but does not consider other factors that could ameliorate or neutralize the degree of blame.

The ability to correctly assign blame is treated as a coping skill in CCT. One method of *blame training* is to teach patients to collect data on internal and external factors that can cause a problem, weigh the data, and then ascribe blame based on that analysis. This way, blaming is done in a scientific manner. This is covered more fully in the section on "forgiveness training" in chapter 7. The two examples below illustrate how this technique works.

Case Study: Grace

Grace has an ability to always see the best in other people. This allows her to forgive others when they err or violate her trust. She does this by believing that external factors are to blame while ignoring internal factors in the other person (e.g., their greed or promiscuity). She also gives too much credit to causal factors that exonerate the guilty party (e.g., "He's had a hard childhood and upbringing and that is why he acts as he does"). Because of this, she rarely gets mad or blames significant others for their faults. She is habitually understanding.

In general, this is a positive coping skill, but she carries it to excess. Problems arise when her husband continues to transgress and commits inappropriate and unethical behavior. Yet she has a difficult time holding him to blame when he deserves it. Because of this she cannot set limits on him or more strenuously call for a change in conduct. Her lack of anger gives him the wrong impression that she is not concerned about his misdeeds. Grace needs to objectively ascribe blame when it is appropriate to do so. In CCT, she undergoes blame training to learn how to do this. She learns to give more weight to his internal factors (his selfishness) and less weight to external factors (his busy work schedule). This approach helped her to set limits on her husband when his behavior was errant.

Case Study: Robert

Robert cannot forgive others easily. He is sharply and quickly critical. He cannot do what Grace is able to do easily. In therapy he undergoes forgiveness training to learn how to pardon others' misdeeds more quickly. To do this, Robert is trained to find external causes for other's behavior, so others' behavior appears more complex instead of unicausal and simplistic. Searching for external factors helps him to realize that internal factors in individuals(e.g., their vanity, greed) are not totally responsible for an undesirable action. In turn, this promotes forgiveness.

Another method of blame training develops a self-questioning ability when ascribing blame. The intent is to soften hard judgments of blame, and seek accurate judgments. See handout 3.3 below.

Handout 3.3: Questions for Assigning Blame

1. Where is the evidence that person X caused this event?
2. How certain am I that person X caused this problem, from 0 to 100?
3. If s/he contributed to the negative event, how much of a role did s/he play? What percentage of the problem did s/he cause?
4. Who else or what else should receive some of the blame as well?
5. What factors external to myself or this other person could also have caused the negative consequence to some extent?
6. What percentage of the blame should other factors receive?
7. Are there positive consequences that results from this negative situation, and what are they? Have I or others benefited some how by the events or consequences?

Anti-imperative Thinking

Challenging absolutistic thinking, referred to as anti-imperative thinking by Ellis (Dryden & Ellis, 1988; Ellis & MacLaren, 1998), is one of the basic techniques in cognitive restructuring. In fact, treatment for absolutistic thinking is one of the hallmarks and dominant contributions of RET to psychotherapy (Dryden and Ellis, 1988). The therapeutic desire is to develop a capacity in patients to dispute and challenge their imperative thinking post-treatment. This requires *training in anti-imperative thinking*. Again, patients are taught the steps in cognitive restructuring: (1) identify the belief about the activating event, (2) convert the belief into a hypothesis, and (3) if the belief is absolutistic, than it is challenged for rationality and realism. At this point, patients need skill in self-questioning, developed by the questionnaire below given to patients.

Questions 1–3 ascertain if the patient is engaging in imperative thinking. Question 4 disputes imperative thinking and offers the idea that it may only be nondesirable. People believe that something is imperative if

Handout 3.4: Working with Imperative Thinking

1. How do I want this situation to proceed?
2. Do I believe that it must proceed in a certain way or that it is vital that something occur or not occur in this situation?
3. How important is it that the situation proceeds the way that I want, from 0 to 100, with 100 being absolutely important?
4. If the situation is rated as vital, why is it vital? Is it vital or just not preferable that the situation go a particular way? Why can't it be considered undesirable?
5. Will I be able to tolerate the situation if it turns out the way that I don't want? What is my tolerance ability in this situation?
6. If I believe that I won't be able to stand it, why can't I stand it? Where is my evidence that I am incapable of tolerating something I don't like?
7. If I believe the situation must proceed a certain way, how do I rate this situation? Do I consider it terrible or awful if it does not go the way that I want?
8. If the situation is rated as awful, why is it awful? What makes it awful?
9. Are there other outcomes that would be more awful? Rate the present situation for awfulness compared to other situations.

they assume that they cannot stand it. Question 5 asks if there is sufficient tolerance to bear an undesireable situation. If a low estimate of tolerance is given, this is disputed. If tolerance is lacking, then it is taught (e.g., frustration tolerance training, uncertainty tolerance training). Question 7 asks if a severe rating is given to a situation rated as vital to occur or not occur. Questions 8 and 9 then proceed into anti-awfulizing. The reason for anti-awfulizing is that a severe negative evaluation of a situation can result in imperative thinking ("This is awful so it must not happen now or ever again").

Problem Solving

Problem solving is considered one of the three basic components of CBT, along with cognitive restructuring and coping skills therapy. However, CCT considers problem solving a coping skill and integrates it into coping skills therapy. Problem solving has developed as part of a general movement in mental health referred to as social competence training, which includes social skills training (Wine & Smye, 1981). Problem solving is also an extension of the self-management or self-regulation movement (Kanfer, 1970; Bandura, 1977; Meichenbaum & Cameron, 1973). Problem solving has the advantage of integrating coping skills into the chosen plan; it generalizes to other situations and enhances treatment maintenance after the conclusion of therapy.

Problem solving is a process that leads to finding the best solution to a problem (D'Zurilla & Goldfried, 1971). This approach has been widely studied with children (Spivack & Shure, 1974). A number of models of problem solving have been proposed (Mahoney & Arnkoff, 1978; D'Zurilla & Nezu, 1982; Spivack et al., 1976). The steps are similar in each of these models:

1. *Problem identification* accurately perceives and appraises something as a problem and gathers information about it.
2. *Alternative solution thinking* identifies short- and long-term options for resolving the problem. This skill requires an ability to *brainstorm,* by suspending judgment until several options have been identified that have a variety and range of ideas (Osborne, 1963).
3. *Consequential thinking* is then used to identify consequences from pursuing the various options that are being considered. This skill requires a *prognostication ability* to "move into the future" to evaluate options by anticipating outcomes, judging and comparing outcomes, and then deciding which is best.
4. The best option is selected. Central to this is the skill in *cost-benefit*

analysis, to decide the overall costs to oneself if an option is selected.

5. *Means-end* is then employed to find the best tactics once a strategy has been selected, by planning a series of steps to achieve a goal.
6. *Verification* is done to assess if the plan is working. This skill requires self-monitoring to assess changes brought about by implementing the plan.
7. *Self-reinforcement* is needed to sustain a plan once selected.

Self-management Strategies

CCT relies on self-management or self-control tactics (Kanfer, 1970, 1971; Rehm, 1977; Rokke & Rehm, 2001). CCT extensively uses them and incorporates them into most every training module. They are used to increase the voluntary control of psychological and behavioral responses. Kanfer (1970) proposes the following three interconnected processes that are involved in self-regulation.

Self-monitoring

This ability raises the level of awareness by being observant of self-processes or emotional responses. Self-monitoring is a twofold process: a) becoming aware of the existence of a state of being, and b) quantifying the magnitude or level of that state. Self-monitoring can be used in different ways. It can be used as part of homework assignments regarding the frequency, intensity, and duration of problems (Meichenbaum, 1977). It is helpful to learn how much someone focuses on a particular thought or subject in a given time span (e.g., how much someone thinks about mistakes) or how much someone engages in a particular behavior in a given time period. For example, Linda is having difficulty with a prolonged grief reaction regarding the death of her husband. She is asked to monitor her thinking and quantify how often she thinks about him each hour, from none to constantly. This allows her to realize that she is overinvolved with his death and will not let him go.

Self-evaluation

Self-evaluation has several uses. One, it determines how much a skill has produced a desired outcome. Two, it estimates if someone can successfully execute a skill or behavior (Bandura, 1977, 1997), which is a major determinant if a behavior will be initiated (Bandura, 1980). Three, it provides evidence as to whether a new coping skill is being utilized, by judg-

1. How angry did you get today, from 0 to 100?
2. How long did you hold on to your anger?
3. If you were angry, did you find multiple causes for why you feel angry?
4. Using the relaxation techniques, how much were you able to lower your level of anger?
5. How fast could you stop thinking about what went wrong, using sensory diversion techniques?
6. What was the best way you were able to divert yourself today from focusing on your anger? How well did it work?
7. How much do you think you are gaining ability to manage your anger?

ing if a skill performance meets a desired standard for that skill. Above is an example where a self-questionaire assesses these matters, regarding an anger management training program.

A fourth use of self-evaluation is to assess how much antecedent or consequential factors are influencing the performance of a skill. Five, it can be used to assess the accuracy or validity of an evaluation. If a patient has a severe, extreme rating for a person or event, s/he can compare the degree of terribleness or awfulness of various people or situations to the one in question (therapist: "You think not gaining your husband's approval is awful, but which is worse, not gaining approval from him, getting cancer, or being audited by the IRS?"). The patient then rank-orders which is the worst or most terrible to gain objectivity.

Another purpose for self-evaluation is to assess reinforcement behavior. Does a person think particular thoughts or performs certain actions that increases the likelihood of a positive action continuing or a negative action diminishing? Self-monitoring is used to assess if there is insufficient self-reward or excessive self-punishment.

Self-reinforcement

Self-reinforcement is used to sustain an action or diminish an action. A person needs to determine what reinforcers will work for him/her. For instance, Jimmy uses cocaine. He treats himself very well, but his drug use is limiting how much he can spend on himself for pleasure items. Each week he does not use, Jimmy takes one-fourth of his money saved by not buying cocaine and spends it on himself. This is his positive reinforcer. If he uses cocaine, he gives one-fourth of his money to an organization or person he hates, a negative reinforcer. Akin to self-reinforcement is verbal persuasion (Bandura, 1997). Both are used extensively in *self-support training* (see chapter 7).

☐ Perceptual Skills

This is an ability to selectively attend or not attend to a given image in a situation. It is an ability to manipulate or deliberately alter the perceptual process, to mechanically place one image or thought in a foreground position in place of another. CCT maintains that perception has not received the attention or support it deserves in CBT. Instead, Gestalt therapy has done most of the work in showing how to use perception in treatment (Perls et al., 1951; Polster & Polster, 1973; Zinker, 1977).

Perception involves the use of the senses to acquire information in a given situation termed the "perceptual field" (Kofka, 1935; Perls et al., 1951). It is the act of noticing and observing using the senses to discern physical images. In addition, there is mental perception, where objects, thoughts, or images are viewed in the mind's eye. According to Gestalt psychology (Kohler, 1959), whenever a foreground image is perceived, other objects or images are simultaneously pushed into the background and receive less attention. Whatever is foregrounded has far-reaching influence on other cognition, emotion, physiology, and behavior.

Perception can be used in an adaptive or maladaptive way. It is an important contributor to mental distress. Anxious or apprehensive people use perception in a negative way, by continuously scanning the perceptual field for danger. Depressed people engage in brooding, which is a preoccupation or "over-focus" with negative matters whereby some images receive inordinate attention, leading to a negative state of mind. CCT shows patients how to manipulate perception to create a desired mental state, lessen an intense negative emotion, or improve relationships with significant others.

Below are some of the ways perception can be used as a coping skill:

- It can be used to tune out or lessen the effects of persistent physical sensations. This has direct benefit for the treatment of chronic pain (Turk et al., 1983). The patient focuses on another object that supplants the pain as the foreground image, which automatically pushes the pain into the background.
- Perception can be used to enhance a desired state. For example, it is a vehicle for heightening appreciation, which CCT refers to as *savoring training* (see chapter 8). This skill increases patients' en-

joyment of something by learning how to relish dimensions of the experience. This has direct benefit for depressives who suffer from anhedonia.

- Perception can be used to decrease stress, by focusing on pleasant bodily feelings or positive elements of a fantasy.
- Perception can increase objectivity, by viewing the situation from multiple perspectives (becoming another person in that situation). It is part of *perspective taking*, which is imagining how another person thinks and feels.
- Perception is used in *psychological distancing training*. A patient views other objects instead of the feared or troublesome image. Once a negative image is not foregrounded, it has less of a negative effect. For instance, instead of looking someone in the eye, which can cause a negative feeling, a person visually traces the lines of that person's face. Used in this regard, avoidance of eye contact and attending to value-neutral objects increase psychological distance.
- Perception can also be used to eliminate or limit a mental image or thought from intruding into consciousness. CCT terms this perceptual shifting. One way this can be done is by halting an image or thought which is called *thought stopping* (Wolpe, 1958, 1973; Mahoney, 1974). A person says "stop" to terminate thinking about something that causes distress. Another method is thought substitution, where a benign, neutral thought or a pleasant thought is substituted for the negative thought. Examples may be imagining the opening of a favorite television show or a relaxing scene.

☐ Emotion as a Coping Skill

While feeling an emotion appears natural and effortless, several abilities are required. First, there is the ability to experience the experience, to fully feel dimensions of the experience. There is the ability to tolerate painful or intense negative emotion. There is the ability to understand an emotion, by using the intellect to provide meaning for the experience and a sense of reality. There is an ability to know when to think about an emotion (a timing skill). If the intellect is brought in too soon, it will interfere with the experiencing of the experience. Feelings have to be managed, which involves several abilities. One is *compartmentalization*, an ability to experience emotions at the appropriate time and place, so feeling an emotion does not interfere with other activities. A second management skill is verbal expression of emotion, which involves *communication skills and tactfulness training*. A third skill is emotional containment, whereby feelings are restrained or inhibited, or emotional attenuation, where a feeling is diluted so it is not so intense. (Chapter 10 provides steps for restraining emotion.)

There is also a behavioral component of emotion, and this is when emotion operates as an action tendency (Izard, 1977). In this regard, emotions have a neuromuscular component, whereby striate muscle action helps to "initiate, amplify, attenuate, or inhibit an emotion" (Izard, 1977, p. 415). As emotions are experienced there is a habitual, overlearned, or hardwired physiological and behavioral response for handling that feeling. The feeling has an action component that is repetitively, mindlessly adopted to attain an end goal. In this regard, action tendencies are coping skills: a pattern or habit that is used to cope with a difficult circumstance.

However, cognition, in the form of executive beliefs, influences and elaborates the action tendency in key regards. First, it converts the stimulus into a symbolic representation so the facial and expressive motor response reflects that characterization. Executive beliefs provide the language for that representation, which in turn can attenuate or concentrate responsiveness (e.g., absolutistic terms are used that intensify motor activity). Third, executive beliefs direct attention to only certain sensorimotor information, which affects how the person views the situation, which in turn influences the action tendency further.

Barlow (1988) lists the action tendencies for several emotions. For fear or panic, the action tendency is to avoid, escape, or take flight. This saves a person from encountering a fearsome situation. For generalized anxiety, the action tendency is hypervigilance. This involves chronic scanning for threat and continuous readiness to take action if a threat appears. For depression, the action tendency is disengagement or withdrawal from a negative stimulus, so it has less effect on the individual. Linehan (1993) states that the action tendency for anger is confrontation and fighting with the object.

The action tendency is both a consequence of the emotion and a manifestation of it. For example, the vegetative aspect of depression is manifested as disengagement. Once disengaged, the depressive quickly realizes that this is a way to cope with a demanding, frustrating world. The action tendency is then reinforced and strengthened by the service it performs.

On one hand, action tendencies are a solution allowing a person to manage potential problems. On the other hand, they are a symptom of the emotional disorder, a component of pathology, and a dominant focus of treatment. For example, in cases of phobias and panic attack, the avoidance response becomes the major focus of treatment, because it prevents learning about and tolerating the feared stimuli. In regard to apprehension, the recurring scanning for danger causes the tense, jittery, uneasy feeling that makes anxiety so unpleasant.

While Barlow (1988) and Linehan (1993) call for suppressing action tendencies, CCT does not want to discard or reject them; rather, it seeks to combine them with other skills to form a new, more useful response set. Because action tendencies are considered to be a problem only when used to excess, CCT teaches patients what is a proper amount of use for that response.

☐ Altering Physiological States

Many skills require a particular level of organ and muscular functioning and a specific amount of energy output. Unless people can alter physical states upon command, they are less able to perform various coping skills. For example, some skills require an energetic, aroused, excited response, so people need to be able to accelerate cardiac, pulmonary, and neuromuscular activity while raising their blood sugar level. Conversely, other skills demand a lower level of arousal, requiring that people decelerate cardiac, pulmonary, and neuromuscular activity. Other tasks demand a steady but low organ output, which is needed while concentrating or studying. Hence, skill needs to be developed in manipulating physiological activity to attain a desired goal. CCT teaches patients how to do this.

One of the primary tools for altering physiology is relaxation. Relaxation training has been a widely used modality for many years, including such techniques as deep muscle relaxation (Jacobson, 1938), meditation (Benson et al., 1974), and autogenic training. It is a basic part of biofeedback training. Relaxation training is an important component of other skills, such as anger management. Behaviorists use it while teaching systematic desensitization (Wolpe, 1958) and deconditioning.

☐ Altering Behavior

This is the level of physical action. The skill can be purely physical or involve a combination of perception and behavior, such as free-throw shooting in basketball, which involves muscle control blended with eye-hand coordination. The skill can be a nonverbal ability, such as moving the face and body muscles to communicate a thought or to express an emotion.

One major behavioral skill is communication: the ability to articulate thoughts or to express emotion. There are communication skills for marriage and the family (Jacobson and Margolis, 1979; Satir, 1967), for parents and children to help them verbalize their emotions (Gordon, 1970), and skills for the classroom teacher (Gordon, 1976). Numerous social skills for children have been identified (see Forman, 1995). The therapeutic emphasis is on sending nonthreatening, clear messages. The training usually includes modeling, rehearsal, and practice in real life (Jacobson & Margolis, 1979).

Closely allied to communication training is assertiveness training. This extremely popular behavioral approach has almost become a social movement. It is a combination of communication skills, values, and philosophy (i.e., it is good to assert one's rights, to be candid, to not be passive or aggressive) (Alberti & Emmons, 1978). It developed from the early work of Salter (1949) and Wolpe (1958). As an outgrowth of assertiveness training, social skills competence (Sprafkin et al., 1993) has developed to train people to deliberately perform behaviors that are positively reinforced and not to practice behaviors that receive punishment from others (Libet & Lewinsohn, 1973).

There are numerous social abilities, and they are developed by coaching, modeling, and practice sessions. There are skills for severely impaired psychiatric patients (Christoff & Kelly, 1985), the mentally retarded (Andrasik & Matson, 1985), marital couples (Wachkman & Wampler, 1985), and children (Ladd & Asher, 1985).

☐ Summary

There are various types of skills that involve cognition, perception, physiological activities, and behavior. In particular, the cognitive skill of self-instruction training receives particular attention for skill building. Other cognitive skills include objectivity, meaning change, anti-awfulizing, blame training, problem solving, and self-management strategies such as self-monitoring, self-evaluation, and self-reinforcement. Skills that involve the emotions deal with action tendencies, which are the behaviors that act out a feeling. Perception is used in various ways to intensify or attenuate a feeling. A physiological skill is relaxation training. Behavior skills include communication and assertiveness training.

4

CHAPTER

Limitations of Cognitive Restructuring

Questions need to be raised about the universality of cognitive restructuring as a treatment approach. Though the approach has received solid support in research, there are situations where it has limitations or other approaches may be preferable. Young (1999) has raised several concerns about it and maintains that critical factors must be present in order for it to work. This chapter identifies problems with cognitive restructuring and discusses how a coping skills approach can overcome limitations.

The chapter is not written to demean or discredit cognitive restructuring as a treatment approach. It deserves its accolades. The problem is not so much with cognitive restructuring per se but with how cognitive-behavioral therapy is practiced today. One major problem has already been raised in chapter 1, which is the issue of balance. In deciding how to treat patient problems, far too much weight is given to changing thinking, with less weight given to coping skills. Cognitive-behavioral therapists immediately focus on how and what patients think and less on how patients cope or need to cope. Instead, this book urges therapists to make the decision about which treatment model to use on a case-by-case basis. Hence, there needs to be understanding about where cognitive restructuring is applicable, where it is inapplicable, where it can be used as an adjunct to a coping skills approach, and vice versa.

Limited Growth Model

Cognitive restructuring, like most mental health models, is predominantly pathology-driven, not growth-driven. Mental health has been and still is largely influenced by the medical model: treat disease, eradicate malady, remove symptomatology. Its focus is on the troubled, the weary, and the sick—the clinical population. In fact, except for a few modalities such as Gestalt, almost every mental health model focuses on defect or what is wrong with people (what is preventing them from becoming who they want to be), instead of what is right with people—their healthy, adaptive responses.

Oppositely, another trend has developed in medicine called social competence (Wine, 1981), which emphasizes prevention: equipping the individual or group with adaptive responses to improve functioning and avoid disease. Simultaneously, the humanist movement promoted the concept of growth.

Cognitive restructuring does have utility as a growth model. It is effective for removing blocks to self-actualization efforts. By changing cognition that is preventing them from developing, people are free to become-in-the-world, as existentialists would say. In addition, cognitive restructuring can supply the beliefs necessary to develop healthy responses, such as optimism, perseverance, altruism, civility, or tolerance. This is part of a trend called "positive psychology" (Dorsey, 2000), which focuses on using psychology to develop virtues.

The problem is, growth involves more than just good thinking. Other skills are required, including affective, perceptual, physiological, and behavioral skills. Likewise, supplying people with good thinking does not guarantee adaptiveness. As Mahoney and Arnkoff (1978) stress, adaptiveness is not necessarily isomorphic with rationality. Adaptiveness, like growth, may require other skills of and beyond rational thinking.

This is not to argue that cognitive restructuring models ignore other levels of being besides the cognitive. In recognition of this, rational emotive therapy has changed its name to rational emotive behavioral therapy, or REBT (Ellis & MacLaren, 1998) to give greater prominence to behavioral interventions. Cognitive therapy (Beck et al., 1979) also makes extensive use of behavior. Young (1999) has broadened cognitive restructuring and extensively uses experiential techniques in addition to cognitive and behavioral techniques.

The issue is really which cognitive-behavioral model is best suited for helping patients grow. This book argues that a coping skills approach offers more to the patient concerned with personal growth because its basic mission is *total response capacity*. Its focus is on *constructing a more fully functioning person*. In doing so, it makes greater use of all of the levels of human experience, such as perceptual and affective skills, which are largely ignored by cognitive restructuring. Hence, *CCT is more of a holistic approach than cognitive restructuring.*

A second problem with cognitive restructuring is that it does not do much with the patient's native or acquired abilities that contribute to pathology. It does not refine, rehabilitate, readapt, or recontextualize dysfunctional responses so that they have better use. It does not show the patient how his/her pathological responses contain benficial, healthy coping skills. CCT does this. In summary, cognitive restructuring offers patients only a limited growth model, while CCT is better suited for the purpose of self-actualization.

☐ Problems with the Insistent Patient

Rigid patients are a challenge for cognitive restructuring (Young, 1999). They have difficulty changing their thinking, even when contrary data are presented that show their beliefs are irrational, unrealistic, or maladpative. The rigid patient has difficulty changing his/her behavior, even when evidence is presented that it is injurious to self or others. Such a person makes a rule and steadfastly, doggedly refuses to bend or suspend it. S/he is certain the belief is valid or that the rule should exist. The insistent thinker engages in absolutistic thinking, inserting into a situation a demand that something must occur.

When demandingness or insistence (as CCT prefers to call it) is encountered in cognitive restructuring, it is treated by chipping away at the rigid loyalty to a belief. Questioning, homework, rational emotive imagery (Wessler & Wessler, 1980), and other cognitive techniques continue to be used in the hope the patient gradually, begrudgingly will come to agree that his/her thinking is irrational or unrealistic. This method of doing therapy follows the "more of the same" solution: when something does not work, do more of it (Watzlawick et al., 1974). When some disputing does not work, do more of it until rationality emerges in the patient. However, if rigidity persists, continued disputation may not change some patients' thinking. This is especially the case when other people or social institutions support that way of thinking.

CCT would deal with insistence differently than cognitive restructuring would. The former offers more flexibility and chance for creativity than the latter. First, CCT defines rigid thinking as a coping skill. The therapist will discuss with a patient where it has applicability and where it does not. CCT does not characterize insistence as resistance, as does cognitive restructuring, so it avoids the pejorative label of noncompliance. Instead, insistence is viewed as a positive response used to excess or in the wrong context. This does not make the patient feel attacked, and so it maintains rapport. Furthermore, CCT will try to make a patient into a "better" insistent person. Chapter 8 presents a case where a rigid, insistent perfectionist is trained to become a better or more proficient perfectionist.

Second, CCT can make use of paradoxical treatment, which it incorporates into its approach. It can recommend that the rigid thinking or behavior be continued. Then patients are asked to monitor how upset they become when they continue to insist that something happen. They are asked to observe the consequences of being insistent and then choose if they want to continue being that way. This makes patients take responsibility for their insistent ways and stops the tug-of-war between therapist and patient.

Third, new coping skills can be added to the present ones. Insistence may be occurring because patients lack sufficient means to attain their end goals. Resolving the coping skills deficit can make it easier for rigid patients to try other ways of thinking and being.

CCT can change rigid thinking indirectly by teaching coping skills that inadvertently change absolutistic thinking. The rigid thinking is not disputed, but by learning new coping skills the patient changes his/her thinking over time. The new skills make the absolutistic thoughts either obsolete or inapplicable. Chapter 7 provides an example of how a new coping skill, psychological pain management, changes the insistent tendency as well as the schema supporting it.

CCT can change insistent thinking in ways other than direct disputation. For example, Herbert was an engineer who hated his job and was ready to retire in two years to pursue his two true loves: playing piano and making pianos for sale. Then he suffered a stroke that cost him the functioning of the left side of his body. His plans for the future ended at that point. He became severely depressed and furious and insisted that this should not be happening to him. He strenuously asserted that life and God had been unfair to him. While admitting that life is not fair, he nevertheless clung to his thinking that it should be. Cognitive restructuring had little effect on changing his thinking. He was what Albert Ellis calls a difficult customer. A behavioral approach also failed, because he refused to engage in activities that could lead to positive reinforcement. He remained focused on and stewed about his losses. He had adopted a philosophy that God was evil. His executive belief demanded denouncing God for what God had taken from him, and by gaining little pleasure from life. This was his way of declaring to God how bad he was.

A coping skills approach was then tried. To complement his executive belief of no pleasure, the therapist recommended *self-denial training,* whereby the patient was to practice denying himself any pleasure in all possible ways. To become adept at self denial, the patient was to have sex with his wife, eat his favorite foods, and go to interesting places but practice self-denial while doing them. He was instructed to gain no pleasure from those activities. Techniques were taught to reduce his overall level of pleasure, such as by distracting himself when doing something that was fun. Essentially, the therapist was prescribing the coping response the patient was already using under the guise of trying to make him better at it—to become more proficient in self-denial. Ironically, self-denial was practiced in such a way as to increase his pleasure, which reduced his depression. Eventually, this strategy demonstrated to the patient the absurdity of his policy and executive beliefs. He gradually adjusted to his losses.

☐ Problems with Unmotivated, Resistant Patients

A common type of patient is one who does not want to be a patient. These patients reject having a problem although they have many. Yet, they often are required to be in treatment by parents, spouse, school, employer, or the court. They come to sessions passive and silent, or aggressive and challenging, but not ready or wanting to work on what got them into trouble. This type of patient poses difficulties not just for cognitive restructuring but for all models of care. For cognitive restructuring, they are a major problem because the approach requires collaboration and cooperation to jointly examine cognition and to do the homework necessary to gain cognitive skills.

However, a coping skills approach can offer this type of patient something other modalities lack. It can appeal to their desire to be more potent and successful in some way, any way. This is attractive to everyone's pragmatic, self-centered side. It is most appealing to sociopathic, narcissistic, oppositional-defiant patients, or those with a conduct disorder. They are often rebellious about being in treatment but covet success and potency. The unmotivated patient is asked if there is some part of their life where s/he wants to function better, such as asking someone for a date, handling teasing, or getting a job. The original presenting problem is initially put aside as the focus shifts to making the patient more adept and facile. This builds a therapeutic relationship and acceptance of treatment. At this point, the resistant patient may be more willing to discuss the presenting problem that brought him/her to treatment in the first place.

Some therapists try to overcome resistance and lack of motivation in resistant children by becoming a "fun guy" who makes small talk or plays games until the patient is ready to participate. This wastes a great deal of time, and in the days of managed care that is untenable. CCT avoids this by quickly focusing on skills that the patient wants to possess. This recruits the patient much more quickly into working on issues.

Cognitive restructuring will work with the unmotivated, resistant patient by addressing his/her thoughts about having to be in treatment. This leads to identifying irrational, unrealistic, maladaptive thinking that underpins the rejection of therapy (e.g., not wanting to go to therapy because it is not fun). Still, this type of approach focuses on what is wrong with the resistant patient, and that may be rejected.

CCT has a different way to treat resistance. One approach is to teach skills resistant patients need to possess if they continue to be resistant or exhibit low motivation to change. Chapter 7 illustrates this approach. A dependent patient who does not want to change her life situation is taught pain management skills, because if she does not change and stays in her present situation, that skill will be necessary. Skills training in pain management helped her to realize the need for change. Another approach is to convert resistance into an assertion that the patient already possesses sufficient coping skills and does not need to learn any more (see chapter 10). Data collection then tests this assertion. Third, resistance is conceptualized as a coping response to preserve some basic way of operating. The focus then shifts to discover what the patient seeks to preserve.

□ Problems with Chronic Relapse

Cognitive restructuring would assert that patients who chronically relapse, due to an addiction or habit disorder (e.g., recurring rages, worrying), do so because a key cognition has not been identified and changed. The presumption is that if the patient can change his/her thinking, relapse will stop. If relapse continues, a cognitive restructurist would then assert that the patient is not yet ready to surrender dysfunctional, disturbed thinking. In this case, "more of the same" is typically pursued. The original error in thinking is disputed over and over in the hope that chipping away at dysfunctional thinking will gradually avoid relapse.

CCT offers a different approach. It declares that the recurring slips are due to disinclination to discard a desired coping skill. CCT would first identify that coping response. The positive elements of the pathological response are highlighted, and then the response is readapted or recontextualized. New skills are added so the relapsing patient does not have to rely solely on old skills to manage life problems.

One option in working with relapse-prone patients is to preserve their policy and executive beliefs in some form but make them less injurious. For example, addicted patients often have low frustration tolerance (Ellis et al., 1988). Their policy is to avoid situations that increase discomfort.

Efforts to avoid or decrease frustration commonly lead to relapse. The addict returns to using because recovery is too frustrating and difficult. CCT tries to work with the patient's policy belief to minimize frustration. To treat frustration avoidance, CCT first cites the benefits of this response and how it helps. The problem of frustration avoidance is then reframed as a coping skills excess (there is *too much effort* to avoid frustration) or a time-fit error (the tendency to avoid frustration is labeled an old response that is no longer useful for recovery). CCT then tries to readapt and utilize frustration avoidance on behalf of the patient. The addict receives *hedonism training,* which entails learning how to minimize frustration as much as possible. This entails learning how to tolerate short-term pain for long-term gain. A number of skills are taught to facilitate *long-term hedonism,* such as discomfort tolerance, value clarification (to identify the most important goals), and end-means thinking (see chapter 9), to form the steps leading to the long-term goal. Other skills are taught (anger management training) to cope with immediate problems causing frustration. Thus, the strategy that leads to relapse (frustration avoidance) serves as a bridge to recovery, a means to avoid relapse.

□ Problems Correcting Deep-Level Structures

There are patients who proceed through cognitive restructuring and agree that their thinking is incorrect, irrational, and unrealistic. Certaintistic and absolutistic thinking is challenged, and the patient admits that his/her thinking is self-injurious and needs to change. Yet bad feelings persist or resurface at a later point in time. Disputing only produces an intellectual but not an emotional recognition of the problem. Deep-level structures—schemas and basic assumptions—continue to exert an unconscious influence. Emotionally, this type of patient continues to believe, deep down, in his/her irrational, unrealistic thinking.

These are patients who suffer from *positional slippage,* a term coined by CCT to describe the process of slipping back into old ways of thinking after the therapist, friends, or family demonstrate that their beliefs are erroneous or harmful. This problem is common among those with personality disorders, whose lives are shaped so strongly by overlearned belief sets. The answer of cognitive restructuring is to assign more homework and dispute more vigorously, in the hope that there will be a rejection of old, deeply ingrained thinking. Old ways of thinking often return, though, once the patient is away from therapy or when a crisis occurs and retriggers conditioned beliefs.

To help this type of patient, there is often a need for greater flexibility than is present in cognitive restructuring technique. For instance, there is a need to embrace experiential, expressive-emotive techniques. These techniques can work with the patient's feelings, the level that supports the irrational, unrealistic thoughts. This is the level that is having the most trouble changing allegiance to an old way of thinking. While rational emotive behavior therapy (Ellis & MacLaren, 1998) has made changes in itself in recent years, it still only recommends a limited number of experiential techniques that appeal more to the intellect than the emotions (e.g., forceful coping statements, forceful taped disputing). Self-instruction training (Meichenbaum, 1977) and cognitive therapy use very few experiential techniques.

CCT, however, spends considerable time helping patients deepen their experience that is an outcome of deep-level structures. The intent is to experience the effect of those structures, so they become more vivid. The therapist wants the patient to feel what it is like to have that schema about oneself.

CCT works with deep-level structures in other ways. One, it can install coping skills that neutralize their injurious effects so they become less problematic. Chapter 8 gives an example of how a patient's schema and policy beliefs are preserved but their effect becomes benign once new coping skills are inculcated. A second approach is to indirectly change deep-level structures by installing coping skills that alter the beliefs over time. Chapter 7 provides an example of this, where the therapist successfully changes the patient's schema by developing coping skills that indirectly change the schema. A third approach is to reexperience the original situation in the past, where the deep-level structure was introjected (swallowed whole without analyzing it). Recalling incidents in the past and describing them in the first person as if they were presently happening facilitates this. CCT will also use the empty chair technique from Gestalt therapy (Polster & Polster, 1973), where the patient talks to a part-of-self that still subscribes to dysfunctional childhood coping skills and old ways of thinking. A dialogue is waged between the parts-of-self that are for and against changing archaic coping responses. This arouses emotion that can challenge allegiance to long-held attitudes.

☐ Problem with Patients in Painful Circumstances

There are many patients who are distressed because they are in situations where there are concrete dangers, difficulties, handicaps, or ill health. The cause of their pain is not imagined but real; their situation would be troublesome to nearly anyone. They have to face residual damage, limitations, penalties, or losses.

Cognitive restructuring can benefit this patient in certain ways. If the patient incorrectly evaluates the situation in an extreme, severe way, then the judgment can be restructured to be more realistic. If the patient imposes demands on the situation to be a certain way, then training in anti-imperative thinking is helpful. If the patient has "I-can't-stand-it-itis" (Dryden & Ellis, 1988), then disputing this position is most helpful. In essence, if the patient makes an already bad situation worse by irrational, unrealistic, maladaptive thinking, then cognitive restructuring can alleviate some of the pain. It can help people face a basically negative circumstance. This is a modulating strategy, one that aims to dial down the degree of pain.

However, the fact is that the situation will remain painful. True, cognitive restructuring can make negative feelings more bearable and less intense, but the situation will still be painful. If forced to live in an ungiving, abusive, nonsupportive, neglectful environment, the person is left with some degree of negative feeling. The person will still have a limiting, depriving, and painful condition. With this type of problem, cognitive restructuring has limited benefit. If the patient's thinking is not worsening an already negative situation, then cognitive restructuring has little to offer.

CCT provides benefit to this type of patient. It can provide the patient who is in objective pain with coping responses to make the painful situation livable. The focus is on increasing competence. Once the patient is more competent, bad situations become less painful. For example, patients with a chronic, incurable, degenerative physical disease can learn how to live a more palatable existence by learning such skills as *diversion training, optimism training, frustration-tolerance training, acceptance training, and savoring* (see chapter 9 for details.) For example, single parents trying to cope learn how to manage their objectively difficult lifestyle by learning such skills as *limit setting, time management, and hedonism training* (see chapter 8). The coping skills model cannot change the reason for a painful situation (e.g., a chronic illness, marital separation), but it can make the situation less onerous and burdensome.

☐ Problems with the Needy or Entitled Patient

One of the basic conflicts in cognitive-behavior therapy is *the struggle between realism and adaptiveness*. Should the therapist emphasize changing unrealistic thinking that causes problems, or improve adaptiveness to the problem that unrealistic thinking created in the first place?

This conflict becomes clear in the treatment of overly needy or entitled patients. Both present with strong needs to be satisfied and a strong drive to realize them. Both engage in absolutistic thinking: that their needs must be met. When their needs are not met, they have a tendency to awfulize, rating the situation as terrible because they did not get what they want. A traditional cognitive restructuring approach is to dispute the absolutistic thinking that satisfying unmet needs is a must, substituting the idea that it is merely preferable. Effort is made to correct the irrational evaluative judgment by declaring that unmet needs are not awful, just undesirable. The unmet need is then compared to other situations that are truly awful (e.g., murder, rape) to show the patient that his/her thinking is unrealistic.

What often follows is a struggle between cognitive restructurists and the needy or entitled patient, who feel discounted by the therapist for not "understanding the importance of my needs." A tug-of-war erupts over quantity: how big is the need? The patient declares it is "really big" and the therapist says that it is not that big. What does cognitive restructuring then do if its viewpoint is rejected? A common approach in RET is to confront the needy or entitled patient and call him/her a "big baby." This obviously is not music to the ears of the needy or entitled, and it breaks rapport.

The overly needy or entitled patient present as the "true believer," the patient who has faith in his/her certaintistic thinking and asserts that his/her thinking is correct. In the case of the needy or entitled, they believe deep down that having particular unmet needs is truly awful and must be resolved by satisfying the need.

CCT takes the patient in a different direction than cognitive restructuring and avoids many of the pitfalls the latter encounters. First, it relabels entitlement thinking and persistence to get what is wanted as a coping skill. Strong efforts to get what is wanted are then applauded. This tactic maintains rapport.

Different strategies are then pursued. One strategy focuses on helping patients realize their needs, which is what they wanted in the first place. A coping skills approach teaches the patient how to get their needs met. Present tactics to attain needs are examined to assess if they are counterproductive. A second strategy focuses on how to respond if needs are not met. This involves *acceptance training,* to come to terms with the fact that the need will not be satisfied, and *frustration-tolerance training,* to learn how to bear the disappointment. Avoiding self-pity is also important, so the patient is taught *self-pity rescue* (see chapter 10). *Forgiveness training* (see chapter 7) is taught to mend the bad feelings against the party not satisfying the need.

Hence, the needy and entitled patient learns how to adapt to life when needs are not met or how to become more potent in the quest for goal attainment. CCT believes that teaching the needy or entitled how to think realistically offers benefit but has limited returns. Instead, *teaching adaptiveness offers more possibilities* because it helps the patient function in a more efficacious way. At that point, the pain from unmet needs (created by unrealistic thinking) does not hurt as much.

☐ Problems with Emotionally Oriented Patients

There is a large group of patients who can be called noncognitive by choice and nature. They are expressive-emotive by nature—much closer to their emotions than to their intellect. Their first response is to feel rather than to think or problem-solve. They like to discuss feelings and emotional response to situations. Cognition is reserved for understanding the causes of problems. Less time is spent on problem solving. This does not mean this type of patient is deficient in intellectual ability. When need be, they may be quite adept at problem solving and planning strategies. However, analyzing cognition is unappealing to them. If forced to engage in cognitive restructuring, they can do it (and may even do it well), but they do not enjoy it. While they can actually benefit greatly from cognitive restructuring, they often reject it, because the focus is not on feeling but on thinking, which is not their milieu. In this case, the difficulty with cognitive restructuring is more one of "product appeal." Because of this, the emotionally oriented patient often shuns cognitive restructuring, instead seeking out the feeling-oriented therapist, who spends considerable time identifying and processing emotional experiences ("So how did you feel when he did that, and what did you feel after that?"). This type of therapist supports and gives voice to the patient's feelings much more than a cognitive restructurist.

However, a coping skills approach can be appealing to the emotionally oriented patient. First, their intense, negative emotions are labeled as a coping skill and are not seen as pathological as in cognitive restructuring. This will make the feeling-oriented person feel accepted. Second, CCT does not discourage or sidetrack emotional expression, as in cognitive restructuring. While the focus does shift in time to become didactic, when skills are taught, considerable time is allocated for experiencing past and present situations. Third, CCT helps emotionally oriented patients become more adept in managing prolonged, intense affect by teaching them how to better express, channel, and contain those feelings. Although CCT is still a cerebral approach, it does focus on what is interesting to this type of patient—talking about and working with emotion directly, as compared to cognitive restructuring, which addresses feelings indirectly by focusing on the beliefs that stimulate emotion.

Problems with the Unaware or Nonverbal Patient

There are many patients who lack awareness of their thinking and its central role in influencing total functioning. This significantly restricts the ability of cognitive restructuring to function. The focus must then be placed on developing awareness of cognition. The most common method is by assigning homework that asks the patient to identify beliefs in specific situations. However, there are patients who will have only limited success in identifying their thinking. This will greatly restrict their ability to participate fully in cognitive restructuring. The therapist can overcome this problem partially by deducing the patient's thinking and then informing him/her about what it is. Hypothesis testing can then begin at that point. However, if patients lack awareness ability in general, then they will still not be able to examine and change their thinking after the conclusion of therapy. They will not be able to engage in cognitive restructuring with themselves, so the total treatment benefit is reduced. CCT can avoid this problem to some extent. It has greater ability to raise a patient's overall level of awareness, because it teaches awareness skills from Gestalt therapy (Polster & Polster, 1973), which is a most adept model for increasing patient awareness.

There is another type of patient who cannot verbalize his/her experience. They lack ability to articulate their experience. Examples of this type of patient include children and adolescents, or patients with a lower intelligence quotient. This type of patient is a challenge for *all* mental health approaches, because talk therapy requires talk.

Either problem—lack of awareness or poor verbal ability—does not mean cognitive restructuring cannot help this type of patient. However, both problems do limit the total benefit of this model.

The unaware or nonverbal patient is not as much of a problem in CCT. All that is required of the patient is an ability to identify a goal; the cognitive coping therapist then supplies the means to the end, selecting and designing the subskills necessary to resolve the presenting problem. Because CCT is so concrete and didactic, the patient does not have to be aware of his/her thinking, because the cognitive coping skills therapist will supply the patient with thoughts (new executive beliefs) or train him/her in responses to acquire a skill. Much less verbal ability is required of patients undergoing CCT.

Summary

Several types of patients are examined for whom cognitive restructuring offers only limited benefits. They include patients who are resistant to treatment, insistent on realizing their thinking, relapse-prone, unaware, nonverbal, in a painful life circumstance, or overly needy, or who have a strong sense of entitlement. The ways coping skills therapy can work with these types of patients are discussed. The problem with cognitive restructuring as a growth model is also discussed.

5

CHAPTER

Theory

This chapter presents the underlying theory that forms the basis for CCT. The theoretical influences on CCT are first presented, followed by the theory of pathology. The reasons for disorder are viewed from a coping skills perspective. A theory of health is then presented, citing key variables that facilitate mental health. Finally, CCT's theory of change is discussed to distinguish it from cognitive restructuring theory.

☐ Theoretical Background

The historical, philosophical, and theoretical contributions to CCT are presented in this section. CCT intertwines several theoretical strands from behaviorism, self-regulation theory, existentialism, Gestalt, Ericksonian hypnotherapy, social psychology, and of course, cognitive-oriented therapies.

Methodological behaviorism has contributed the rigor of evaluative research and empirical validation to CCT (Kendall and Hollon, 1979). Behaviorism seeks to witness change, measure it, and validate that it is happening through the senses. Because of this, it prefers observable, measurable goals, self-observation, and overt behavioral change as the end result. However, behaviorism (Homme, 1965) also believes that unobservable "mentalistic" processes, what Cautela (1967) calls covert behavior, can also be measured, evaluated, and reinforced. Self-regulation therapy (Kanfer, 1970, 1971; Goldfried and Merbaum, 1973; Mahoney and Thoresen, 1974), which grew out of behavioral therapy, takes a similar position. Likewise, CCT emphasizes *monitoring* and *evaluating* change in each skill that is learned. Patients regularly observe and measure how successful they are at learning and incorporating new responses.

Behaviorism emphasizes *performance-based therapeutic procedures, such as training and conditioning* to develop behavioral capacity. It stresses *exposure-based treatment,* where the patient confronts what s/he fears or has difficulty managing (Kazdin, 1978; Bandura, 1969a). CCT agrees with behavioral therapy that performance-oriented treatment protocols must be arranged to promote active practicing of coping skills to gain proficiency. Coping skills therapy is based on *training*. After patients have learned a new skill, they are exposed to a feared or troublesome situation to test management ability. CCT has extended behavior therapy's covert conditioning model to include cognitive techniques in training modules. However, CCT does not believe that behavior change alone is sufficient to bring about enduring change. Broadened awareness is also necessary.

Gestalt therapy (Perls et al., 1951; Polster & Polster, 1973) has contributed important variables to CCT practice. Gestalt is an outgrowth of both the existential-humanistic movement and cognitive psychology (Kohler, 1947). *Awareness* is the centerpiece of Gestalt practice and is explicitly assumed to be both necessary and sufficient to bring about change. Treatment is holisitic and the treatment goal is to broaden and deepen awareness on multiple levels—affective, cognitive, and physiological—to the point that the patient can no longer evade who s/he is as an individual. At that point change supposedly occurs automatically. The study of *process*—how one proceeds in the world—receives major attention and is used as a vehicle to broaden self-awareness. Gestalt also believes in practicing new behaviors, which is why it emphasizes *experiments*. While experiments are not designed to be as rigorous or as exacting as a training paradigm, they do offer the opportunity to perform and learn new behaviors, and to expose oneself to the feared, avoided situation. Gestalt therapy has incorporated Gestalt psychology's theory of perception and uses it to guide interventions.

Likewise, CCT also uses this theory of perception to guide its interventions regarding perceptual skills. CCT helps patients to reorganize their perception, to learn how to highlight some objects instead of others to change affect. CCT also emphasizes holistic treatment and seeks to develop skills on multiple levels: cognitive, emotional, and physiological. There is a major focus on awareness. Experimentation is encouraged, especially to test skill development. The technique of process has been incorporated into CCT practice, to identify the patient's present coping skills and ones that need to be added.

While CCT agrees with Gestalt that awareness is a necessary and vital component of treatment, CCT does not believe that it alone is sufficient to bring about change (although for some patients this is certainly the case). CCT believes that for the majority of patients awareness must be coupled with behavior change; hence, it emphasizes training and conditioning as well.

To emphasize one point, cognitive restructuring also focuses on awareness. Ellis's ABC paradigm (1973) directs the therapist to identify the activating event (A), beliefs (B), and the resultant consequences (C). Cognitive restructuring features charting of beliefs and emotions (Beck et al., 1979), which acts to broaden awareness. However, the cognitive level receives much more attention while other levels of response receive only superficial, intellectual consideration. By contrast, CCT is much more awareness-oriented in general, wanting patients to have a broad, detailed, and comprehensive understanding of their total self.

Milton Erickson's work has also influenced CCT. He has proposed the concept of *utilization,* which means utilizing the patient's construction of self, including his/her traits, values, needs, abilities, beliefs, and interests (O'Hanlon, 1987). Erickson has emphasized therapist *flexibility* to accept and use alternative explanations and approaches to resolve the presenting complaint. Lastly, Erickson has developed *paradoxical therapy,* where patients are prescribed symptomatic behaviors in order to change the presenting problem (Haley, 1973).

CCT uses the idea of utilization when designing treatment plans and certainly makes use of the patient's present coping skills whenever possible, including the skills that are part of disorder. CCT agrees with Erickson that therapists must be highly flexible and not dogmatic. Hence, CCT is an eclectic model that varies with the presenting problem. It does not automatically move into cognitive restructuring or coping skills therapy, but uses either selectively, depending on the presenting problem. CCT uses paradox with patients as well, such as prescribing the use of a coping response that is not working to encourage the patient to suspend its use and try something else.

In addition, several theories from social psychology have contributed to CCT practice, including attribution theory, cognitive consistency theory (Heider, 1958; Rosenberg, 1960; Festinger, 1957), incentive theory (Edwards, 1954), and attitude change theory (Bem, 1965). For various types of problems these theories are used in differing ways.

In regard to philosophy, self-regulation therapy, existentialism, and cognitive theory have influenced CCT. Self-regulation therapy maintains that people have the capacity for self-control by setting their own goals and regulating their own interests. CCT too believes in self-regulation, by supplying patients with the tools needed to manage their lives.

Existentialism goes much further than self-regulation therapy and strongly emphasizes the central role of the individual, who is conceived of as having the freedom to choose how s/he wants to be. Based on this belief, it places a primary emphasis on self-actualization, will, decision making, and responsibility (May, 1961). Decision making means taking responsibility for one's being-in-the-world. Existentialism pushes patients toward self-realization and integration to reach their potential. The individual is expected to accept his/her role in shaping his/her own destiny, to decide if s/he prefers health to disorder, rationality to irrationality. CBT in general agrees with the existential perspective and maintains, "The client is the architect of their own misfortunes, and that they therefore have control over their thoughts and actions" (Dobson and Block, 1988, p. 30). How people think creates their disease as well as their cure. Because of this, Ellis (1973) puts cognitive-oriented therapies into the humanistic movement.

This existential-humanistic philosophy is embraced by CCT. It too promotes *self-actualization*. It uses *responsibility* in two different ways. One, the patient is asked to take responsibility for the coping skills they prefer to use and for resisting change. Two, CCT wants patients to be able to respond, and encourages this by developing enhanced coping responses to facilitate freedom. Without adequate skill development, CCT believes, patients will not be free to shape their own destiny. Self-actualization is strongly emphasized, and it is accomplished by broadened skill acquisition.

Last but not least, the cognitivist tradition in mental health certainly exerts an enormous philosophical, theoretical, and practical influence on CCT. CBT is a *mediational model,* maintaining that cognitive events mediate behavioral change. The ability to mediate between stimulus and response is the central value and common denominator in all cognitive-behavioral approaches. In fact, Dobson and Block (1988) say, "Only in instances where cognitive mediation can be demonstrated, and where cognitive mediation is an important component of the treatment plan can the label 'cognitive-behavioral' be applied" (p. 7). Modifying the mediational process becomes the primary focus of treatment.

There are basic assertions that form the core of all cognitive therapies. While behaviorists seek to change behavior as an end result, CBT seeks to change cognition with the presumption that behavior will follow. Cognitivists maintain that people are capable of monitoring and altering their own thoughts and can know about their cognitive processes. Second, cognitive assessment can be done by self-observation and can be measured and charted, as behaviorists have asserted. Third, a cognitive change results in a behavioral and emotional change. There is interdependence between them, with cognition having the most important influence. Finally, cognitive appraisals, interpretations, and assumptions about the stimuli affect the response to the stimuli (Ellis, 1962).

CCT agrees with each of these assertions. It theorizes that people use self-instructions (which CCT calls executive beliefs) to shape responses. Self-instructions mediate between stimulus and response. Kendall and Hollon (1979) position coping skills therapy between behavioral and cognitive therapy. However, because of the focus on executive beliefs, CCT is much closer to the cognitivist tradition than the behavioral tradition.

☐ Rationalism Versus Constructivism

Within the cognitivist tradition, substantial differences have emerged in the past generation. One perspective has been called the realism or rationalism tradition, representing the work of Ellis (1962), Beck (1976), and Meichenbaum (1977), among others. The other viewpoint is termed constructivism, which includes the work of Guidano and Liotti (1983), Guidano (1987), Kelly (1955), Piaget (1970), Mahoney (1988), and others. This section summarizes some of the philosophical, theoretical, and practical differences between them. The CCT position on those issues is then presented. The following discussion is indebted to Mahoney's (1988) analysis of these two branches of CBT.

Function of the Brain

In regard to the function of the brain in therapy, rationalists seek a realistic, rational brain to control and direct emotion and behavior. Their mission is to form accurate, valid mental representations. The treatment task is to make mental representations correspond to reality, so the former reflect the latter. They want to empower the parts of the brain that reason, philosophize, and collect data to come to know reality. There is a dominant concern that a belief be true, rationally defensible, and empirically justified. While this is also important to constructivists, they want patients to use their brain to organize their experience into viable mental representations that are flexible, adaptive, resilient, and aid personal development. The realism of the construct is not as important as its usefulness. The central concern is on the consequences of a belief and what practices the belief supports or suppresses (Neimeyer & Raskin, 2001).

CCT is involved with both functions of the brain. It wants a patient able to embrace reality, and focuses on this when it teaches acceptance and tolerance training. At the same it focuses on the consequences from using a coping skill and how executive beliefs support, guide, and encourage various forms of functioning. When working with mental representations, *the focus can be on either the realism or the viability of a representation, whichever allows the patient to attain his/her goal.* The policy and executive beliefs do not have to be valid representations of reality, but they do have to be practical and aid adaptation. Realism is stressed, such as when the skill of *acceptance* (of reality) is taught, but only if it advances the treatment goals. However, if realism hinders goal attainment, then it is not stressed and other skills receive attention, such as *optimism*, which can ignore or distort reality.

CCT seeks to develop a *pragmatic brain*, one able *to construct instrumental responses* that can lead to goal attainment. It appeals to one of the basic functions of the brain: to plan, design, and formulate means to an end. It wants the brain to review coping responses for how well they can lead to goal attainment, take responsibility for dysfunctional coping, and then construct viable responses by training the brain to execute a desired skill.

Body-Brain Relationship

Pertaining to the body-brain relationship, rationalists believe in cerebral primacy and rational supremacy, meaning intellectual processes direct the organism's response. The intellect is given more weight than affective process and is given more credit for causing and changing disorder and health. Affect and behavior are mostly understood to be postcognitive. Constructivists are more holistic, citing the inseparable link between mind, emotion, and body.

CCT gives primary credit to cognitive functioning in the form of executive beliefs as the driver behind affective, physiological, and behavioral responses. Working with policy, executive, and operational beliefs, *CCT arranges cognition to support, develop, and maintain needed coping skills.* However, CCT also believes that the perceptual process, emotion, physiology, and behavior can influence or affect cognition as well. CCT studies and extensively works with these other aspects of human functioning. CCT gives more credit to the emotions than rationalists do by maintaining that feelings are a primitive form of knowing, similar to Guidano (1987). They are viewed as an intuited ability to rapidly assign meaning to the situation. CCT agrees with Greenberg and Safran (1987), who say, "Emotion can be thought of as an economical signal through which multiple sources of information relevant to survival can be experienced . . . by integrating the evoking stimulus with relevant memories, images, and expressive motor and autonomic behaviors." At the same time, *the intellect ratifies, justifies, and elaborates upon emotional responses to form an inte-*

grated coping response. CCT views coping skills as interdependent, complex constructs with interacting components. For instance, when the problem of brooding is addressed, it is referred to as a cognitive-perceptual-affective structure, where each level interacts with and affects the other. Insistence is viewed as a cognitive-perceptual activity. As a generalization, CCT practitioners are more holistic than rationalists are.

Conceptualization of Problems

Both rationalists and constructivists would argue that problems are a result of how people think. Specifically, in regard to intense negative affect, they would define it as a problem and a manifestation of a disorder resulting from irrational, unrealistic, and maladaptive thinking. Rationalists seek to correct, change, ameliorate, or eliminate intense, negative affect. Problems in general are viewed as bad or aspects of pathology. Constructivists consider intense negative affect not as a problem but as a type of primitive knowing (Guidano, 1987). Constructivists have a "more positive and progressive conceptualization of affective intensity" (Mahoney, 1988, p. 374). When encountered in therapy, the focus is not so much on changing intense affect but on understanding it, such as learning about its origin or what intense feeling means to the individual. Constructivists see problems in general as an opportunity for growth, as troublesome but not necessarily bad or pathological. Problems are considered to be a demand on the current adaptive capacity, as a call for self-actualization and development.

CCT conceptualizes problems as a difficulty in coping (see "Theory of Pathology," below). Agreeing with both rationalists and constructivists, CCT maintains that problems in coping are largely the result of how people think. While policy beliefs can certainly lead to difficulties, the main problem is due to dysfunctional or inappropriate executive beliefs. Changing or contextualizing executive beliefs becomes a dominant focus of therapy.

In regard to intense negative emotion, CCT believes that this form of emotion can be a useful coping skill for goal attainment, depending on the situation. For instance, rationalists would consider rage to be an outcome of irrational thinking, a reflection of pathology, and something to be changed. CCT would not invalidate rage by calling it pathological and would try to preserve it—but only for an appropriate time and place. It would consider rage or any intense negative feeling as a way to meet a need. The only issue is whether or not affective intensity offers the best result.

Certainly CCT wants to manage, minimize, or eliminate the presenting problem. However, it does this as part of a growth perspective, following its existential base. *CCT does not see the patient as having a "pathology" or a problem but rather as having a "crisis in growth."* CCT believes that people get into trouble because their means of management—*their inveterate coping responses—turns out to be dysfunctional and ill suited for goal attainment.* The antidote is growth. In fact, CCT does not like to view any problem as pathological per se, preferring to look at it as a coping response that needs to be recontextualized, restructured, readapted, or supplemented with other skills.

Work with Affect

Rationalists do not explore emotional experiences to any major degree. Once affect is identified, the work of treatment shifts to cognition, which receives the greatest amount of attention. Emotional expression and experiencing during therapy are not encouraged. Patients remain in an intellectual mode while discussing issues. Present-day affective problems receive the most attention. Constructivists encourage emotional expression and experiences are explored in detail, especially the origin or context for the beginning of a belief. Affective problems in earlier times are explored.

The traditional use of coping skills therapy with affect has been to manage or channel feeling. Coping skills are formed to contain and express emotion in such a way that affect becomes nonproblematic. For instance, relaxation techniques are commonly taught to attenuate affective intensity, or assertiveness training is taught to build potent, facilitative communication.

When CCT works with affect, it seeks to be more flexible and takes a broader approach than traditional coping skills therapy. Affect is seen as an indication of need, a sign that a goal has been set or has not been attained. The issue at that point is whether the coping skill can attain the goal. CCT first views affect as an expressive motor behavior and action tendency. The focus is on making affective expression more capable of meeting the patient's needs. CCT may examine affect in early-life situations to reveal the background for why a particular coping skill was developed. CCT may want the patient to reexperience early life scenes to recognize and realize—on an emotional level—why there is such loyalty to a coping response in the present.

Similar to rationalists, a great deal of the work with affect in CCT stays on a cerebral level. There is an analysis and understanding of present affective skills and the executive beliefs that manage and structure the expression of emotion. Building better affective skills is done in a didactic fashion. The process technique (discussed in chapter 6) is used quite often in CCT. It helps the patient operate in the role of a nonemotional observer.

However, CCT is not averse to intensifying the affective level given the treatment task. CCT agrees with Freud (1964) that for certain problems there is a need for catharsis or abreaction. Feelings may have to be expressed with sufficient intensity if the patient is to move on in treatment. In such a case, time is given to allow patients to vent and express their feelings. CCT believes, though, that expression of intense affect is a skill. If this skill is lacking, then the focus shifts to skill development. The need to mourn is encouraged in treatment, and patients are also shown how to do it effectively. "Experiencing the experience" is a treatment technique used for various purposes. CCT tries to preserve the patient's natural emotional responses, whatever they may be, but also to make them more adept and functional.

Resistance

In regard to resistance, rationalists conceptualize resistance as a motivational deficit, ambivalent about change, or avoidant. It is the result of irrational thinking that needs to be identified and changed. Resistance in general is defined as something that needs to be overcome. Constructivists view resistance more positively, as a self-protective activity to guard against vulnerability and to maintain the integrity of the self.

CCT largely agrees with constructivists in this regard. While *resistance* may be due to irrational thinking, it may also be *a way to cope*. For instance, depression is disengagement, which certainly is a way to cope with the world. Hence, resistance needs to be understood carefully to know why the patient utilizes that method of responding. CCT may deal with resistance as a coping skill used in the wrong context. In that case, an appropriate time and place is found for the resistant response, so its utility is preserved. Sometimes resistance occurs because of a crisis in growth—there is a lack of key coping skills. In such cases, resistance is a way to avoid entering a situation the patient feels unready to manage. In that case, other skills are taught so that resistance does not have to be used. CCT uses the technique of reframing when encountering resistance, saying that the intention behind the resistance is good but how the resistance is practiced is not beneficial.

Relapse and Regression

Rationalists view relapse and regression as a return to irrational thinking, as a failure to maintain rationality. Relapse is seen as something to be avoided and minimized. Constructivists see it more positively, as a limit in current capacity but also as an opportunity for growth.

For CCT, *relapse tells* the therapist that there is a crisis in growth, that *the patient is stunted or stymied in his/her ability to grow and needs to rely on old, dysfunctional responses to manage*. In this regard, *relapse* and regression is a cry for help and an effort to use *dysfunctional means to satisfy a need*. Hence, CCT views relapse in a more positive light, as a return to using a coping response that had benefit in a different time and place, has benefit but is not as useful as other responses, or is a beneficial skill but is used to excess. It would show the patient how to satisfy his/her needs in other ways so relapse is not necessary. CCT would seek to preserve whatever skills are part of regression but supplements them with other abilities. In general, CCT sees relapse positively, as a chance to grow, as patients learn where and how much to employ their abilities.

Role of Insight

Rationalists think of insight into irrational, unrealistic beliefs as both necessary and sufficient to bring about change (although they utilize behavioral techniques to supplement insight). Constructivists also see insight as important and encourage self-exploration. However, they also stress emotional and behavioral work as important for change as well. Expressive-emotive techniques are used extensively (Young, 1999).

CCT also stresses insight as a means to change, especially when dealing with historical coping patterns or time-fit errors (see below). However, influenced by behaviorists and Gestalt, other variables are given more credit as a cause of change, including conditioning, training, performance-based interventions, awareness, and expressive-emotive techniques.

Intervention

In regard to intervention, rationalists are largely ahistorical and symptom focused. The main goal of treatment is the elimination of problems. By and large, rationalists present a form of treatment that is short-term and most appropriate for managed care. Constructivists are more historically focused, focusing on where and how deep cognitive structures develop. There is less emphasis on alleviating symptoms. Hence, the form of treatment advocated by constructivists is generally longer-term.

In this regard, CCT is more similar to rationalists, by being *mostly ahistorical and problem-focused*. It is designed to be a *short-term form of treatment*, so it is compatible with managed care. Yet with some patients, if need be, CCT can take a historical perspective. It will try to understand where long-term coping responses have developed and why they are still influential (see chapter 10). This is most important when working with time-fit errors (see "Theory of Pathology," below).

Guidano (1988) charges that rationalists only work to change surface structures while constructivists seek to change deep cognitive structures as well. Whether this charge is true or not is open to debate. Regardless, *CCT focuses on both surface and deep-level structures* and will work with either as long as they attain treatment goals in the shortest time possible. CCT gives patients new operating beliefs, which are mostly surface structures. In regard to executive beliefs, which operate mostly on a semiconscious level, substantial effort is made to identify them and change them as need be. In regard to policy beliefs, which are primarily unconscious, there is an attempt to change them either directly, by disputing them, or indirectly, by organizing a different response set that will eventually alter their very nature.

Therapeutic Relationship

In regard to the therapeutic relationship, rationalists act very much like a technical instructor and guide patients in how to think rationally and realistically. Constructivists put much more emphasis on establishing a supportive, therapeutic relationship with the patient.

CCT often follows the rationalist lead in this regard by acting as a technical instructor and teacher in how to cope. At other times, the cognitive coping therapist is very much supportive, nurturing, and caring, especially when problems about ineffective coping skills and unmet needs are explored.

In conclusion, CCT shares similarities with both. In regard to theory, it probably is closer to constructivism. In regard to technique and method, it has a closer relationship with rationalists.

□ Theory of Pathology

Having discussed theoretical background, let us now move to study CCT's theory of pathology. Overwhelmingly, the literature on coping skills therapy focuses on one main cause of pathology—a coping skills deficit. Yet there are several other causes of disorder. CCT emphasizes six causes of pathology:

(1) a coping skills deficit,
(2) a coping skills excess,

(3) a contextualization error,
(4) a time-fit error,
(5) a sequencing error, and
(6) an irrational, maladaptive coping skill (IMCS).

We will now examine each of these.

Coping Skills Deficit

A coping skills deficit occurs when there is an absence of a significant skill that is needed to manage in a given situation. There can also be a general skills deficit when someone lacks an ability that is required for most life situations, such as social skills or assertiveness.

Addressing the issue of a coping skills deficit, CCT makes several assumptions about the nature of human beings. *Symptoms of pathology (e.g., poor self-image, anxiety) are a result not of life problems but of an inability to cope with life problems.* Trauma does not cause pathology nearly as much as does an inability to cope with the trauma. The reason childhood conflicts, abuse, or deprivation linger or have long-range effects is not because of the abuse or deprivation itself. It is due to a lack of skill development; the vulnerable child is the skill-deficient child. The abused or traumatized child reaches adulthood ill prepared for what lies ahead. The inadequate personality is the skill-deficient personality.

CCT views life as difficult, distressing, and potentially debilitating—if skill development is inadequate. CCT maintains that most people will endure some form of deprivation, hardship, or trauma during their lifetime. Yet the nonpathological population has sufficient coping skills to minimize the negative effects from virulent circumstance. In comparison, the pathological population lacks skills and as a consequence suffers much more. The reason life is more onerous and taxing for them is because their pool of coping skills is inadequate for the task at hand. Without adequate skill development, they cannot ameliorate or manage the toxic effects of life problems. The pathological population is out of control, literally, because they lack the skills necessary to control the outcome of the situation. Their feeling of inadequacy is real. Their skill level is not adequate to attain their goals. Conversely, *pathology recedes or disappears once people know how to resolve and cope with their own problems.*

A coping skills deficit may occur in different ways. Some coping skills deficits are broad, where patients lack significant abilities in major areas of their life—for example, key social skills may be lacking. In other cases people may have general coping ability but lack a specific subskill or microskill that causes them to struggle across situations. In this case the task is to fill in the links in the coping skills chain. A third problem is when there is adequate skill development in general but deficient skills for a particular context or relationship. Here there is a mismatch between person and place.

Such is the case when rational people enter irrational environments. For example, Jody is a gentle, sensitive, caring person who was effective in most facets of her life until she took a job with a domineering, critical boss who overwhelms her. In this context she lacks the tenacity, push, and aggressiveness to hold her own with him. Her job becomes overwhelming and her self-image is jolted, not because she is inadequate generally but because she is inadequate for a harsh, demanding situation.

Existentialists have paid particular attention to coping skills deficits. They refer to this problem as "not becoming-in-the-world." This is the problem of the truncated self, which is a crisis in self-actualization. The self-actualization process is the continuing effort to overcome a skills deficit.

The cause of a skills deficit can be a lack of learning, poor role models, or an introjection (Polster & Polster, 1973). Introjection is a concept used in both the psychodynamic and Gestalt literature, but the latter uses it to refer to a rule or proscription about how to think, feel, or act that is swallowed whole at an earlier age. (This book will present the Gestalt version of this concept.) Introjections continue to control the individual long after the original context, prohibiting, curtailing, or circumscribing the development of coping skills. CCT will work with introjections similarly to Gestalt, by examining where an introjection is valid and where it is not.

Coping Skills Excess

A coping skills excess occurs when a person has a useful, helpful, appropriate skill but uses it excessively, either across situations or in a particular context. The coping skill becomes that person's general way of handling a life event, an all-purpose solution. This type of problem is more of an error in deployment—the skill is not utilized properly. Action tendencies are a coping skills excess because they are a habitual response for handling an emotion. Paranoia is another example, where a useful solution—suspiciousness—is used to excess. Rages can also be an example. There are situations when going into a rage may be helpful, such as a situation where the issue is grave and someone must emphasize a point strongly to make others take the point seriously. In this case the rage is adaptive, making others listen and change their behavior (although there are better ways to accomplish the goal). However, some people carry ragefulness too far and make it a regular way of expressing anger. They explode indiscriminately when the situation does not warrant it. In such a case their rages are a coping skills excess.

Watlawick and colleagues (1974) would refer to a coping skills excess as "more of the same or when the solution becomes the problem" (p. 31). They maintain that people have the commonsense idea that when they have a perfectly good coping skill but it is not working, doing more of the same thing will gradually fix the problem. For instance, when told it is cold outside, what do people do? Add more layers of clothing until they are warm. Generally, the "more of the same" solution usually involves the opposite of the problem. This is the eternal struggle of "more versus less" (de Shazer, 1985). If kids make too much noise, tell them to be quiet. If that does not work, tell them more loudly until they stop. The way to gain quiet is by making more noise than those who are making the noise.

The "more of the same" solution becomes a problem when it prolongs or exacerbates the original difficulty. The classic example is when the use of punishment causes more harm than good. The cycle goes as follows. An oppositional child is punished but continues to act out. The parent reasons that the punishment is not successful but is still a good approach, so s/he punishes more until the child capitulates and ceases acting negatively. However, many children at this point feel resentful and act out more. The solution—the coping skill of punishment—then becomes the problem.

On an emotional level, a coping skills excess can occur when one feeling becomes the predominant mode of expression for others. This happens when there is difficulty experiencing or expressing one particular emotion but little difficulty experiencing or expressing another emotion. When this happens, the troublesome feeling is experienced or expressed by the preferred emotion. For instance, sadness, frustration, or disappointment may come out as anger, as anger becomes the all-purpose emotion and response pattern for other feelings.

When encountering a coping skills excess in treatment, often there is difficulty persuading the patient to surrender its use. Although the solution has caused countless difficulties, there is fierce loyalty to behavioral solutions. One explanation for this is the phenomenon of intermittent reinforcement (Bandura, 1969a), which is shown to be more reinforcing than a continuous reinforcer. The solution works sometimes but not all the time. The infrequent or intermittent success with a solution more strongly reinforces its use. A second explanation is that the coping skill actually becomes a fundamental aspect of the person's personality. The coping skill embodies the individual and reflects who s/he is. It is an extension of the self. In that case, stopping the use of a coping skill feels like abandoning the basic core of one's being. The person is caught in a bind:

give up a coping skill that is causing problems and feel better, or continue using the skill that is self-destructive but preserves identity.

For example, Nancy is a warm, soft, yielding, loving person. When she had children she acted this way with them, believing that she could influence their behavior by being accommodating, gentle, loving, and giving. With her daughter, this solution worked quite well. However, it did not work with her second child, who was stubborn, defiant, and oppositional. What was Nancy's solution? She continued to do more of the same and stayed gentle, yielding, and giving, hoping that he would eventually receive enough love and comply. With him, the "more of the same" strategy did not work. He could not be loved into submission. Nancy was told to try a new approach, tough love; that involved being firm, setting consistent limits, and withholding rewards until he complied. This was most difficult for her because the new coping response did not mesh with her personality and felt like she was giving up who she was as a person.

Contextualization Error

There are two types of contextualization errors. One type occurs when *the assigned meaning for the situation is not supported by the facts*. A statement is understood and its meaning makes sense only in a given context—the situation or the environment where the statement is made. In this case the situation provides the background or rational for the statement. Someone is "contextually correct" if their meaning or definition of the situation is supported by the facts in the situation. For instance, someone believes the situation is threatening because there is evidence that others are hostile and unfriendly; the meaning matches fact, so there is no error.

A contextualization error occurs when this is not the case. Such is the case when there's a misperception: the person's impression or understanding of the event is incorrect and is not warranted because the facts do not support it. This is true in the case of generalized anxiety disorder, where danger or threats are perceived but none exist (Barlow, 1988). The meaning (the situation is dangerous) is not supported by the facts and does not match the situation. Likewise, depressed patients perceive a situation negatively when the facts do not support the negative appraisal (Beck et al., 1979). These are errors in the processing of information. This type of contextual error is most suited for cognitive restructuring.

The second type of contextualization error happens when the choice of behavior does not match the context. *The coping skill does not match the situation, and the situation does not support the use of that skill. It is inappropriate for that context.* Because of that, utilization of that skill does not make sense.

A contextual error can occur when someone uses a skill across situations as an all-purpose solution for everything. For example, a person is intimidating to anyone who does not give him what he wants. In some contexts, intimidation is useful, but it lacks value when used everywhere, because there are many contexts where other solutions are preferable. A second example is the avoidant personality who generally acts cautiously and guardedly around others. This type of behavior is warranted around strangers or hostile people but not around supportive, caring people who are not a danger. In the latter situation, the coping response does not match the context but is nevertheless used across situations, to excess.

There can be contextualization errors in both meaning and action. An example is the "cardiac cripple," who incapacitates him/herself out of fear of another heart attack. In general, people are supposed to be inactive, worried, and call for help if they perceive signs of a heart attack. However, many cardiac patients often experience physical signs of a heart attack (i.e., angina, tingling) when they are not actually having one. The situation is incorrectly defined as dangerous when the facts do not support that assumption; meaning does not match fact. These patients incorrectly believe that they are on the verge of a heart attack when they are simply having symptoms of heart disease. At this point they maladaptively adopt the coping skills of a heart attack patient. They become acutely alarmed, call for help, and seek hospitalization. They lead inactive lives, curtail most of their physical hobbies and activities, and worry extensively. This type of coping response is not justified given their condition. In essence, the wrong coping skill is used for their situation.

The task of treatment is to evaluate whether or not a habitual response fits the context where it is deployed. CCT refers to this as a *contextual search*. Patients are told not that their skill is objectively bad but that it is used in the wrong setting. A discussion occurs about where it is best to use that skill, so the patient does not discard that ability but uses it in an appropriate context.

In a contextual search, the mission is to match the appropriate skill for a given context. Another type of intervention is to match the best skill for a given context. CCT refers to this as *contextual sorting*, where skills are categorized by viability and utility for a specific situation. Skills are sorted and rank-ordered by which is the best to use in a given situation.

Time-Fit Error

A time-fit error is a particular type of contextual error. There are many coping skills that were appropriate for a certain time in a person's life, such as in childhood or in the military. In the correct age or stage of life the coping skill is realistic and adaptive. The skill made sense and was possibly an efficient way of dealing with that situation. *Problems arise when a skill continues to be used at the wrong point in time.* In that case the skill does not fit, becomes maladaptive, and is nonutilitarian. *A basic error is committed when coping skills are not updated to remain appropriate and timely for the next stage of development.*

For example, William was teased by his peers in grade school. He also lived in an unpleasant environment at home, where there was significant conflict and contention. If he asserted himself with his father, he would be disciplined harshly. To cope as a young boy, William learned how to tune out students and family members. He trained himself to be oblivious to others' words and actions. In turn, this coping skill was reinforced: children left him alone when they realized their teasing had minimal effect. William continued to utilize obliviousness as a life skill in adulthood and was unmindful of his wife's concerns and criticisms, which resulted in marital problems. Is obliviousness a bad coping skill? No—in the right time and context, it can be beneficial. But in the wrong time and place, it can be devastating. William also had another skill developed in childhood. With a harsh, potentially violent father, he became nonassertive or passive. This coping response helped him avoid altercations with a father who could hurt him physically. However, as an adult, assertiveness is much more helpful than passivity. The context for William's life has changed—he is no longer living with a harsh, reactive parent—but he continues to be passive. His skills have not been updated for his present situation.

Jody provides another example of a time-fit error. Her parents were sensitive, caring people who weighed their criticisms carefully when they spoke to other people. Living with them, Jody did not learn how to filter out their comments because they were not verbally abusive. Using her parents as role models, Jody became a sensitive adult who takes people's statements seriously. Her problems began when she took her first job out of college. She works in an atmosphere with a backbiting, gossiping set of coworkers and a boss who is critical, mean-spirited, and insensitive. Jody does not know how to cope. She finds herself continuously becoming upset because she takes everyone's routine, critical comments to heart. At this time in her life, her skill of sensitivity is a handicap. This skill—which is a good one in general—does not fit her working environment. In CCT, Jody's therapist suggests "obliviousness training," to learn the same skills that William naturally learned as a child. Jody needs to become adept at tuning out her coworkers and filtering out her boss' impertinent, disrespectful, inappropriate comments. She needs to match her coping skill to the appropriate context, so she is sensitive only with sensitive people and does not take others' comments so seriously when they are not deliberately meant to harm her.

Generally, time-fit errors are deeply ingrained from past reinforcement or early social learning and are taken for granted as appropriate. Patients are usually not aware that they are even in operation, because they are mostly unconsciously deployed over many years automatically and nonchalantly.

Treatment of time-fit errors in part parallels the work of constructivist therapists. First, the pattern of using the old coping skill has to be identified. The reason for using a response needs to be understood. The patient reviews the original context where the skill was learned, and then decides if s/he wants to preserve it. Sometimes the patient needs to reexperience the feelings s/he had when s/he first developed that skill, and then compare the feelings s/he had in the past to the present to learn if the situations are different. Afterward, there will be "elaboration of alternative models of self . . . such that the deep structures can adopt a more flexible and adaptive articulation" (Guidano, 1988, p. 307).

Sequencing Error

A sequencing error occurs when a viable skill is used in the wrong sequence. There is a problem with the chaining of skills, which results in a life problem. For example, Billy likes to play after school. He puts off doing his homework until late at night, when he is too sleepy to study. Play and studying are both appropriate coping response, but they are deployed in the wrong sequence (study needs to precede play), and that is what causes a problem. Oppositional children immediately dig in their heels and refuse to perform an action before they even know what it will be like. Stubbornness is a useful coping response, but they use it in the wrong sequence. Oppositional children decline an activity before gathering evidence about it. At a later point in time the oppositional child learns about the activity. However, investigation and experiencing of the activity needed to occur before decision making. Disinclination and stubbornness should be deployed in an appropriate sequence, when there is knowledge that an activity will be unpleasant. Anxious people first look for danger before they know something is dangerous. Scanning for threats is appropriate after a threat is identified. Until then, spontaneous involvement with a situation should occur prior to scanning for danger.

Irrational, Maladaptive Coping Skills (IMCS)

An irrational, maladaptive coping skill (IMCS) is a configuration of subskills that by themselves, in the right time and place, may not cause problems, but when put together into a whole or chain of subskills cause significant distress and suffering.

The specific subskills individually may not be harmful and can even be quite useful, but the combination of them becomes virulent; in essence, the whole becomes greater than the sum of its parts.

Before presenting the components of an IMCS, there is a need to first understand the thinking of CCT as compared to traditional cognitive-oriented treatment. Rational emotive therapy (Wessler & Wessler, 1980) makes an explicit assumption that irrational beliefs are composed of at least two of the following three components: (1) awfulizing (an extreme, negative rating), (2) demandingness (a demand that something must occur), and (3) a general tendency to review situations with evaluative judgments. The latter is an intellectual habit—to grade or rate. Problems arise when the rating is severe, extreme, and negative. Also, a problem arises when a person is equated to their rating (reductionistic thinking). RET maintains that combinations of the three lead to pathology.

CCT looks at these three tendencies and does not believe that they individually or in combination are totally to blame for pathology. CCT does believe that they are contributing factors causing distress but asserts that pathology results from a more complex combination of subskills, what CCT terms an irrational, maladaptive coping skill (IMCS). It is the IMCS that awfulizes the patient's situation. When people feel awful, it is not just because of an intellectual rating or demandingness but because of a cognitive-affective-perceptual response. CCT maintains that the RET explanation of pathology (absolutistic thinking and awfulizing) is too simplistic of an explanation.

The subskills of an IMCS will now be described. The reader may wonder if any of them is truly a coping skill. Remember that each can be useful if not used to excess and in the right time and place. Also, a coping skill does not have to be beneficial to receive that designation. It only has to be that person's habitual or general way of attaining a goal or responding to an event.

Tendency for Evaluative Ratings

There is a natural, normal human tendency to evaluate and rate situations as good or bad, right or wrong, helpful or hurtful, and so on. If done correctly, this habit produces minimal distress. Yet this tendency can cause *vulnerability* to disorder if done incorrectly, when the rating is rigid, extreme, severe, or negative, and when evaluating is performed excessively. The result can be pessimism, catastrophic thinking, or a judgmental nature.

Correcting extreme evaluations may involve cognitive restructuring or coping skills therapy. On one hand, extreme, negative evaluations are due to faulty thinking, which can be corrected most readily by hypothesis testing (cognitive restructuring). On the other hand, they can be due to a coping skills deficit—the person may routinely evaluate matters incorrectly, so there is a lack of ability to grade and rate. In that case there is a need for evaluative judgment training (see chapter 8 for discussion).

Insistence

CCT agrees with RET (Dryden and Ellis, 1988) that extreme ratings can cause an initial, negative feeling that intensifies with the presence of *absolutistic thinking*, which *issues a demand on the object (self or others) that something must or must not occur.* This is the act of insistence, and it is a cognitive-motivational ability: to keep resolutely to a task, to persevere, to be tenacious in thought or action. During insistence, a policy is made, but it is structured as an imperative—something must or should occur. There is often an emotional component to insistence in that the demand is made vehemently. Task completion is overly valued. Ellis (Dryden and Ellis, 1988) refers to insistence as "demandingness" and states that it does not have to cause a disorder but perpetually keeps the individual in jeopardy and increases vulnerability, especially if the issue being insisted upon is irrational, unrealistic, and nonutilitarian. CCT prefers to use the term of insistence instead of demandingness, because the latter does not accurately portray the persistent, fervent nature of the demanding individual as s/he remains resolute and unshakable that something must happen. Demandingness is a pejorative term and does not capture the positive aspects of this potential coping skill.

Agonistic Activity

Insistence becomes much more of a problem when *something is reviewed incessantly, as part of an agonistic self-dialogue that keeps the absolutistic belief alive and pressing* on the individual. The *agonistic activity is a cognitive-motivational construct.* The intention is to make the object take a policy belief seriously and then vigorously work to achieve it. The activity rallies the individual to do something when motivation sags. Arguments are made and reasons are given for why something must occur. No obstacle, limitation, or handicap is allowed to deter goal attainment. If the agonistic activity involves others, then the self persists in a dialogue to get others to attain the goal. Conflict continues with anyone preventing or frustrating that endeavor. Various tactics are used for this purpose, including pleas, persuasion, demands, pressure, self-pity, exhortation, reasoning, encouragement, or confrontation. *The agonistic activity is what largely contributes to the driven nature of the individual.*

The agnostic activity is not the same as obsessing, which is intrusive, excessive thinking about something. The agonistic activity can involve obsessing but it can also be a reflective, chosen activity.

The exact self-dialogue varies with the belief. In someone with an achievement orientation, the person combats with the self to remain loyal to the absolutistic belief that competence must be obtained or that error should not occur. The enemy is the imperfect self who is not diligent enough, careful enough, or competent enough. The self-instruction is to motivate the self to always do better.

In the policy belief "Life should be fair," the argument rages against a higher power (fate, God, fortune, more powerful other). The demand for fairness is not a mere assertion but an ongoing contest similar to a courtroom drama where the self repeatedly addresses the jury in fantasy. The accused is the higher power, who is criticized without mercy on the witness stand. Of course, the self is also the jury and finds the higher power guilty as charged—as being unfair, which is not allowed under the rules.

Consider the policy belief, "Life should not be frustrating and I should not have to endure discomfort." In this case the agonistic activity works to diminish anything that causes discomfort. Self-arguments are prepared to persuade the self to avoid the unpleasant situation. For example, recovery from drug addiction is certainly frustrating, so it is mentally impugned and discredited repeatedly to facilitate relapse without guilt.

Extreme ratings, insistence, and the agonistic activity certainly do cause intense negative feelings, but they do not have to result in severe distress, nor pathology. People can still avoid disorder if they have an ability to "drop it and move on." That is, they are able to redirect thinking and get involved in other pursuits. However, this does not occur if "squelching" is present.

Squelching

This is a cognitive-perceptual-physiological activity that operates in tandem with the agonistic activity. On a cognitive level, there is a refusal to entertain another way of thinking or another course of action. The present policy belief is reaffirmed and loyalty to it is demanded. *Alternative policy and executive beliefs are suppressed or repressed.* The individual refuses to adapt to data that argue for an alternative coping responses. On a perceptual level, the self ignores other images in the perceptual field. This keeps the demand on the object alive in the foreground, thus preserving figure-ground constancy. On a physical level, a simultaneous action occurs in the neuromuscular system. Muscles tighten as thoughts or intentions arise that are contrary to the policy belief. The muscular activity suppresses any physical inclination to take another course of action. For example, a husband is cold to his wife after an argument. His policy is revenge: make her feel bad for hurting his feelings. When she tries to make-up, he tightens muscles in his face and throat to hold back words that could facilitate reconciliation. He tightens his arms to prevent touching her. Squelching is similar to Gestalt's concept of a retroflection (Polster & Polster, 1973). When people adhere to or swallow imperative beliefs (introjections), they are literally gripped by their belief as muscles tighten to prevent another way of being. They stay frozen as long as the standoff continues between the part-of-self wanting to act differently and the part-of-self loyal to the introjection.

Brooding

Once a person insists that something happen (or not happen) and evaluates the situation as awful, this encourages *brooding* about what has (or has not) occurred. Brooding makes any violation of the absolutistic belief harder to tolerate and *adds emotion to the agonistic argument*. It *supplies emotion to the intellectual rating of "awful,"* so someone not only thinks something is awful but feels that way as well. This is a *cognitive-perceptual-emotional activity*. Cognitively, the individual ponders something in a serious, somber way. The loss or presence of something is considered grave. The focus of thinking is narrow as problems are dwelled upon and reviewed incessantly. Brooding replays the agonistic argument but with intensified feeling (e.g., "I shouldn't have made that mistake. Why? Why did I do it?"). The brooder mentally or verbally expatiates about the issue in great detail, preserving figure-ground constancy. Emotionally, the person frets, feels agitated, anxious, or resentful, and has a dismal, gloomy mood that can easily turn into sulking, self-pity, or sullen behavior.

Castigation

The final variable that contributes to pathology is castigation. This is predominately a *cognitive-emotional activity, but it has perceptual and motivational aspects*. Brooding usually precedes and accompanies castigation. Once there is preoccupation (figure-ground constancy) with a problem or shortcoming, the narrow focus on disappointment results in or encourages castigation, disparagement, and/or revenge seeking. (The tendency for brooding and castigation is not caused just by cognition. People can have a genetic predisposition to brood and become preoccupied with matters [attention narrowing], and these activities do encourage or stimulate revenge seeking.)

Cognitively, the person attributes blame to an object or thing. However, the blaming is done not in a platonic, benign manner but in a hostile, angry fashion. The person criticizes and damns the self, others, a higher power, or an institution. If blame is attributed to oneself, the self-dialogue is self-punitive. The person punishes him/herself for a supposed misdeed with scathing self-denigration. The attitude toward self stays disrespectful and derogatory. If others are blamed, then the person may punish someone else in fantasy with excoriating self-dialogue, or punish them outright with revengeful behavior. The revengeful behavior can also include passive-aggressive behavior.

Emotionally, self-castigation results in psychological pain. Because the self-castigation is a repetitive activity, normal activities are interfered with or responsibilities are undertaken but with agony from self-punitive thinking. Pleasure is derived from hurting oneself for being such a disappointment, for not delivering what should have occurred. If the castigation is directed toward another person, then there is a feeling of glee as the hated object suffers.

How is castigation a coping response? It is a way to handle anger by siphoning off the frustration and helplessness that occur when someone does not get what is wanted. The frustration does not simmer inside but has an outlet. Bringing pain to the object soothes the disappointment. Hurting oneself or others feels good in a perverse way. Self-castigation splits the person into two parts. One part hates and punishes oneself (the aggressor part-of-self), while another part experiences the hatred and feels tortured (the victim part).

In summary, an IMCS follows this flow of events:

1. The situation is perceived.
2. It is given an extreme degree of importance (an incorrect evaluation), so if something does not occur, the consequences are evaluated as awful or terrible.
3. The person insists that an action must occur.
4. Arguments are made to continue the insisted-upon activity (the agonistic activity). These arguments fuel further insistence that action occur or not occur.
5. Simultaneously, alternative policies, ideas, and actions are squelched. Emotional inclination to pursue another course is squelched.
6. If the mandated goal is not obtained, the person broods. This results in a feeling of bitterness and remorse.
7. The person castigates him/herself or others for not attaining the demanded goal.

Subskills of an IMCS: Alone and in Combination

If we view *each of the subskills of the IMCS individually, any one of them can be beneficial in an appropriate context or with another positive coping skill.* In general, CCT maintains that almost any given behavior can be useful if we find the adaptive, helpful components of a behavior and combine it with other skills.

Consider self-castigation, which on the surface appears to be a nonproductive, harmful behavior. By itself, though, it can have benefit if used in a measured, prudent manner and in the right situation (although there are probably other, nonpunitive ways to get the same result). A self-attack can drive a procrastinating, inactive person to accomplish a desired goal, and in this regard it is motivating; everyone at times needs a good kick in the rear to get going. Self-castigation can also be used to keep oneself in line—to refrain from self-injurious, odious behavior. This is useful for someone who engages in destructive thoughts or actions.

Likewise, other skills of the IMCS have utility. Brooding contains a useful skill—preoccupation—that is needed to remain focused on a task until it is completed. Insistence is a most helpful action for limit setting and taking a stand against something that is unethical or unproductive. Insistence or demandingness is quite motivating and is a major reason for accomplishment, by refusing to not give up or let go of a goal until it is realized. It motivates precise, committed work. People who lack drive to attain a desired goal need the agonistic activity, because it summons various arguments to push oneself or others to do what is needed. Even an extreme rating such as "awful" can have a motivating capacity. Which sounds more motivating: "It is awful if this happens, and we must do something about it" or "It will be more desirable if this happens, so let's try to change things"? Squelching maintains resolution to accomplish a goal by crushing impulses to do anything else. It keeps people on task.

None of the subskills of the IMCS, when used alone, have to result in pathology. RET (Wessler & Wessler, 1980) maintains that awfulizing is egregious and pejorative. CCT believes that the extreme negative rating of "awful" by itself does not have to result in intense negative feelings. It can remain just an idle intellectual exercise. There are countless people who use extreme ratings in their speech but do not brood and castigate themselves or others when something does not turnout their way. When disappointed, they experience only minimal distress, if any. *If the other subskills of the IMCS are not added to the mix, then the label of "awful" is nontoxic.* It is the *interaction and combination of the above subskills of the IMCS that really result in pathology,* turning the label of "awful" into a feeling of awfulness. *Any given subskill of the IMCS may cause some degree of distress for short periods of time, but distress does not have to result in disorder and impairment in role functioning.* Pain becomes long-lasting and intense only when some or all the subskills of the IMCS are combined.

For example, a women evaluates her ex-husband's behavior as awful and believes that he must absolutely not act the way he does toward her. Thinking this way, she will feel distressed, at times even severely distressed. But if she allows herself to be diverted into other activities, does not brood about his behavior, and does not engage in agonistic arguments about him "not having any right to act the way he does," then the distressed feeling will subside over time. Due to the absolutistic thinking and extreme labeling, she will still be vulnerable to further distress, but again, the distress does not have to result in pathology.

The nonclinical, nonpathological population also utilizes some of the subskills of the IMCS at various times to manage their feelings or to cope with their problems. For instance, they too get down on themselves for a while (self-castigation) or brood momentarily, but the self-hurting diminishes after a while because they do not engage in *sustained* brooding, insistence, self-castigation, and agonistic activity. They too may insist on things occurring in a certain way, but after a while they surrender their demands and move on. The clinical population lacks this flexibility, does not go with the flow, and instead remains fixated on their problems.

Let us now look at some of the subskills in different combinations, similar to a multiple regression equation. Predictions can then be made regarding the consequences of the interaction.

1. *Insistence on something occurring plus agonistic activity without brooding, self-castigation, or no extreme negative evaluations* (*no awfulizing*). No pathology, but there will be mild to moderate stress secondary to goal attainment, because the person is driven to accomplish a demand. The absence of brooding avoids slipping into self-pity and the absence of self-castigation avoids self-torment while the agonistic activity is occurring.
2. *Severe negative rating placed on person or event without brooding, self-castigation, or agonistic argument; insistence on something happening dissipates over time.* Mild distress or no distress. Dwindling insistence and lack of squelching allows person to move on to other matters.
3. *Severe, negative rating placed on person or event plus insistence that something happen, without brooding, self-castigation, or agonistic argument.* Mild to severe distress that can recur at times but is generally short-lived. Due to absence of brooding and self-castigation, person will not feel so tormented.
4. *Insistence plus agonistic action plus preoccupation with not attaining a goal and brooding; absence of castigation and extreme negative rating.* Distress can build but will probably stay at a moderate level; pathology unlikely. The most likely scenario includes tension and agitation, but the person will not feel like a failure because of absence of self-castigation and negative rating.

5. *Insistence plus brooding, self-castigation, extreme negative self-rating, and squelching.* Severe, longer-lasting pathology.

Theory of Health

For CCT, mental health depends on having the capacity to solve life problems and accomplish goals. This requires a broad skills armamentarium to cope with the range of daily difficulties human beings have to address. All day, every day, there is a need to deploy a number of life skills to address routine irritants (Egan and Cowan, 1979). Skills insulate people from stress and trauma and lead to a sense of self-efficacy (Bandura, 1977) and perceived control, which increases self-esteem. Negative stimuli are believed to be less aversive when sufficient skills are present (Geer et al., 1970). There is less anxiety overall when there is a perception of control (Phares, 1969). Coping skills therapists do not believe human growth is limited genetically; people can become who they want to be if they know and practice the technology for change. CCT basically holds a very optimistic view of human nature.

Healthy people use the skills they already possess at the right time and place. They can accurately gauge when a potent skill from one context is not appropriate in another context. They know when it is time to learn new skills to adapt to a new situation. They update past skills and discontinue using old ones when they are no longer warranted or efficacious. They have learned how to use a skill in an appropriate amount and not to excess. They know what skills need to be mixed and matched in a certain sequence. Finally, they are able to judge when a solution is causing part of the problem. They are able to be objective and judge themselves dispassionately and fairly when they decide that a favored approach has become part of the problem.

In summary, the cognitive coping therapist has several questions that need to be answered as treatment proceeds:

- Which subskills need to be included in the coping skills chain?
- What subskills need to be deleted from that chain?
- What coping skills need to be shifted to other contexts?
- What skills need to be updated to be applicable to the present?
- What skills need to be altered by taking the useful parts of them and then combining them with other skills?
- When is cognitive restructuring mandatory to facilitate a change in coping skills?

In the previous section, components of an irrational, maladaptive coping skill are discussed. Conversely, what is a healthy way of responding, especially when disappointed with the consequences of a situation? Below is a list of skills that CCT believes is important for achieving mental health. Together, they comprise a rational, adaptive coping response.

Acceptance

This is an ability to live with something considered less than ideal. It is an ability to define one's limits as a human being and live within them. It is an ability to set realistic goals. Acceptance requires forgiveness—an ability to pardon oneself, others, higher powers, or institutions for not delivering what is expected. Acceptance allows people to adjust to reality and admit reality into one's life, even if it is undesirable or disappointing. It stops absolutistic thinking and insistence that something or someone must be different. It is the antidote for what Ellis (Dryden and Ellis, 1988) calls "I-can't-stand-it-itis." It stops the agonistic arguments and the endless motivational tactics to change something when it cannot be changed. An accepting person comes to terms with not getting what is wanted, making mistakes, not receiving fair treatment, losing a coveted relationship, or not gaining approval from a significant other.

Tolerance

This is an ability to withstand or bear something that is less than ideal. It is an ability to tolerate what is beyond one's control, what the individual cannot affect or change. Tolerance means enduring, but without consternation or self-pity. There is patience with painful circumstances and the ability to persevere in them—for however long they are painful. Tolerance allows someone to continue the "good fight" and not surrender when such a strategy is chosen. There are several types of tolerances: disapproval tolerance, helplessness tolerance, discomfort tolerance, and failure tolerance.

Self-assurance

People can acquire a skill in something through training, increasing their overall level of ability, and yet lack self-confidence. They still may not believe that they can affect the consequences of the situation, what

Bandura (1977) calls self-efficacy. Something else is needed: to know that one knows something, that a given level of proficiency has been attained (Mahoney, 1974). That special knowledge is self-assurance. It accompanies self-efficacy. In part, it is a cognition, where someone believes that sufficient skills have been developed or are present. Identity is then extended and self-image is formulated. Self-assurance leads to a feeling of security and peace-of-mind. A lack of self-assurance can lead to a state of learned helplessness (Seligman, 1975). To acquire self-assurance, self-monitoring and self-evaluation are needed in order to gather data that an ability is being developed and confirmation that this is so.

Mourning

Coming to terms with life often necessitates mourning. Anything that is considered important or vital but is not attained will lead to a feeling of loss. Mourning a loss is important for recovery. While mourning is a natural response, it does require skill in several regards. First, there is an ability to feel the sadness and experience it without becoming overwhelmed by it. There is an ability to use the intellect while grieving to gain an objective understanding of the loss. There is an ability to mourn the loss and still become engaged in other areas of life. This is compared to people who are not able to feel emotion in general or cannot feel intense emotion in particular, or they feel intense emotion but to such an extent that they become incapacitated by it. When faced with a loss, they become preoccupied with it or avoid their emotions altogether. They may not be able to express their sadness to others or cannot terminate grieving because they cannot find resolution for their pain.

Use of Descriptive Judgments and Accurate Value Judgments

In general, CCT agrees with RET (Wessler & Wessler, 1980) that it is better to avoid evaluative thinking and the continuous rating of self or others. Sensory-based descriptive judgments are preferable to evaluative judgments to understand and improve most situations. The former do not criticize or castigate anyone, but merely describe the situation or what could be different. They produce substantial information that is useful for *problem solving*. Oppositely, evaluative judgments yield little information beyond the rating, while arousing negative feeling without producing a solution.

If evaluative judgments have to be made, they need to be accurate. A healthy person is objective when he/she can fairly compare gradations of badness according to rational, reasonable criteria. When extreme ratings are given, they are reserved for only a very limited set of situations (e.g., murders, holocausts). Further, a healthy response resists reductionistic thinking that can develop out of a rating (I equal my mistake).

Perceptual Shifting

Perceptual ability is an ability to shift attention to other matters and other goals when appropriate. This allows the individual to compartmentalize, which is an ability to mentally put aside a disappointing situation and to refocus on other pressing matters. This stops the preoccupation with the problem, which is at the heart of brooding and obsessing. Perceptual shifting stops the agonistic activity and the berating and condemning of self or others. Focusing on something else short-circuits the endless negative self-dialogue. This is a cognitive-perceptual ability. A decision is first made to shift attention elsewhere, and then perceptual skill is needed to ignore certain images and instead focus on value-neutral or positive images.

Problem Solving

A healthy person has good problem-solving ability. This means s/he is able to avoid taking action impulsively and instead engages in alternative-solution and means-end thinking. S/he is able to entertain several options, decide if any of them have harmful consequences, and then pick the best one(s) for a plan.

Self-Support

Finally, healthy people are able to motivate themselves or others in supportive, encouraging ways. Using self-support, they are aware of their positive attributes and take pride in their accomplishments (see chapter 7 for fuller discussion).

Let us now examine some combinations of irrational and rational coping skills:

1. Insistence (demandingness) plus awfulizing, plus tolerance of negative situation, followed by acceptance and gradual ability for perceptual shifting: episodes of distress but no enduring pathology; and
2. Insistence plus awfulizing, plus brooding, plus self-castigation, fol-

lowed by acceptance: frequent distress that can develop into pathology that will recede over time.

Theory of Change

Explaining change is a very complex proposition. No single variable can usually explain or predict it. Because of this, a theory of change needs to operate similarly to multiple regression, where several variables are selected to determine how much each is able to explain and predict a given result. This section presents CCT's beliefs about the relative efficacy of the components of cognitive-behavioral treatment. It compares cognitive restructuring to coping skills therapy in order to answer the question of how much of a patient's distress can be reduced by cognitive restructuring or coping skills therapy. More specifically, to what extent do irrational, unrealistic thinking or coping skills problems explain and predict pathology?

1. *Pathology is more a result of how people cope than of a problem in how people think.* More of the patient's pathology is a result of an irrational, maladaptive coping skill, errors in skill deployment (a contextual or time-fit error), a skills excess, or a skills deficiency, rather than irrational, unrealistic thinking. CCT is not arguing that the latter is inconsequential. Certainly, if a person thinks in a dysfunctional way, s/he will have problems. However, CCT maintains that more of the pathology and a greater degree of suffering can be explained by problems with the coping response. Dysfunctional schemas and absolutistic thinking do cause a person to become vulnerable in times of crises or over the course of his/her life. However, how people cope as a result of a schema or how they respond to their absolutistic thinking is the more serious problem.

CCT does concede that a great deal of work in cognitive restructuring focuses on the subskills of the IMCS. This is why, according to CCT, cognitive restructuring is successful. It stops self-castigation, brooding, squelching, and the agonistic activity, which in total prolong and intensify the damage from absolutistic thinking and awfulizing. However, cognitive restructuring is only one way to alter the problematic components of the IMCS. A skills orientation is another way. By altering the set of coping skills one way or another, patient thinking can change as well.

2. *Changing the executive beliefs will lead to more benefit than changing the policy beliefs.* Certainly, changing an irrational, unrealistic, maladaptive policy belief is helpful. However, how a person plays out a policy is what causes most of the problem. For instance, there is a policy to not make mistakes. The executive beliefs may either handle mistakes benignly and

forgive or crucify the individual when a mistake occurs. *Executive beliefs detail the response to the policy infraction.* The executive beliefs contain *the self-instructions for how to play out a policy,* or how to respond specifically. They influence the exact content of thinking (the operating beliefs). Because of that, CCT maintains that there is *more* benefit in focusing on and correcting executive beliefs. Also, a change in executive beliefs can also correct the policy belief, while still providing the patient skill development.

In addition, many patients are unwilling to change their policy beliefs and prefer to preserve their absolutistic thinking. In fact, a case can be made that in today's economy, corporate values encourage irrational thinking. Employees do drive themselves to gain approval from significant others in the workplace (e.g., boss, team members) because bureaucracies in industry and government make advancement intricately connected to positive ratings. Employees do make advancement and excellence absolutely important, because this is the predominant ethic and is demanded in the business world. In 1937, Karen Horney wrote *The Neurotic Personality of Our Time,* saying that "normal" is actually neurotic. Her comments are still quite appropriate today.

At issue is how a person responds when s/he does not get what s/he wants, when he becomes frustrated. People need to know how to cope when they do not reach their goal, even if it is an irrational, maladaptive goal. People need skills so they are less vulnerable when they choose to think irrationally, so they suffer less from their irrational beliefs. Given the crazy expectations that exist in our culture, isn't it better to equip people with the skills that are necessary to survive in an irrational world? Adaptive, useful executive beliefs provide this.

3. *Change can be produced by altering only components of an irrational maladaptive coping skill, rather than changing the entire skill.* Change the parts of the whole and the whole is changed. Change some of the parts of an IMCS and the disorder changes as well. Change the sequence of skills (rational or irrational) and change can occur as well. As Haley (1987) says, "A therapeutic change can be defined as a change in the repeating acts of a self-regulating system—preferably a change into a system of greater diversity" (p. 112). To CCT, this means broadening how the system copes by adding or rehabilitating presently used skills.

Change does not require a total correction of dysfunctional thinking if other coping responses are in place or if there is an absence of other maladaptive skills. (Chapter 8 makes this point at length in a case study of a depressed perfectionist.) Certainly, an irrational way of thinking makes someone vulnerable to pathology, so changing those thoughts may be useful. However, suffering can be avoided or ameliorated with the right combination of skills added or subtracted from the mix of skills placed in the right sequence. Hence, if a desire escalates into a "must" at some point in the future, teaching the patient a rational, adaptive coping skill can ease the degree and length of distress.

For example, Lisa gets distressed when she receives disapproval. In part, this is because she rates the situation as awful and demands or insists that she receive the approval she covets. Is she doomed to develop a pathology, due to her absolutistic thinking and awfulizing? CCT would argue that Lisa can continue to think that disapproval is awful and demand that she receive it. She will still be upset when approval is not forthcoming, but her distress can be minimized and remain short-term, providing that she does not engage in brooding, self-castigation, or self-agonistic arguments. *The key is limiting other responses that make dysfunctional thinking even more virulent than it has to be.* Further, she can be taught how to be a successful approval seeker by learning some of the subskills of a rational, adaptive coping skill. With those skills, the risk of distress is reduced even more. Those skills for Lisa include:

- *Mourning plus self-support.* "I did not get approval and I feel the loss, but I am still a good person anyway" (self-support).
- *Acceptance.* "That's reality that I did not gain approval and I have to live with it."
- *Perceptual shifting.* "I won't dwell on my disapproval and I'll put my mind on other things in the meantime."
- *Problem solving.* "What can I do to get approval in the future?"

One may ask at this point, "Why not just eliminate the irrational thinking at the root of her problem? That will resolve her difficulties." That may be best for some patients, but there are many patients who elect to fight for approval, or the need for approval is so firmly ingrained that removing it is very difficult. In this case, a skills orientation may be preferable.

4. *What separates the nonpathological population from the pathological population is the absence of an IMCS along with the presence of key coping skills.* Both cognitive restructuring and coping skills therapy make assumptions about the nonclinical, nonpathological population and the clinical, pathological population. CCT believes that the former may also think in an irrational, unrealistic way. CCT theorizes that the nonpathological group also engages in awfulizing, demandingness, and habitually uses evaluative judgments. Yet they are not perpetually upset or intensely distressed for long periods of time. As RET (Dryden and Ellis, 1988) maintains, people can think irrationally and not have significant emotional disturbance.

From the standpoint of CCT, the causes of personal distress and relationship dysfunction are due to the presence of harmful, excessive, or missing skills. CCT strongly agrees with Meichenbaum's claim (1977) that both the clinical and nonclinical populations think irrationally. He maintains that the primary difference is "the coping mechanisms they employ, may be what distinguishes clinical from nonclinical populations . . . it may not be the absence of irrational thoughts per se but rather the set of management techniques employed to cope with such thoughts and feelings that characterizes the nonpatient populations" (p. 191). Meichenbaum too takes the perspective that when a patient alters his/her coping skill repertoire—and not necessarily his/her beliefs—pathology is altered.

Some pathology and change can be predicted and explained by the table below. Irrational thinkers with poor use of coping skills will have the most severe problems. However, *rational people who have skill problems will also have significant difficulties.* Conversely, people who think irrationally or rationally but have rational, adaptive coping skills will have minimal to no pathology, respectively.

	Irrational Thinkers	Rational Thinkers
Irrational, maladaptive coping skill, major skill deficits and excesses	Moderate to severe pathology present (Lower Global Assesment of Functioning)	
Rational, adaptive coping skill, few skill deficits	Mild to no pathology; higher functioning (Higher Global Assessment of Functioning)	

5. *Therapists need to judge on a case-by-case basis if cognitive restructuring or coping skill treatment should be the primary emphasis for a particular patient.* Cognitive restructuring has almost become the automatic way of operating in CBT. This is unfortunate, because that means cognitive-behavioral therapists are approaching cases in a mindless fashion. For instance, there are many practitioners who utilize REBT and automatically zoom in on such variables as absolutistic thinking, awfulizing, and "I-can't-stand-it-itis" with full confidence that this will be the cure-all. From a CCT point of view this is unfortunate, because every case is different, and some patients require more of a skills emphasis than a change in cognition, or vice versa. CCT maintains that cognitive restructuring is a most robust and powerful treatment tool. However, it is not necessarily the best or first choice for all patients. Likewise, CCT may not be the first choice for

some patients; cognitive restructuring, Gestalt, ego-supportive therapy, or something else may be a better option. In essence, CCT does not want to join the long list of treatment approaches saying, "Follow me, I have all the answers." There have been far too many past gurus that have done this to market their approach, and I think it has turned many in the mental health profession into single-minded determinists and true believers who try to fit every patient with the same size coat.

☐ Summary

Cognitive coping therapy combines theory and technique from other treatment approaches, including behavioral therapy, self-regulation therapy, Ericksonian therapy, Gestalt, existentialism, social psychology, and of course cognitive-oriented therapy. CCT shares many common practices with the two major forms of cognitive therapy, rationalism and constructivism. CCT focuses on six basic causes of pathology: (1) coping skills deficits, (2) coping skills excesses, (3) contextualization errors, (4) time-fit errors, (5) sequencing error, and (6) an irrational, maladaptive coping skill. The latter consists of the following: extreme evaluative ratings, insistence, an agonistic activity, squelching, brooding, and castigation. CCT maintains that combinations of these subskills of the IMCS is what causes pathology, not the subskills alone. The theory of health promotes the following subskills: acceptance, tolerance, self-assurance, grieving, descriptive judgments, perceptual shifting, problem solving, and self-support. The theory of change maintains that pathology is not so much the result of people's policy beliefs—even if they are irrational and unrealistic—as it is a result of how they cope. CCT believes that more benefit can be gained from working with the patient's repertoire of coping skills than from working with irrational thinking alone.

6

CHAPTER

Methodology

This chapter will present an overall view of how CCT operates in practice. There are four distinct phases in treatment: (1) an education phase, (2) the identification and utilization of the patient's present coping skills, (3) the teaching of new coping skills, and (4) the practicing of new skills in combination with present skills. The cognitive coping therapist moves back and forth between each of these phases but may focus more on one phase than another, depending on the problem, patient, and situation. Each of these phases is repeated as each new problem is addressed.

☐ Education Phase

In cognitive-behavioral therapy (CBT), there is a deliberate attempt at the beginning of treatment to educate the patient about the concepts and practice theory underlying this approach. The patient is given a conceptual framework in lay terms to understand the causes of their symptoms and pathology. For instance, cognitive restructuring therapies such as RET (Ellis, 1962; Dryden & Ellis, 1988) or Cognitive Therapy (Beck et al., 1979) inform patients that they are having problems because of how they think and that change can be predicted if the content or process of thinking is changed. Key variables of the practice theory (i.e., belief, assumption, hypothesis) are defined. The roles of patient and therapist are explained.

CCT also has an education phase at the beginning of treatment. Several areas are discussed. CCT uses its practice theory to explain symptomatology and disorder as a crisis in coping. Dysfunction is attributed to an absence of key skills, an improper deployment of skills, or the use of an inefficient skill. The philosophy of CCT is presented, that problems are a result not of pathology but of a crisis in growth, and that growth occurs through skill development, either on a personal or systemic level. Key terms used in treatment are defined, such as *coping skill* or *contextualization error*. The roles of patient and therapist in CCT are defined. The former is given the role of student while the latter is given the roles of teacher, coach, and director. The director's job entails a variety of duties: assigning practice skills for various contexts, arranging for record keeping, and orchestrating the blend of old and new skills. *The nature of a coping skills approach* is discussed, with the explanation that it *is structured and prospective in nature*: goals are declared, and coping skills that can attain the goal are identified and practiced until proficiency is reached. The therapist knows the direction of treatment and works to get there. He/she creates a process and steps to reach the end goal. Finally, the patient is informed early in treatment about the conditions for progress. As a training paradigm, CCT stresses that practice is crucial for making and sustaining progress, and the responsibility falls to the patient to practice and utilize necessary skills.

In actuality, an education phase recurs throughout therapy. When introducing each new coping skill, the therapist educates the patient about the role of that skill in their life, its benefit or utility, and the consequences of using it. This is part of the induction that accompanies the introduction to every skill, to increase acceptance of it and motivation to practice it.

☐ Utilization of Present Skills

CCT is a goal-oriented form of treatment. At the beginning of therapy, patients are asked what their goals are. To attain them, the focus immediately shifts to present functioning. While CCT spends considerable time addressing coping skills deficits, it makes a major effort to understand the use of skills that are already in operation. How do they contribute to the presenting problem, and how do they need to be changed? How and where can present skills have use?

Basic Propositions

In CCT, a major part of treatment is to identify how people engineer their lives, and the ways they have chosen to reach their goals. If those ways are counterproductive, CCT does not want to abandon or dismiss present functioning but rather seeks to utilize it somehow on behalf of treatment. With this goal in mind, CCT makes the following propositions:

1. *There is no such thing as a bad coping skill.* At the risk of inviting attack or cross-examination from other approaches, CCT makes the bold assertion that *virtually any response has utility, providing it is used by the appropriate person, in the right amount, and in the appropriate time and place.* For instance, knowing how to be affectively flat and emotionally impassive may not appear to be desirable abilities, but parents of children with oppositional-defiant disorder or conduct disorder can tell you how invaluable these skills are. When correcting their children, overreaction or any negative emotion typically results in a far more onerous, difficult interaction. However, knowing how to delete emotion from the voice results in much smoother contact.

Knowing how to create "vexatious internalizations" seems like a strange coping skill. They are representations of self that can be readily activated about intense, conflict-ridden memories that cause a person to feel remorse and regret (Millon, 1996). When used to excess by guilt-ridden individuals, vexatious internalizations will cause depression and unnecessary suffering. Yet people who are affectively callous need to be trained in how to feel guilt and remorse upon command, to help them deliberately feel bad about their treatment of others. This is necessary for creating a conscience, which is part of the treatment of narcissistic and antisocial personalities. Their therapy involves training them in how to feel anguished and how to summon vexatious internalizations upon demand.

2. *Pathology and symptomatology contain invaluable skills.* The task of CCT is to make use of what the patient brings to treatment. This is a three-part task. First, the cognitive coping therapist has to *extrapolate or tease out the positive skills contained in a pathological response pattern*—to separate the wheat from the chaff. Each pathology has benefit if the helpful aspects of the pathology can be isolated and identified. Therapists too often ignore worthwhile abilities because they are part of a disorder; in essence, they throw out the baby with the bathwater. Two, *skills formed by the pathology need to be "readapted,"* which means altering them *so they have utility*. Finally, *the positive elements of the pathological response need to be combined with new skills* to form potent, appropriate, socially beneficial abilities.

People are quite loyal to their solution set and do not believe that they are contributing to their problem. They focus on the benefits of their responses, which allows them to cope with difficult, noxious, or threatening circumstances. Their response may not be the best of solutions but it does offer help in some way, and the patients know it, consciously or unconsciously. This is why they use these coping responses repeatedly and resist abandoning dysfunctional behavior. Hence, CCT asks, why not *use the skills patients bring to treatment and incorporate them into the treatment plan?*

For example, narcissistic personalities are interpersonally exploitative. While this is not a socially desirable behavior, it does contain entitlement thinking, which has benefit and is most important for becoming independent and assertive. However, problems begin when entitlement thinking is combined with a lack of empathy and imperturbability. In that case there is a lack of concern about others and overconcern about "what is coming to me." Hence, narcissistic patients have to be trained in how to use entitlement thinking so it helps rather than hurts themselves and others.

Any problematic skill by itself can cause problems but in combination with other skills has merit. For example, antisocial and sadistic personalities are affectively callous, and that causes interpersonal problems. However, this coping response is most important for making hard, difficult decisions, and is especially needed by managers. If it could be combined with a sense of priorities, empathy, and compassion, then its deleterious effect is neutralized.

3. *Any skill has value if used in the proper amount.* CCT maintains that *the problem is often not the skill itself but the dose of the skill*—the amount it is used. Any skill loses worth if it is used to excess. For example, problem-solving skills are most helpful, but if a person practices them to excess, he/she becomes ponderous, loses spontaneity, and avoids taking action when needed. Being behaviorally guarded is an ability to scan the situation warily to spot danger or threats to well-being. In the right context this skill is most helpful, especially for sociopaths. For instance, in the context of substance abuse, family members can benefit from being behaviorally guarded with a family member who is addicted, to prevent or inhibit behavior that can cause the addict to overreact, become violent, or abusive. However, when behavioral guardedness is used to excess, it can cause people to become avoidant, tense, anxious, overly controlled, and overly contained.

4. *A thought, action, or physiological response does not have to be maladaptive if it is reshifted and readapted.* If all skills have use, should they be utilized? Not necessarily, because some skills are superior to others for a given situation. Some skills are better for attaining a desired goal with a particular person. Part of *the mission of CCT is to identify and select the best skills for a given situation.* Everything depends on time and place. Situational factors will dictate which skill is best.

In other cases, the skill is not effective only because it is used in the wrong sequence. Changing the sequence may be all that is needed to make the inveterate response benign or even beneficial.

Readapting a skill involves personalizing it. Someone else's skill may not fit or mesh with another's personality, so it must be *adjusted for that individual.* For example, a timid person with a social phobia can utilize some of the ways of an aggressive person, who challenges people's boundaries and compels them to perform a desired action. While this way of acting does not mesh with the social phobic's personality, it can be incorporated if it is readapted, so the desired behaviors are done in a softer, quieter, but firm manner.

5. *Dysfunction is not so much a matter of ineptitude or an inadequate personality as a lack of knowledge, experience, and training and a failure to learn from past mistakes.* CCT maintains that part of the reason for dysfunction and feelings of ineptitude is actually a lack of refinement of skills or trying to make a poor solution adequate. A patient may have a problem because he prematurely judges his abilities before they are practiced enough. He feels inept because of inexperience performing a skill. Reassurance needs to be given that when any new action is performed initially there will be mistakes, but with experience, knowledge, and training there is enhanced precision. Hence, ineptitude is reconceputalized as lack of proper training.

☐ Assessment of Present Skills

Taking the above ideas into consideration, at the beginning of therapy CCT wants to discover the patient's overall abilities, or what behaviors can be converted into skills. There is a need to know about response tendencies and general orientation to situations. To assess this, four methods are utilized: (1) a coping skills inventory, (2) process, (3) a historical analysis, and (4) use of solution-oriented questions.

Coping Skills Inventory

In the first few sessions, the therapist wants to learn how the patient copes at work, at home, in personal life activities, and in relationships. An inquiry is made about how the patient handles situations, conflicts, emergencies, problems, and feelings, and where he/she is successful. The following questionnaire has been designed to give a quick sketch of the patient's response patterns.

Coping Skills Questionnaire

1. When someone hurts my feelings:
   a. I forgive and forget quickly.
   b. I take a while to forgive the person who hurt me.
   c. I carry a grudge for quite a long time.
2. When I get angry with someone:
   a. I keep my feelings to myself.
   b. I communicate how I feel.
   c. I let the other person have it with both barrels.
3. When I feel sad:
   a. I continue to interact with others but keep my feelings to myself.
   b. I withdraw and stay to myself.
   c. I tell other people about how I feel.
4. When I have problems that need to be dealt with:
   a. I only think about them when it's appropriate.
   b. I worry about them.
   c. I become preoccupied with them and cannot get them out of my mind.
5. When I am upset and stressed:
   a. I have a hard time concentrating and maintaining my responsibilities.
   b. I maintain my responsibilities with a lot of effort.
   c. I quickly compose myself and maintain my responsibilities.
6. When I am stressed:
   a. Any little thing can put me over the edge, interfering with my duties.
   b. I do what I am supposed to do but feel upset inside.
   c. Very little changes because I stay calm both inside and outside.
7. When I am disappointed:
   a. I cope with it and move on.
   b. The feeling stays with me for a while.
   c. I get depressed.
8. When I am frustrated:
   a. I get quickly upset.
   b. I stay calm for a while until frustration builds, then I lose it.
   c. I keep my cool and stay calm.

9. I can handle:
   a. Little disappointment.
   b. Moderate amounts of disappointment.
   c. A lot of disappointment.
10. When I do something successfully:
    a. I give myself praise and savor my success.
    b. I don't make a big deal out of it but feel good inside.
    c. I don't notice it very much and move on to other matters.
11. When other people praise me:
    a. I relish the compliment and think about it.
    b. I say thanks and go on to other matters.
    c. I feel awkward because I hate being complimented.
12. When other people criticize me:
    a. I take it to heart and feel very bad.
    b. I ignore it completely and am indifferent.
    c. I consider what they have to say and then make up my own mind about what's right.
13. When I make a mistake:
    a. I think about it for a long time and get upset.
    b. I get upset for a while but move on to what needs to be addressed.
    c. I don't think about it very much.
14. When I have to make a decision:
    a. I am very quick to take action.
    b. I give the problem some thought and then take action.
    c. I take a long time and ponder what to do next.
15. How much stress can you tolerate in general, from 0 to 5? ___
16. How much anger can you tolerate before you blow up, from 0 to 5?________
17. At work, what are your greatest strengths? _________
18. With your family and friends, what are your greatest strengths? _________
19. People have told you that you need to do the following in order to be more successful: ____________

The various items reveal different skills. Item 1 indicates if a person has an ability to forgive quickly. Items 2 and 3 show the person's communication abilities. Item 4 indicates whether the patient has a cognitive termination ability (to stop a recurring thought). Items 5–9 show the stress management capacity of the person. Items 10 and 11 indicate whether the person has a self-enhancement ability. Item 12 indicates if the person has cognitive objectivity or if s/he defines him/herself using another's criteria. Item 13 shows if the person broods. Item 14 indicates if the person has an impulsive style of decision making and needs help with problem solving.

Illuminating Process

One of the primary methods for identifying coping skills is by illuminating process. Process-oriented interventions are extensively used in Gestalt therapy (Zinker, 1977). CCT maintains that it is an excellent method to learn about response patterns. Process describes what is occurring on multiple levels at a given point in time, and includes the coordinated activities of thought (reason and problem solving), emotion and action tendencies, perception (sensory activity), physiology (management of body), and behavior. It can focus predominantly on one level such as cognition, as in the case of cognitive restructuring, or oscillate between levels of being. Process reveals the subtle and imperceptible nuances and vicissitudes of responses. It is interested in how something or someone operates, to learn its general nature. Processing illuminates what leads to a particular state of affairs and what follows afterward. It focuses on how something becomes what it is. It makes static entities into dynamic operations.

Process concerns two areas. One is the mechanism of action that makes something happen—how affect, cognition, or physiological activity influences the response. A second concern is about mechanisms of action that inhibit or prevent a response. This is the counterresponse ("What thoughts keep you from acting?").

The following examples illustrate how to frame process questions. Notice the extensive use of "how" and "what" questions.

Client (C): I am very confused about what to do next.

Therapist (T): How do you confuse yourself? What do you do so you become uncertain?

The question focuses on what the patient does to create confusion, the process leading to uncertainty. The intent is to discover the mechanism for making things uncertain or scrambled.

C: I'm worried that things aren't going to turn out right.

T: What are you doing to scare yourself?

The question responds to the patient's dire conclusion, to discover what he does to scare him/herself. The focus is on the process leading to the pessimistic conclusion.

C: I don't have any confidence in myself.

T: What do you do to lose confidence in yourself?

The question focuses on the process of how the patient diminishes self-confidence. Loss of confidence is discussed as an active process and not a fixed state.

C: I am not an organized person.

T: How do you stay disorganized?

The question indirectly makes a point that disorganization is organized. The question focuses thinking on how it occurs, as if there is a "plan" for becoming disorganized. This posits the idea that disorganization is within one's control.

C: I feel badly about myself.

T: What are you doing to lower your opinion of yourself?

The question is making the point that there are activities leading to negative images of self. The intent is to discover how the person lowers his/her view of him/herself.

C: It has been a good week.

T: What have you done to make it go well?

The question makes the point that success or good feelings do not occur by accident but by specific actions.

Now, let us examine how to use process to discover a person's present coping skills. A portion of an interview involving a spouse abuser is presented. In the interview, the therapist (T) secures information about how the patient responds on multiple levels. This will give information on how the abuser, John (J), copes when challenged or angry.

J: My wife just pushes my buttons and I go off on her.

T: But there are times when you don't "go off on her." What occurs when you don't become violent, when you put the brakes on your urge to hurt her?

The therapist focuses on how John curtails the response to violence—on what skill he uses to contain explosiveness. The therapist explicitly assumes that there is a counterresponse operating at various times, because he is not violent on all occasions, only at select times. After gaining information about this, the therapist returns to the issue of what happens to the counterresponse at the moment of rage eventuating into violence. That is, why doesn't the counterresponse to violence work to control his behavior when conflict arises with his wife?

T: How do you become violent?

J: What do you mean? I just have a hair-trigger temper and she knows it. She just pushes me until I cannot control it anymore.

John, like most spouse abusers, believes that he is controlled by a demon force—his wild temper—that resides inside himself, and it takes over and dominates him. He uses this as an excuse for abusive behavior. Instead, the therapist will show that John has a coordinated response pattern that facilitates aggression and that he does not try to utilize self-control when angry with his wife.

T: How do you lose your ability to police your urges? That's what I want to know. For instance, you say you love your wife. Those feelings would keep you from hurting the person you love. What happens to your feelings of love when you get mad?

J: I don't think about it then. I just get mad.

T: So you push those feelings aside?

J: That's right. My anger just boils to the surface.

T: And you flow with it? You give it free reign?

J: It [the violent behavior] just pops out.

The therapist continues to make the point that there is a commissioned response pattern of intended violence, for which John needs to take responsibility. However, John fights against this by asserting that his anger is beyond conscious control. In essence, John is saying that he possesses no coping pattern to contain aggression, only a spontaneous, uncoordinated eruption of behavior that he cannot manage.

T: But what happens to the rest of you at that moment when you are all anger? How do you keep yourself from noticing other factors, such as your wife's terror and your children's fright when you are violent? How do you ignore their feelings or their opinion of you?

J: She just pisses me off. That's all I am thinking about.

T: So you are only thinking about the wrong she has done against you?

J: That's right.

T: So your hurt is all you are focusing on. I am not judging you. I just want to understand what happens at the moment of violence. You seem to create a form of tunnel vision or a narrowing of attention.

J: You can say that.

T: What's on your mind as you get angry?

J: I think about what she has done against me. I think about her big mouth.

T: So you remain focused on her negative qualities and how she has hurt you. That's the only thing on your mind. Your perception narrows, and when you do this you become angrier. How do you keep other thoughts out, such as your fear of consequences from getting violent, or the thought that the relationship is falling apart? These are thoughts that can help you to pull back and control yourself.

J: I don't think about those things.

T: So you have one internal image of your wife as bad and hurtful—a real devil—and all other thoughts are pushed into the background.

The process inquiry has now revealed a maladaptive coping skill that involves a perceptual process—tunnel vision—that freezes the foreground/background image. Positive images of his wife are pushed into the background, so they have little effect. His foreground image remains fixed on negative representations of his wife and his own hurt feelings. This fuels the push for revenge. He turns off problem solving and consequential thinking, which can slow reactivity. Through the process inquiry, the therapist gains information about how John responds when he becomes violent. He learns what makes the counterresponse to violence inadequate. Due to his tunnel vision, John does not respond to other factors that can ameliorate his anger. After learning how John's perceptual activity operates, the focus turns to the counterresponse to violence, or what he can do to inhibit aggression.

T: Let's talk for a moment about what you are doing when you don't get violent. Think of times when your wife is upsetting you but you don't get violent. What is happening on those occasions?

J: Well, I don't want the kids to be scared of me. I remember how scared I was when my dad used to yell at my mom.

T: So when you don't get upset, you deliberately focus on images that can inhibit your anger, such as the vision of your kids scared of you, or a memory of yourself when younger.

J: That's right.

T: So we have now identified one way to control yourself. You can use your perception—how you look at things—to contain yourself. We can work on building an inhibiting ability to keep your cool when upset.

In forming process questions, the therapist needs to avoid sounding judgmental or evaluative. Processing is an exploration without value judgments or bias about right or wrong. If the patient detects the therapist's values, this will curtail disclosure. Instead, the therapist needs to be guided by his/her curiosity. In general, the process inquiry examines present functioning. The next technique assesses functioning over time.

Historical Analysis

When learning about how patients respond in a given situation, an important consideration is whether or not their response is part of a longstanding pattern. A historical analysis can discover the continuity or discontinuity of coping skills. It is used to study habitual, routine, automatic responses to a stimulus. The analysis puts into perspective the present response to learn if it is part of a timeline, if it is part of normal operation for that particular problem or context. A historical analysis is a way to identify time-fit errors (a coping skill used earlier in life that is no longer applicable).

The analysis can be done in different ways. One way is to trace the use of the skill over time. After identifying a present response, the therapist can ask if the patient normally responds that way. The patient is asked to think of other situations in the past that were similar to the one in the present and how s/he coped in that context. Was the present skill used on that occasion?

To illustrate, Ann is suffering depression from a marital separation. Her primary focus is on her marriage, but the therapist is interested in how she copes with losses in general. He asks her to trace how she has responded to losses throughout her life. A pattern emerges to show that her present way of coping is typical. She takes the feeling of loss and transforms it into anger and then displaces it onto others. Displacement is her coping response. It eliminates the sadness temporarily, which is her main concern. It is not an adaptive response, but it is her historical response.

Learning about discontinuities in coping skills also can be helpful; that is, why has a skill been abandoned or changed. Asking some of the following questions can discover this:

- Your present coping skill was not used at other times in the past. Why not? Were there circumstances preventing its use?
- A past coping skill seemed to help you, so why did you stop using it in the present situation?

Wendy gives an example of why it's important to learn about junctures where patients change skill selection. Her presenting problem is job stress, but the therapist wisely asks her about how she has coped with stress historically. She did cope relatively well until her mother died when Wendy was just sixteen. Since then she has had several periods of mild to moderate depression. On those occasions she becomes promiscuous and has a series of short but destructive relationships. When sad, she attaches herself to highly dependent, needy males who try to control her life. The therapist theorizes that Wendy has never worked through the death of her mother and copes by gaining temporary closeness with men who also need her desperately. Based on that theory, the therapist makes an inquiry to learn if Wendy has adequately mourned the death of her mother. Wendy reveals that she remained cold and impassive at the funeral and afterword. Consequently, the therapist moved to teach her how to mourn "effectively" (see chapter 7 for details).

Another method of conducting a historical analysis is to make a biographical sketch of the patient's life, learning about coping responses at various life stages or critical junctures (e.g., after separating from the family of origin, after getting married). The focus is twofold:

1) *Skill continuity:* does the patient continue to employ the same skills over time, and
2) *Skill discontinuity:* is a skill terminated upon entering a new life stage.

If healthy, adaptive skills are identified but are not presently being used, then the therapist can assess how they can be resurrected and employed for coping with a present problem. There is benefit in identifying healthy, rational, adaptive skills from the past, because they are still part of the coping repertoire even though they are dormant, not dominant, or infrequently used.

Use of Solution-Oriented Questions

Solution-oriented therapy (de Shazer, 1985, 1988; Selekman, 1999) has developed several questions that are most helpful for identifying present coping skills. They pinpoint when someone is successful, which indicates that coping skills are being utilized but without a patient's awareness.

Pretreatment question

"So what have you noticed that's better since you first called me for an appointment?"

The question refers to what coping skills were summoned after the initial appointment was made that helped things improve.

Exception-oriented question

"When does this problem not happen?"

"What are you doing differently that's making things go better?"

"To get that positive situation going again, what will you have to do again?"

"What do you want your __________ [parents, spouse, etc.] to continue doing that's helping you get along better?"

"What have you been doing that is good for your family?"

"How did you manage to take this important step to turn things around?"

"How did you get yourself ready to change?"

These questions ask about times when the person coped instead of not coping.

Coping sequence question

"How come things are not worse?"

"What are you doing to keep things from getting worse?"

These questions ask about when the patient copes.

General questions

"What do you think other therapists have overlooked or missed about you?"

"What skills or talents do you have that would benefit other people or families?"

(As an aside, CCT would be an invaluable addition to solution-oriented therapy, which lacks a training model for skill acquisition.)

In addition to identifying specific skills for managing emotions or relationships, a cognitive coping therapist may also identify major *life coping strategies*. These are strategies for organizing one's life in total, to achieve a major goal. They are similar to scripts in transactional analysis (Berne, 1961; Steiner, 1974). They contain both policy and executive beliefs.

☐ Techniques for Working with Present Skills

Once the patient's skills have been identified and there is an understanding of how they operate, attention turns to evaluating their use. We will now examine several techniques for doing this:

(1) incentive analysis,
(2) contextual search,
(3) reframing,
(4) taking responsibility, and
(5) prescribing the symptom.

Incentive Analysis

Engaging the patient in a calm, deliberate, dispassionate discussion, the therapist wants to know about the relative merits of a skill. This is termed an *incentive analysis*. The patient is first asked what his/her goal is and then what his/her means for achieving that goal are. Next, s/he is asked to evaluate how much s/he has to gain or lose by performing that action; this is done by listing the pros and cons, the advantages and disadvantages, of a response. The lead question is: "When you do perform that action, how does that help you and how does that hurt you?" or "What do you gain and lose by being that way?" Even responses that are considered dysfunctional or nonproductive receive this approach. There is an underlying presumption that people do not continue to utilize a chosen response unless it is helpful in some way.

Incentive analysis theory comes from social psychology, and it holds that people make decisions by trying to maximize subjective utility. Subjective utility is based on both the value of a particular outcome and the probability that an action will produce that outcome (Edwards, 1954). The implicit assumption behind the technique is that people are rational and capable of making decisions based on their calculations.

The analysis is used to increase the potential for rational, wise decisions. It increases objectivity. It is an appeal to the intellect and forces people to put emotion aside for the moment. While CCT does not presume that people are rational, it does assume that they have the capacity for rationality. The purpose behind the analysis is to help the patient ponder and realize the consequences of his/her behavior and what motivates him/her to act, feel, or think in certain ways. The analysis wants the patient to consider his/her total and most important needs, and what is the best way to satisfy them. It helps the patient evaluate whether his/her skill is unproductive, inappropriate, or harmful in some way. It confronts and helps the patient grasp reality: how much a particular response is worth. For the person committed to an unwise course, the analysis raises uncertainty that the chosen path is advisable. For the patient loyal to an irrational belief, value, or action, the analysis chips away at their loyalty.

An incentive analysis is a technique for treating a coping skills excess and time-fit errors. If patients use a response to excess or are continuing to use a coping response from the past that does not fit the present circumstances of their life, the analysis can show shortcomings in that skill. It reveals the disadvantages in continuing with a particular response.

Contextual Search

A *contextual search* is an indirect way to confront inappropriate deployment of a coping skill. It is used for treating a contextualization error. After a skill is identified, the patient is asked where that skill is most helpful and where it is not beneficial. It is used for treating time-fit errors. After a skill is identified, the patient is asked when that skill was first used and whether it is still helpful for the present situation. Before asking this, though, the patient is told that his/her coping response has benefit and is useful—but only in the right situation and at the right time. This confirms a fundamental belief that everyone's coping responses have worth in the right time and place. This also positions the therapist as nonrejecting and a nonantagonist, someone who understands what has value to that person.

A contextual search can be combined with an incentive analysis. After identifying a response pattern, the patient is asked what the advantages and disadvantages are of employing that skill in different contexts. Once an appropriate context has been identified for a skill, the therapist prescribes utilizing that ability for that setting.

If the patient is not using the skill in the proper context, this quickly becomes obvious. The search forces the patient to see reality without being confrontative. For instance, in the case of John, the abusive husband, the therapist first states that violence has use in particular circumstances. The objective is to find the proper context for its deployment, such as wartime or when physically attacked. The point becomes obvious that family members do not pose a physical menace, so spousal abuse is not warranted.

A variation of a contextual search is *contextual sorting*. This technique categorizes appropriate skills for a given situation and then rank-orders them. The skills are compared and contrasted for viability.

Reframing

If CCT considers all coping skills as potentially positive, how does the cognitive coping therapist address ones that cause damage to the patient or others? One way to do this is by reframing the maladaptive, injurious coping response. This shows the silver lining in the destructive, nonutilitarian way a skill is employed. The intention is not to discard a skill but to help the patient use it in the appropriate time and place.

There are several ways to perform reframing:

1. *Find a positive intention for a negative thought or action* (Bandler & Grinder, 1982). For example, a parent physically abuses a child. The parent is told that the abuse is bad but the intention behind it is good, to correct the child and to help him respect authority. The parent is told to preserve the intention but to change how it is enacted. As another example, a husband physically abuses his wife when she acts disrespectfully toward him. He is told his behavior is wrong but his intention is good, because he seeks to be treated respectfully, which is the right of everyone. The focus of change then becomes the method of gaining respect.

2. *Declare that the thought or action has benefit, providing it is not used to excess, in the wrong context, or at the wrong time.* In essence, the assessment of the coping skill error becomes the reframe. For example, a domineering boss acts in a callous way with his family members. The therapist tells him that there is benefit in being tough at work, but he is using this coping skill in the wrong context—the family. The boss is told to continue being tough where it counts (thus the behavior is being prescribed) but to use another skill for contexts where toughness is not helpful.

3. *Provide a new use or significance for a negative coping skill.* In using reframing, the intention is to have the patient see the positive aspects of a negative behavior. Because patients derive benefits from aspects of their disorder, pushing the patient to admit that his/her coping response is bad and must be changed turns the therapist into an adversary. This results in a break in rapport. It is far more helpful to discuss when and where a seemingly negative coping skill is practical or adaptive.

For example, Tom has had numerous affairs during the course of his marriage, not because he is unhappy in his relationship but because he "just likes to play around." His wife has recently discovered the last one and has threatened to leave him if this happens again. He does not want to lose her but admits that he has a most difficult time being loyal to one woman. He has been to therapy a few other times for this same problem because he knows it is wrong, but he cannot stop himself from being promiscuous. Each time a previous therapist has told him that he is selfish and exploitative, and each time he has dropped out of treatment after hearing this. His narcissism does not allow him to hear negative thoughts about himself, although he admits that these other therapists are correct. Essentially, these therapists win the battle but lose the war, because Tom terminates therapy.

The cognitive coping therapist has the task of building a therapeutic relationship and stimulating Tom to work on his problem. To do this, the therapist chooses to reframe Tom's behavior. While Tom is selfish and exploitative, telling him so without finding the merits of those responses only alienates him from treatment. He hears the reality about himself but is not given a direction for future growth. The therapist informs Tom that he is concerned with his own interests, takes advantage of the situation for his own good, and has a strong sense of entitlement. These actions are labeled as worthwhile—providing they are done in the right amount. The diagnosis is now a coping skills excess. Tom uses these basically good actions too much. The therapist does not want Tom to stop his ways, because they have merit when performed at an appropriate level. Hence, by taking a coping skills orientation, Tom is confronted about his excessive, egregious, harmful behavior without alienating him from therapy.

At the risk of trivializing Tom's destructive behavior, the therapist reframes the urge to have affairs as "indifferent pleasure seeking." This means nonchalantly, insouciantly following his own desires without caring about how he affects others. Following the rule that all coping skills are good, even ones that appear odious, the therapist asserts that indifferent pleasure seeking is basically a positive activity in and of itself, providing it is done in the right amount in the right context (e.g., eating alone in a restaurant). However, Tom is warned that if it is done to excess, this response pattern will cause him to become a nonthinking hedonist, a menace to himself because he only values the stimulus of the moment without considering long-term consequences; i.e. specifically, the ending of his marriage. Using reframing, the therapist maintains rapport between him and the patient. At the same time, the therapist suggests skills that need to be combined with Tom's present ones, such as *empathy* and an *ability to become affectively anguished* to feel the pain he causes other people.

Taking Responsibility

CCT emphasizes this concept from existentialism. It is used with patients who are having a difficult time surrendering the use of a coping skill. The purpose of the incentive analysis and contextual search is to make the patient aware that s/he is using a skill inappropriately. For some patients, though, this information does little to terminate their habitual response. To change their behavior, time is spent detailing the consequences of employing an irrational, maladaptive coping response. Then the patient is asked to take responsibility for the negative consequences s/he causes. Often this halts pejorative behavior. Patients dislike admitting publicly that they are willing to let a harmful occurrence happen deliberately.

Choice is emphasized when using this technique. The patient is told, "You have a choice in this matter regarding how you want to be. You can continue to use this approach. I just want you to take responsibility for your choice. Is this how you want to be?"

Prescribing a Coping Response

Sometimes patients have difficulty surrendering an inappropriate, harmful coping response because it benefits them in some way. Sometimes patients are not aware of the ramifications of using a particular skill. To treat these problems, CCT suggests prescribing the coping response that is already in operation. At the same time, the therapist recommends needed companion skills. For example, Jill, and avoidant personality, hesitated to use the social skills taught by the therapist to become involved with others. The therapist then prescribed further avoidance of social contact. At the same time the therapist recommended to Jill to learn how to be a successful schizoid personality who does not need social contact. To accomplish this, Jill was asked to learn how to cope with loneliness and become adept at not needing others. She revolted against this course and practiced social skills training.

The purpose behind a paradoxical intervention is to incite revolt. Patients may have an easier time rejecting a response when it is "forced on them" by another person. Rebelling against what the therapist demands causes the patient to pursue a more beneficial course of action (Weeks & L'Abate, 1982).

The prescriptive technique is commonly used when a patient's presently used coping skill is included in the treatment plan. This makes the response officially approved of by the authority in charge. It makes an unconsciously used response conscious and deliberate. Prescriptions are also used to learn more about how present skills operate. The therapist prescribes the skill in use and asks the patient to monitor what happens afterword.

The Use of the Past

When conducting a historical analysis, past events and people are discussed. This can lead to an inquiry about why a skill was practiced at an earlier age. The cognitive coping therapist has a choice at this point. S/he can gain just enough background material to understand how past events shaped present coping responses, and then move back to working on present coping skills. Or s/he can engage the patient in an extensive discussion about early-life events and how they influenced the formation of policy and executive beliefs. The more severe the disorder, the more the latter strategy needs to be pursued. Generally, the treatment of personality disorders requires some work with the past (see chapter 10).

Often there is a need not only to identify deep cognitive structures that began at an earlier age but also to feel the emotions associated with those structures (Guidano and Liotti, 1983). Early-life conflicts may need to be recalled and the emotions associated to them will have to be reexperienced. This provides a background for why childhood coping responses began as they did. It will illuminate why patients formed the policy and executive beliefs that they continue to use in the present. The need for the policy beliefs may have to be reexperienced. This is part of working through feelings connected to the development of schemata and basic assumptions. Time is then needed to allow patients to vent and feel the circumstances that spawned the deployment of their coping responses. Finally, credit needs to be given to those old responses that lubricated passage through difficult times, even if they are counterproductive in the present. This will increase understanding of why loyalty to archaic skills is so strong.

The following format can be used when working with the past:

1. Identify present coping skills.
2. Discuss when they were first used in the past.
3. Discuss the events and people involved in the initial use of the skill—who it was used with and why. Discuss the use of that skill over time.
4. If the patient has intense feelings when discussing this, ask about those feelings.
5. Have the patient reexperience the original feelings when he first used that skill ("Feel what it was like when you acted that way with your dad"). Give time for catharsis if necessary.
6. Discuss others' responses to that coping response when it was used in the past.
7. Have the patient reexperience how s/he felt as a consequence of others' responses ("Feel how you felt when your dad got upset with you when you did that.")
8. Inquire if people in the present feel the same way about that coping response as people in the past did.
9. Give credit to the old coping skills, to facilitate the patient's appreciation of them.

☐ Learning New Coping Skills

CCT continuously wonders what coping skills need to be learned to attain the stated goals. When new skills are discussed, CCT emphasizes the following values to the patient:

- Become a whole person by integrating new responses. Embrace self-actualization and growth.
- Learn from others: friends and foes alike, people like you and people who are the opposite of you.
- Explore and be flexible to try out new skills.
- Take risks and do not rely solely on old patterns of behavior.

Assessment: Identifying Needed Skills

In CCT, two assessments are conducted. One identifies the patient's current coping skills, as discussed above. The other assessment identifies what needs to be developed. This addresses the issue of a coping skills deficit, the search for the missing ingredients, the pieces of the puzzle that need to be put in place. Self-actualization and growth are then stressed. This raises several questions.

- What coping skills are needed to attain the patient's goals or to resolve the presenting problems? What's missing or lacking?
- If a new skill is put in place, is it enough to attain the desired goal? If it is not enough, then what else needs to be added to the mix?
- What is needed to facilitate acceptance and utilization of the new skills?
- Do the new skills fit the personality of the patient and the context of the person's life?
- If a general coping skill needs to be added to fill a deficit in functioning, what are the subskills of that general ability? What are the microskills of the subskills? This is a *component analysis,* which is vital when constructing a skills package. What is the *sequence* for deploying those old and new skills?
- How should therapy *utilize and blend present functioning with new skills?*

CCT uses several techniques to identify new and needed coping skills: (1) the coping skills inventory, (2) process questioning, (3) questions from solution-oriented therapy, and (4) the use of role models. The coping skills inventory has already been discussed above. We will now describe how process is used to identify needed skills.

The Use of Process

Processing not only identifies the components and operation of existing coping skills but also points out new ones that need to be added. It identifies what does not exist—the holes in one's being-in-the-world. It pinpoints maladaptive or nonutilitarian responses that have to be squelched, readapted, or recontextualized.

The following example shows how a dysfunctional response is readapted to help a patient function better. Tricia comes to therapy due to work stress. The therapist inquires about how she feels around her boss. She responds that she feels frightened around him, although he does little that is frightening. To identify why she has this response, process questions are asked. The therapist asks, "How do you frighten yourself—what do you think that leads to a feeling of fright?" Tricia responds that she imagines that her boss finds mistakes in her work and will demote her. She is essentially deluding herself, so the therapist utilizes her delusional ability. She continuously makes assumptions. The therapist suggests *"selective delusional training."* She is to consciously, selectively delude herself that her boss actually likes her but cannot express his feelings (which the therapist believes is actually the case). She is to delude herself that her boss goes back to his office and thinks positive thoughts about her. She is to imagine that he feels happy when she sees her. Tricia is given a strategy: "When you begin to feel insecure and there is no reason to justify that feeling, make a leap of faith and delude yourself with positive ideas." Overall, this plan makes Tricia feel less tense seeing her boss, so she makes fewer errors. Consequently, work stress is reduced. Basically, the therapist prescribes the response (making assumptions) she already is pursuing but turns it into a coping skill.

Questions from Solution-Oriented Therapy

Questions from solution-oriented therapy yields substantial information about what new skills need to be inculcated (Selekman, 1999). Below are some of those questions:

"Why now" questions

"What brings you to therapy now instead of some other time?" This will pinpoint present problems that new skills may help resolve.

Presupposition questions (O'Hanlon & Weiner-Davis, 1989)

"How will you know when your problem is solved? What skills will you need to have to make you think, 'Now things have really improved'?"

"If you gaze into a crystal ball and see that things are going better, how will you be acting or thinking?" (de Shazer, 1985)

"What would be a sign of progress to show that you are heading in the right direction?"

Miracle questions (deShazer, 1988)

"Suppose when you go home tonight a miracle occurs and your problem is solved. How will you tell a miracle has occurred? What will be different?"

"How can you make this miracle occur?"

"If I were a fly in your house watching you after the miracle has happened, what kind of things will I see you doing?"

These questions lead the patient to explore what is needed to resolve the present problem. From this, new skills can be identified and practiced.

Finding Role Models

Another way to identify needed skills is to *find role models that can guide the patient in how to act.* The patient is first asked whom s/he knows or knows about (e.g., a public figure) who is able to attain the treatment goal or perform a desired skill. Second, the patient is asked, "How do they do it?" and "What do they do?" Both patient and therapist share ideas in a free-floating, guessing session. This necessitates *stimulating the patient's curiosity* about how the role model functions. Third, the patient is asked to compare how he/she operates vis-à-vis the role model and to note differences, without becoming defensive or feeling inadequate. The therapist inquires if there is any facet of the model that is admirable and worth emulating. If the patient identifies a skill the model possesses, this leads to contract making: "Would you be interested in learning how to perform that skill?"

In a way, this technique operates similarly to RET imagery (Wessler & Wessler, 1983), where the patient is asked to state how s/he wants to feel after an activating event occurs, and then to identify how s/he would have to think to feel that way. This means listing the rational, realistic, adaptive beliefs needed for goal attainment. The main difference between RET imagery and the role model technique is the breadth of the inquiry. CCT focuses on role model's total functioning—action tendencies, perception, and physiological reaction—as well as cognition. All need to be acquired before success can occur.

In selecting role models, the attitude and feeling toward the role model are important. If ambivalence about the model exists, the patient will not embrace the model's skills, no matter how meritorious they are. Some patients may dislike copying another person out of fear of losing their own identity. The therapist has to stress that only a response is being copied—not the whole person.

A desirable role model is one who shares qualities and behaviors with the patient. This helps to build liking and identification with the model in general, which encourages the desire to act like him/her. At the same time, the model needs to be different in key regards, so the patient has someone to learn from. An opposite personality may be rejected even though s/he has useful skills to emulate. Yet opposite models offer exciting directions if presented properly.

George's treatment illustrates a case study using an opposite role model. George is a warm, sensitive, caring manager who has a difficult time setting limits on his raucous, challenging employees. His need for their approval compromises his ability to take command. The therapist asks him if there is anyone he knows who is able to set limits well. George mentions a fellow manager named Richard, but George dislikes him intensely because Richard is abrasive, cold, and intimidating—his opposite. Because of his antagonism toward Richard, George rejects everything about him, including his admirable qualities. The therapist asks George to explore Richard's qualities to assess if there is anything he can learn from him without becoming him in total. George states that he can learn how Richard sets limits firmly and resolutely without feeling conflicted or guilty, and is able to remain unaffected by worker pleas to change a task they must perform.

Exploring further, George explores Richard's qualities of abrasiveness and intimidation. The therapist appeals to George's curiosity about Richard: what allows him to act abrasive, and how does he do it? The therapist asks George if there is anything good about these negative qualities, to separate the wheat from the chaff, the beneficial from the maladaptive. George admits that he would like to be more powerful like Richard, who has an ability to challenge and penetrate others' boundaries and limits, confront others, coerce when needed, and seize control of situations, although he does this in a negative way, which scares other people into submission. The role model technique works to appeal to George's desire for self-growth to acquire the positive aspects of Richard's negative qualities. To do this, the therapist builds a coping skill package to increase George's power, including:

1. *Assertiveness training:* to confront without being disrespectful
2. *Limit setting:* to know how to coerce another into doing something
3. *Imperviousness training:* to overcome George's hypersensitivity to disapproval from others, which occurs when he challenges their limits
4. *Diminution training:* to reduce George's fear of what will happen if he loses approval

In working with George's opposite role model, the therapist had to discuss where the negative traits of the model have utility. Following the principle of CCT that every skill has value, the therapist discussed when a seemingly negative skill or trait had benefit. George is asked if there are ever times in his personal or professional life when being abrasive or intimidating has benefit. George is able to identify work situations when a variation of those responses can be useful. Several of his male employees act "rough and tough." George reasons that he does not have to be abrasive with them, but he can act rougher to earn their respect. When they become overly challenging, a measured use of intimidation can coerce them to back off.

There are two other ways to perform the role model technique. One method is to simply have a free-floating discussion about how the role model would handle various problems the therapist raises. A second method utilizes the empty chair technique from Gestalt therapy (Polster & Polster, 1973). The steps are as follows:

1. The therapist identifies the polar side of self or an opposite personality.
2. The patient assumes the role of the opposing part-of-self and discusses how he/she operates, citing what is good about that opposite way of being.
3. Then the patient switches and becomes him/herself, and shares feelings about the opposite part-of-self.
4. A dialogue can then occur between the two until there is a greater understanding of each part-of-self.

An important point in using this technique: highlight the fact that the patient can be a role model to other people because he already possesses skills and talents others desire. This helps to build self-esteem.

In summary, the following steps can be followed in working with role models:

1. Identify the model.
2. Overcome resistance to being like the model.

3. Show similarities between the model and the patient.
4. Encourage curiosity about the model's outstanding skills and how they operate.
5. Identify the model's skills and how they operate.
6. Form a contract with the patient to work on developing those skills.
7. Educate the patient about how to perform the needed skills.
8. Discuss how the patient can be a model to others, highlighting the steps in how the patient performs those desirable abilities. Identify who can benefit from acquiring the patient's skills.
9. Contextualize where the negative skills of the model have utility, so the patient learns where they can be performed.

☐ Forming the Coping Skills Package

Once the new skills are identified, the next task is to gain acceptance of them. This is the task of marketing.

Marketing

There are different responses to the presentation of new skills. Some of the therapist's ideas will be new and fresh, and the patient will readily embrace and incorporate them into his life. In other cases, the patient is familiar with the new skills but has eschewed them previously. In other words, the patient does not buy the treatment program. In such a case, the treatment task is to sell the program. This means marketing, to gain acceptance of the new skill or to redeploy an old skill.

CCT engages in marketing in two ways. One, when introducing any new skill, subskill, or microskill, there is a need to induct the patient into accepting the skill. During the induction, the cognitive coping therapist presents a cogent argument for learning a new skill and complying with the treatment regimen. The benefits of incorporating and practicing a skill are given to the patient. The induction phase is a part of each new skill presentation.

Second, the therapist markets the training module by finding an appealing title for it, naming the skill something the patient can relate to easily. The name is like a handle, something the patient can pick-up quickly without resistance. This entails utilizing some facet of the patient's life, as Erickson (O'Hanlon, 1987) suggests, and naming the training after it. Two case examples below illustrate this.

Example 1: Bill is a technically oriented, abrasive person who lacks awareness of his effect on others. To remedy this situation, the therapist wants him to reflect on his behavior before he acts and adjust his actions beforehand. This is to help him lessen his negative impact on others. The therapist calls this "calibration training," using a scientific word because it is appealing to Bill.

Example 2: Megan is a computer programmer who has a problem with incessant worrying. The therapist wants her to practice thought stopping and attention diversion to control this problem. He calls it "pressing the escape key," a computer term for terminating an instruction. Her problem with obsessing also involves continuously ruminating about her mistakes. To treat this tendency, the therapist tells her to mentally "press the delete key." When she does this, the errors she worries about vanishes from her mind. Again, he utilizes a term she is familiar with, so she will embrace that skill more readily.

Because of this, the therapist's name for the training module is often different from the one given to the patient. For example, Rick is a headstrong, macho-type person who needs to learn how to submit to other people's wishes and needs. The therapist designs a training module that requires submissiveness. He does not use this term with Rick because he will reject the idea. The therapist wants to change the name to make it more palatable. He asks Rick, "Whom do you know who has the ability to bend to other people's needs when needed yet is tough and strong?" Rick thinks of Tom Cruise, so the name "Tom training" is applied to the practice sessions. When Rick needs to submit to others, he tells himself to be Tom Cruise, which makes bending to the will of others more appealing.

The best friends of a cognitive coping therapist are a dictionary and a thesaurus. The therapist must be precise with word choice and select words that capture the intent of the coping skill but are interesting and acceptable to the patient. Many times a cognitive coping therapist will open a dictionary and read the definition of a word in the middle of a session. The right word captures the intent of the training module and gives a vivid and clear meaning of a skill.

Teaching

After the patient agrees to practice the new skill, the therapist teaches it to the patient. This is a formal presentation. It includes a rationale for why the skill is important and an explanation of how it can make a difference. The basic steps in performing the skills are given. The therapist models the skill in the session and then has the patient perform the skill outside the office.

If self-instruction training is used in the session, then the therapist writes out the self-dialogue with the aid of the patient. Each contributes to the finished product. The therapist says the self-dialogue out loud and then to him/herself, followed by the patient saying it out loud and then to him/herself (Meichenbaum, 1977).

After the skill is presented, two other areas need to be discussed. The patient should be asked to estimate how effective a skill will be for resolving the presenting problem. This is an approximation of the subjective utility of the skills package: how much value the skills have to the patient and the extent to which the skills will produce the desired effect. The subjective utility helps the therapist predict the level of motivation to practice the new skills. A low subjective utility (i.e., the patient thinks the skills package has modest value but in all probability will not do that much to ease symptoms) means noncompliance is more likely. Next, the therapist has to discuss what can interfere with practice. The patient may know in advance what can interfere with skill acquisition, and this needs to be identified in advance. Problem solving will have to be done to overcome obstacles in the way of practice sessions.

When the therapist is ready to blend the present skills with the new skills, two key issues must be considered: the interplay between the patient's schemas and the new skills, and the interplay between the present skills and the new skills. It is necessary to form a match between each, so one complements the other. The next two sections address these basic concerns.

Form Schema-Skill Match

Cognitive-behavioral therapy has traditionally dealt with schemas by trying to change them when they exert a negative influence (Beck et al., 1979; Young, 1999). For some patients, CCT agrees that there is a need to do this and will use traditional disputing tactics on occasion. In other cases, CCT uses two other methods.

First, *CCT does not directly challenge the schema but keeps it intact, while recommending coping skills that can alter its pejorative influence.* In this case, the therapist designs the skills package so that it *inadvertently* disputes and changes the schema. *The therapist utilizes the patient's schemas and basic assumptions to support the use of the new skills.*

The following is an example. Patients with an insufficient self-control schema (Young, 1999) assume that they are unable to exercise self-control. They assume self-control is impossible if they are too frustrated.

They have an absolutistic belief: "I must have minimal frustration in life." In treating the problem, one approach is to dispute the patient's thinking directly ("Is it true that you cannot manage frustration?"). Another approach is to *implant coping skills that complement the schema but eventually and indirectly dispute it.* This is done in the following way. If the patient believes that s/he cannot control him/herself if too frustrated, then it makes sense to learn stress and anger management to help tolerate frustration. This strategy will decrease the overall level of discomfort, which matches the absolutistic belief to have minimal frustration. Indirectly, the skills dispute the self-control schema. By practicing the above skills, the patient learns self-control even while having heightened frustration. This challenges and changes the basic view of self as too inadequate to tolerate frustration.

A second approach is to *minimize the schema's pejorative effect by learning coping skills that empower the person.* The intent is to preserve the schema but improve the patient's basic ways of operating. Chapter 9 is an example, where the schema about perfectionism is preserved but skills are learned to become a "better" perfectionist. In so doing, the skills package lessens the injurious effect of the schema.

The tough love movement offers an example of *how to change the harmful effects of a schema while keeping it intact.* The tough love approach makes recommendations for treating children with oppositional-defiant disorder or conduct disorder by setting firm limits, punishing, and disciplining. Many parents of children with these types of disorder have difficulty embracing this approach. This is because they have a self-sacrifice schema, which means that others' needs are more important than their own and that they should not cause their loved ones any pain. Thinking this way, these parents feel in conflict with the practices and recommendations of tough love. This results in noncompliance with treatment recommendations. To avoid that, therapists who recommend tough love can market their approach as "loving behavior" but with a new twist. Parents can love and care for children with behavioral problems and still put their needs first—by depriving and punishing them. Thinking this way, loving and giving behavior now includes limit setting and discipline. This forms a match between schema (sacrifice for others) and new skill (tough love), so parents can perform the needed behavior without consternation and self-conflict. The self-sacrifice schema remains in effect but no longer prevents behavioral management of the child. In essence, CCT takes advantage of the schema to ensure compliance.

In another example, narcissistic patients have a grandiosity schema that proclaims that they are superior to others. This belief frequently results in difficulty putting others first. At the same time, a tendency exists to exploit others for the narcissist's own good. To treat this situation, the therapist can take advantage of the narcissist's schema to change his behavior. Appealing to his arrogance, the narcissist is told, "Only a superior person can placate others and be conciliatory even when he believes the other person is in the wrong. Others will extol your virtues if you attend to their needs first. You will show your greatness by being humble and giving." Thus, cooperation and helpfulness are marketed as a way to prove the narcissist's superiority and sterling virtues. In this example, the schema is held intact but now works for the benefit of the treatment plan.

In addition, the new skills need to mesh with the patient's personality to be accepted and practiced. For example, a man with compulsive personality disorder comes to therapy with his wife, who complains that he is too rigid and unyielding. He will not try anything new. The therapist suggests flexibility training for him but structures the program to be congruent with his personality. The therapist suggests trying new behaviors and varying his routine, but as soon as he finds behaviors or activities that he likes, he makes them part of a routine. This approach gradually widens the scope of activities that he will pursue.

Form New Skill/Old Skill Complement

The inherent definition of a coping skills deficit is that old skills by themselves are not enough to attain life goals. On the other hand, the new skills, by themselves, may also not be enough. *To construct a whole person, both old and new skills have to be included in the skills package and must complement and mesh with each other.* CCT wants patients to understand that they already possess part of the means to achieve their goals; these simply need to be blended with new abilities.

To illustrate this point, consider Lisa, an avoidant personality who is single. While she has extensive social anxiety and distrusts others, she seeks acceptance from them. While she maintains her distance in social situations and guards her privacy, she nevertheless yearns for involvement, especially with men. Past therapists have attempted to teach her social skills, but she feels too scared and anxious in social situations to practice them and has made only mild progress in treatment. Entering CCT, social skills and assertiveness training are also suggested to Lisa, but this time her old skills are utilized to complement and advance the treatment regimen. Specifically, Lisa has an ability to be behaviorally guarded. She scans the environment for potential threats. The therapist encourages her not to suppress this ability, especially in the difficult world of dating. Instead, he teaches her a new skill—*social oscillation*—that employs behavioral guardedness. In social oscillation, the patient swings toward others and practices social skills. Then, as others respond, Lisa is told to pull back psychologically and use behavioral guardedness to assess the situation, to scan for any threat or sign of danger. If none are found, Lisa is told to mentally oscillate back to the other person and reestablish the relationship. In this case, behavioral guardedness, her present skill, becomes part of the plan to learn new relationship skills and to ease insecurity while practicing those social skills.

In the case of depression, disengagement is both a symptom of the disorder and a coping response. It helps keep the depressive from having to deal with social situations that tax their already depleted psychic energy. It mentally removes the depressive from the scene, so present stimuli are not as impactful. CCT reasons, why not use disengagement to help the depressive? To do so, the depressive is told that s/he already possesses an important ability to manage difficult situations: disengagement. The depressive is asked to get involved in social situations, but when they become too stressful, to disengage to lessen stress. When the patient feels less upset, s/he can become reinvolved. Basically, this is the same technique of social oscillation used with Lisa. The goal is to keep the depressive involved in the situation in order to reap reinforcement from others, which can eventually ease the depression (Hoberman & Lewinsohn, 1985).

There is a lack of understanding of how old skills work to protect, help, and serve the patient. Therapists ignore responses that lead to pathology because they do not know how to utilize them in treatment. One of the egregious mistakes therapists make in working with coping skills is not respecting or using the patient's present abilities to advance the treatment goals. Therapists often commit a blunder by not validating old skills. Honoring old coping skills is one way to boost patient self-esteem, by telling the patient that s/he already possesses powerful abilities that are needed by other people.

Packaging of Skills

As new skills are identified and practiced, they have to be put into a sequence with old skills, to be performed in an orderly way. The connection and interplay between old and new skills has to be discussed with the patient, so s/he understands and accepts the sequence of performance. Further, the patient must accept the context and time for using the skills package. To aid this effort, handouts are used extensively, listing the sequence for deploying each subskill. The therapist presents written information about how, when, and where to use the skills. Self-monitoring and self-evaluation sheets are given to the patient to support the use of the skills package.

The cognitive coping therapist needs to continuously ask, the "What if . . . ?" question. Once the patient performs a particular skill, what will happen next? Is the package of skills enough to attain the treatment goal? What can cause the patient to resist or abandon a skills package? What can get in the way of success? These questions hopefully will identify any skills that need to be included in the skills package.

Resistance to the skills package is conceived of not as a bad thing but as information. If the patient resists, two factors may be causing it. One, another subskill or microskill needs to be added to the mix. CCT assumes that once the patient has sufficient skills, then resistance will cease (because the new skills package offers success while incorporating present abilities that the patient seeks to preserve). Second, resistance can be due to a failure to induct the patient properly into using a skill. Resistance informs the therapist that the patient does not understand or like something about the skills package or how it affects present functioning. If this is the case, the therapist must review the induction into a skill to discover objections or concerns before performing it. This is an education issue.

☐ Practice

During the practice phase, the therapist needs to emphasize one of the basic tenets of CCT: *Dysfunction is not so much a matter of basic ineptitude or personality disorder but rather lack of knowledge, experience, and a failure to learn from one's mistakes.* This sets the tone for further work that features training and repetition. The therapist should also emphasize that the patient is beginning a time of experimentation and must be flexible, because the skills package may be altered several times to find the best mixture of skills and the best sequence for performing them.

CCT varies in how structured it is at various times of treatment. When coping skills are being taught, therapy is quite structured, and the therapist is definitely in the role of teacher and the patient is the pupil. There is also a structure to each session. After a coping skill is taught, a self-evaluation questionnaire is designed to measure how effective it is. At the beginning of the next session, the therapist reviews the questionnaire to ascertain if the skill was practiced, and if so how efficacious was the skill over the course of the week. The homework assignment is also reviewed to assess its effect. After that, the session can return to being a free-floating discussion.

Homework

To develop proficiency in a skill, homework is always assigned. The behavioral influence on CCT is apparent at this point. Proficiency and success are considered to be the outcome of exposure to the problematic situation. By exposing the patient to situational determinants, treatment is able not only to test the efficiency of the skills package but also to modify it as needed. Anxiety about performing a skill will lessen as the person is exposed to what they fear (Barlow, 1988).

Self-evaluation is used extensively along with practice sessions. The patient is asked to fill out a questionnaire on a scheduled basis for each coping skill s/he is working on, which serves as a reminder to perform the practice session. The self-evaluation form measures how much the skill is able to make a difference. The patient monitors his/her response before and after using the skill and charts the changes. The evaluation forces the patient to become aware of the efficacy of a skill.

The evaluation form has another benefit. The therapist can use it to identify irrational, unrealistic cognition. If the patient reports little success using a coping skill or is resistant to it, then the influence of irrational, unrealistic, or maladaptive cognition is considered. If patient beliefs are considered to be a hindrance, cognitive restructuring may be employed at that point.

If other people are involved in causing a problem, they are sometimes asked to continue doing what is vexing or troublesome to the patient. This gives the patient opportunity to practice the needed skills. For instance, children are told to continue being defiant so their parent can practice limit setting or anger management. Spouses are told to continue enacting negative behavior so their spouse has opportunity to practice skills for coping with those actions. This also has a paradoxical benefit, in that other people may rebel about performing a behavior prescribed by the therapist, because it takes away control from them (Weeks & L'Abate, 1982). The prescription makes public that someone is performing a contrary, problematic behavior.

Imagery

Through imagery, patients can gain practice in using a specific skill. Imagery has two benefits. First, the patient has an opportunity to practice the skill mentally before doing it behaviorally. Repeated imagery sessions forge desired habits. Second, the patient sees himself using the skill successfully, which will buoy self-confidence and compliance with the treatment program. Prior success in imagery lays the groundwork for success in actuality. Imagery helps gain acceptance of the skill and forms the belief that the skill can be efficacious.

Ecological Check

Learning new skills will have a dramatic effect on both the patient and others. The homeostasis in the family and the workplace will be altered. The skills package may be perceived as a threat to homeostasis. In turn, maneuvers will be initiated by family members and friends (e.g., threats of separation, intimidation tactics) to return the environment to its previous balance. Other people will resist the changes the patient is trying to make. They will seek to force the patient to drop out of treatment or encourage resistance to using a skill. The self-evaluation questionnaire will keep the therapist informed if there are problems in the environment. If the patient is making little progress, then the therapist can ask about others' responses to the skills package.

To stay abreast of these forces, an ecological check is performed throughout treatment. CCT takes a systems orientation. Patients are routinely asked to include significant others in treatment. If others are not directly included, the therapist must vigilantly notice their influence on the patient and the patient's influences on them. The cognitive coping therapist must be aware of how the patient's new skills are being received by others. If problems are brewing, then this has to be addressed as part of the skills package. For example, if others are opposed to a skill, then imperviousness training (see chapter 7) may be included to help the patient remain indifferent to other people's complaints. If the complaints are considered valid, then the skills package may be modified. The problem may lie in how the patient is performing the skills, and this needs to be considered.

Interplay with Cognitive Restructuring

Cognitive restructuring is actually used at various points when practicing CCT. As practice sessions proceed, the therapist will note the degree of progress. If progress is slow or is not occurring, then the therapist has options. One, s/he may determine whether the skills package is adequate. A key subskill may have been omitted. A second option is to assess the patient's thinking, to learn if a belief is hampering progress. If so, cognitive restructuring can be used at this point. Sometimes cognitive restructuring is used to gain acceptance of a skill. In actuality, cognitive coping therapists move back and forth between a coping skills model and a belief change model.

Many people subscribing to cognitive restructuring may have a difficult time with this model. When they identify an irrational, unrealistic,

Outline of Cognitive Coping Therapy

As a way to summarize the facets of the approach, the following outline is presented of the methodology of CCT:

A. Education phase: teaching about approach and inducting the patient into philosophy of treatment. Areas to educate the patient about include:
   1. Cause of pathology
   2. Key terms
   3. Roles of patient and therapist
   4. Nature of treatment
      a. Underlying philosophy behind CCT
      b. Expected outcome of therapy
   5. Criteria for progress

B. Utilization of present skills
   1. Assessment
      a. Coping skills inventory
      b. Illuminating process
      c. Use of questions from solution-oriented therapy
   2. Deployment of skills
      a. Incentive analysis: identifying pros and cons of each skill
      b. Contextual search: identifying where a skill has use
      c. Historical analysis: identifying past skills and their efficacy
      d. Prescribing the skill
   3. Reframing present skills positively
   4. Encouraging the taking of responsibility
   5. Prescribing a coping response

C. Learning new skills
   1. Assessment of needed skills
      a. Coping skills inventory
      b. Use of process
      c. Questions from solution-oriented therapy
      d. Finding role models
      e. Learning from one's opposite model
   2. Marketing new skills and the coping skills package
   3. Teaching of new coping skills
   4. Form schema-skill match: reframe how new skills has value and fits with schema and basic assumptions about life and self
   5. Form new skill/old skill complement
   6. Package new skills
      a. Implant new skills in sequence with present skills
      b. Connect new skills to old skills conceptually
      c. Contextualize where to perform new skills package

D. Practice
   1. Homework: performing new package of skills
   2. Imagery
   3. Perform ecological check
   4. Use of cognitive restructuring as needed to assist practicing of skills package

maladaptive thought, their orientation is to immediately dispute it. Challenging dysfunctional thinking is basic to them and even sacrosanct in cognitive-behavioral therapy. CBT therapists reading this book may protest when they read the case studies, "Why didn't the therapist just dispute the beliefs directly?" This is because they emphasize cognitive change over a coping skills change. Their orientation is not to search for the coping response. For them, cognitive restructuring is the dominant means to the end, and even an end in itself in many cases. Their bias is strong that a change in thinking is the superior way to approach a case. However, there are other ways to remove the virulent effects of negative, irrational belief besides just disputing it. Coping skills therapy is one such way.

7

CHAPTER

Treatment of a Dependent Personality Disorder

One of the most common types of patients seen in therapy is the long-suffering, dependent spouse in a stable, unsatisfactory marriage. While fearing to separate, the spouse cannot adjust to the difficult, debilitating relationship, too angry to live with it yet too fearful to change it.

The treatment for this group of patients, generally diagnosed as dependent personality disorder (DPD), is discussed. This chapter illustrates how to work with an irrational maladaptive coping skill and a coping skills deficit. Two general coping skills are presented for the patient's care: psychological pain management and independence training.

The chapter shows the interdependence between policy, executive, and operating beliefs. It discusses how to induct a patient into using the above skills, how to market them, and then how to train those needed responses. It demonstrates how the Ericksonian concept of utilization is used in CCT. The use of self-management strategies (Kanfer, 1970) to implant coping responses is demonstrated. The differences between a coping skills therapy and cognitive restructuring is presented, regarding how each would approach this type of case. Further, the chapter shows how to change a schema without disputing it directly, by creating a skills package which indirectly forces the patient to alter his/her basic policy beliefs.

Joan

Joan is an eternally abused, deprived housewife. She has had dysthymia for many years, which is mostly caused by her dissatisfying relationships with family members and friends. Her days are spent in silent suffering, feeling angry and bitter toward the loved ones in her life. Changing others' behavior is most difficult for her, due to her unassertive, passive-dependent personality.

She has been married for twenty-eight years. She describes her husband as self-centered and only involved in his work, male friends, and personal interests. He can be verbally abusive, but mostly ignores and neglects her. He has a volatile temper when angry and intimidates her into doing what he wants. She feels bullied and frightened by him, forever tolerating his neglect and abuse.

They have tried marriage counseling on a few occasions without much success, because June only used the sessions to complain about his behavior but did little to assert herself outside the sessions. When therapists pressed her to assert herself or become more independent, she resisted and eventually dropped out of treatment.

June works full time but is not invested in her career, which has always been secondary to her role of housewife. Her pay is not enough to support herself, so she remains financially dependent on her husband. She has three children. Her two oldest children, both boys, are grown and on their own. She describes them as "carbon copies" of their father: self-involved, neglectful of her, and exploitative. Her only joy in life is her teenage daughter, who is about to leave for college. Knowing that she will be alone with no support when this happens, she comes to therapy.

Like most other patients with DPD, June does not seek treatment to become more self-reliant and autonomous, but to make her unsuccessful, symbiotic relationships more fulfilling. She is hoping the therapist will know how to do this. She is content to stay dependent on her primary caretakers if they would only do their "job"—support, guide, encourage, and love her in the way she wants to be loved.

In the first few sessions, June spends considerable time complaining and ventilating about her family while sidestepping questions about what she can do to make a difference. She is frightened and unwilling to confront her family and push for change. She does not want to shift her focus from her negative relationships to pursue other interests. While she does not like living with her husband, she does not want to live without him either.

Cognitive Assessment

June has two interrelated schemas that form her policy beliefs. They are characteristic of DPD in general, and act to impair her autonomy and ability to perform independently. Young (1999) describes them as dependence and subjugation schemas. The dependence schema maintains that she cannot manage life's responsibilities without guidance, love, and help from others. There is faith in the idea that her decisions lack worth and that others must chart her course. There is a belief that without others' love and involvement, the self cannot survive. Overall, there is a basic belief that she is helpless and cannot act independently.

Supporting this thinking is a subjugation schema mandating that control be surrendered to significant others to avoid their anger, rejection, and abandonment. June subjugates her needs to others and does not express her preferences and emotions, especially her anger. Young (1999) describes this type of person as "other-directed" because they excessively focus on the desires, needs, and feelings of others at the expense of their own needs—in order to gain love and approval and to avoid retaliation.

As a consequence of these schemas, June has developed the *following policy beliefs*. One, "I will turn to others to direct me in how to resolve life problems." Two, "I will get my significant others to support me and care for me." Three, "I will subjugate my interests to others and make them most important; others will come before me."

Coping Skills Analysis

To execute her policy beliefs, June has mindless habits in thinking, perceiving, and behaving that can be referred to as a *dependency coping skill.* She habitually promotes others to think and act on her behalf. Information is processed to make her believe that she is incapable of independent action. Table 7.1 below presents the executive and operating beliefs of a dependency coping skill.

The executive beliefs cause her to hesitate and feel anxious when tackling new tasks without others' support. If others do not deliver what's expected, June feels depressed and angry. She fixates on their failure to take the lead and give her what she needs. Essentially, the executive and operating beliefs act as an impression management structure. The executive beliefs create perceptual constancies. They create a view of self as too inadequate to be independent and needing to be dependent in order to survive. A positive expectation about dependency exists along with a

TABLE 7.1. Dependency Coping Skill

Executive belief	Operating belief
Turn to others for help and guidance.	I can't do this. I will ask my husband what he thinks.
Continue to insist on support.	I must get his help in this matter.
Don't trust my own capacity.	I solved this but I doubt if it's right. I don't think I can handle it.
Trust in the capacity of others.	My husband will know what to do. He's sharper than me at these things.
Disbelieve in independence as an adequate way to live.	I won't make it alone. I must have my family's support.
Don't tell others I'm upset with them.	They'll pull away from me if I say what's on my mind. I hate it when others are mad at me.
Influence on perception: Notice self-failings Give little attention to achievements.	I sure screw things up.

negative expectation about independence. At the same time, a positive impression exists that her primary care providers are more adequate than she is, thus supporting the contention that their support is vital.

Behaviorally she makes herself feel inadequate by not being self-supporting and by self-downing. This results in a poor self-image and insecurity, which makes her cling to others for support. She does not trust that she can become independent, and so she makes little attempt to be autonomous. Thus, she has less evidence that she can cope on her own. In turn, this creates a need for others, which validates the wisdom of her policy belief.

June has an irrational, maladaptive coping skill (IMCS). She insists that others take care of her and broods when they do not. Supporting her insistence is an agonistic activity, where she argues with herself that she is too inadequate and that others are better prepared to assume control. The agonistic activity keeps the dependency schema alive and active.

When others do not meet her expectations there is extensive anger and frustration. To cope with her anger about others' errant behavior and neglect, June, like so many patients with DPD, has a revenge-seeking coping skill. She has the following policy belief: certain actions of others that are awful and wicked should be severely punished. The following executive beliefs carry out this policy belief.

TABLE 7.2. Revenge-seeking as a Coping Skill

Executive beliefs	Operating beliefs
Look how he hurts me.	He doesn't care about me.
Focus on his negatives.	The man is a louse and a brute. All he does is take.
Condemn him for how he treats me.	He's such a creep; to hell with Him.
Fantasize him suffering.	I see him upset and miserable waiting for me to please him but I reject him.
Deprive him passively.	I don't feel good, I cannot have sex, cook your own dinner tonight.
Influence on perception.	
Focus on his mistreatment, push other thoughts aside.	Look how he has hurt me. He always does.

A revenge coping skill directs her to stay focused on her disappointments in others. It directs her in how to gain revenge on others, by vilifying, condemning, and castigating them in fantasy. She is too frightened of others' rejection to criticize them in person. In addition, she directs herself to be passive-aggressive, by omitting to do things others want.

In summary, June has an irrational, maladaptive coping skill that features brooding, insistence, agonistic arguments, and castigation. Together, they create her dysthymia, strengthened by her maladaptive coping responses. Should the therapist change them directly or indirectly?

The Treatment Plan

At this point, the therapist has secured enough information to form an initial treatment plan.

First Option: Cognitive Restructuring

One cognitive restructuring option is to challenge her descriptive judgment about her husband and sons. Are they as depriving and exploitative as she pictures them? This intervention tests the validity of her descriptive judgments, which is a favorite approach of cognitive therapy (Beck et al., 1979). If the perception is unrealistic, then cognitive restructuring can be used to change her assumptions, which would allow her to feel more positively about her family.

The problem is that June has evidence that her family members and friends are depriving and abusive. Her belief is realistic to some extent. Her family is depriving and does disappoint her regularly. Her husband and sons are self-absorbed and abusive. However, let us suppose that June's perception of them is inaccurate *to some degree*. In cognitive restructuring she will collect evidence that her significant others are not *as bad* as she believes. So what? The fact is, her relationships are still basically negative. Hence, what she really needs is help in coping with her negative relationships.

Another descriptive dispute is to challenge her judgment that she is too inadequate to be independent of her husband and sons. Her self-image is unrealistic to some extent, because she is more capable than she believes. Challenging this viewpoint could give her self-confidence to become assertive or more independent. The problem is, she is inadequate in many regards and lacks many skills needed for greater autonomy. That being the case, a coping skills approach would be preferable because it would provide her with the skills necessary for independence and/or assertiveness.

A second option is to challenge her extreme evaluative judgments and absolutistic thinking—a common practice of RET (Dryden and Ellis, 1988). June feels enraged at her family members, in part because of her awfulizing, where she rates them in an extremely negative way. She has absolutistic thinking, that her family *should* be more accomodating, loving, and giving. When others do not meet her absolutistic demands, she becomes enraged. In this case, correcting her absolutistic thinking and irrational, extreme rating will make her feel *less* sad and angry. This could ease her desire for revenge.

The problem with this strategy is that she does live in a negative, depriving environment. Even if she forms a more appropriate level of sadness (has moderate instead of severe sadness), she will still be sad to some extent. Even if she changes her thinking that her family's treatment of her is not awful but unfortunate or undesirable, she will still be deprived and abused, and that does hurt. The causes of her pain are real and not illusory. Hence, from the standpoint of CCT, coping with her pain is a greater treatment consideration. Learning how not to be so affected by her negative relationships is vital, and that is a coping skills issue.

Second Option: A Behavioral Approach

A reality therapy (Glasser, 1965) approach would maintain that June should take concrete, specific steps to overcome her dependency, such as acquiring new hobbies, making new friends, getting a better-paying job, and in general becoming more independent. Behaviorists (Hoberman & Lewinsohn, 1985) would argue that she should refrain from actions that reap negative reinforcement (e.g., alienating others by her continuing demands that they accommodate her) and pursue actions that garner positive reinforcement. Because her family mostly offers punishing interactions, rewarding interactions and activities will need to be found outside the home. This means becoming more independent of her family. Also, behaviorists would recommend assertiveness training to alter how her family treats her.

However, June, like so many patients with DPD, feels too frightened and insecure to become more independent, adventuresome, and assertive at the start of therapy. Also, June is too angry, passive-aggressive, and vengeful toward her loved ones to consider refraining from actions that will frustrate them. Instead, she wants others to shape up and become better caregivers. She wants her rewards in the home and with her family.

A major problem with reality and behavioral therapy is that they ignore the influence of entrenched schemas. Encouraging independence and even assertiveness places her in opposition to her dependency and subjugation schemas. Suggesting that she challenge these two ingrained schemas in the early phase of therapy, which behaviorists would recommend, will result in increased anxiety, resistance, and flight from treatment. Oppositely, CCT is cognizant of and respectful of patients' schemas and often does not challenge them directly, but works to change them indirectly, which is what will happen with June.

Third Option: A Coping Skills Approach

This approach accepts her thinking as accurate—that she does live in a painful situation. Given that, she will need various coping skills to manage difficult, painful life circumstance. At the same time, June cannot act independently until she possesses the coping skills to do it and feels more secure in herself—something that behaviorists and reality therapists ignore. Improving self-image and raising her self-esteem involve skill development. Behavior change alone is not enough.

The therapist presents to June her options: (1) change her life circumstances (assertiveness training), (2) coexist with her present situation (pain management training), or (3) become autonomous from present relationships (independence training). June rejects assertiveness and independence training. This is not at all uncommon for a patient with DPD, who is too frightened of retaliation or abandonment to attempt assertiveness, and who also feels too threatened to leave her caregiver. Because June wants to stay in her present relationships, she realizes that she will need help tolerating an adverse environment. She selects pain management training. This has several advantages:

1. It utilizes her desire to coexist with and stay dependent on her present relationships. Indirectly it overcomes her resistance to becoming independent and assertive.
2. It moves her from a passive role of whining and complaining about her difficulties to becoming active and learning how to tolerate the difficult people in her life.
3. It indirectly encourages her to learn other coping skills. Pain management helps her to realize what her future will be difficult if she does not become more assertive or more independent of her neglectful, abusive relationships.
4. It directly corrects her irrational, maladaptive coping skill.

Cognitive restructuring is used with June to support the use of coping skills. However, it did not function as the main form of treatment. CCT does not believe that cognitive restructuring should be initiated automatically for all patients because a coping skills plan may be capable of changing schemas and basic assumptions indirectly.

□ Strategy One: Pain Management Training

Pain Management Theory

Let us now turn to a brief description of pain management for physical pain, to show how it is similar to a plan for treating psychological pain. Psychological strategies for controlling physical pain have been employed for centuries. For example, the ancient Stoics as well as Spinoza recommended indifference to pain and overcoming it through reason. In modern times cognitive-behavioral therapy has been active in the treatment of physical pain (Meichenbaum, 1977; Turk et al., 1983).

Meichenbaum's model of physical pain treatment (1977) uses Melzack and Wall's (1965) gate control theory of pain. Gate control theory discusses three components of physical pain: sensory-discriminative (physical aspects), motivational-affective (negative feelings about pain), and cognitive-evaluative strategies (i.e., how pain is evaluated). Meichenbaum provides strategies to deal with each of these three components. For the physical level, relaxation exercises are recommended. For the motivational-affective level, attention diversion and imagery manipulation are employed to change negative feelings and to shift the focus away from painful stimuli. For the cognitive level, self-instruction training is the vehicle to alter patient thinking about pain and to change maladaptive responses.

CCT incorporates each of the three components of gate control theory. Psychological pain management in CCT has five components: (1) relaxation training, (2) acceptance, (3) perceptual shifting, (4) mourning, and (5) forgiveness.

After educating June about the facets of psychological pain management, homework is assigned. She is to self-monitor her pain level hourly to develop *self-awareness*. She is asked to complete a form where she rates her degree of psychological pain from 0 to 5, with 5 being extreme distress.

June receives quick *relaxation training* such as deep breathing and progressive muscle relaxation. This addresses the physical level of psychological pain: her muscular tension from getting angry and frustrated. She is given the assignment to use the exercises when the level of psychological pain is at a moderate to severe level (3 on a scale of 1 to 5). The patient is then asked to rate the degree of pain following the relaxation exercise (e.g., 4/2, with 4 being the level preceding relaxation and 2 being the level afterward). This increases self-efficacy (Bandura, 1977) by helping her realize that she can lower her own pain level.

Acceptance Training

Just as acceptance is a key component of rational, adaptive coping skills in general, it is fundamentally important for psychological pain management. It is used with June to challenge one of the components of her irrational, maladaptive coping skills—*insistence*. She insists that her family change to act as she demands.

Acceptance is presented as a skill that can be acquired through mental training. Acceptance is considered a cognitive-quasi-affective structure. Cognitively, it is a report or position on what is reality. Emotionally, it is a feeling of grace, calm, a feeling of peace of mind.

The first step toward gaining acceptance is recognizing that a given state of affairs exists and will have to be tolerated. This means assent that something is reality, acquiescence to that truth, and concession that it will not be rejected—even if that actual condition is not liked, approved of, or wanted. Next, reality is admitted or received into one's life, if not favorably or willingly then at least with forbearance. This entails coexistence with that condition and bearing up under its the weight.

Yet when presenting the concept of acceptance to patients, there is often confusion and misunderstanding. *People often equate acceptance, which is an internal activity, with surrender, which is a behavior*. People assume that if they accept a condition, then they are simultaneously approving of it as well. The following dialogue addresses these issues and shows how to market and induct a patient into being accepting, while also disputing absolutistic thinking. The therapist uses a repetition strategy, over and over confronting June's irrational, maladaptive coping skill of insisting that her caregivers act as she expects them to act.

T: You have told me in many ways how your husband, family, and friends disappoint you and anger you. {June nods in agreement.] You tell me that you are surrounded by neglectful and depriving people. If that is the case, if that is the reality of the situation, are you able to accept that reality?

J: How can I accept that? Look at how they treat me. I don't want them to treat me that way. It's not right how my husband and sons act. It stinks. [She continues to be insistent.]

T: That's fine. You can prefer that they treat you differently. You are totally free to rate their behavior negatively when they treat you badly. You are free to disapprove.

J: I do.

T: Disapproving in and of itself will not cause you significant pain. You can disapprove of something as awful and still not feel bad, as long as you don't accompany the negative rating with lack of acceptance. That's when you get into trouble.

J: I don't understand.

T: When you rate your family's behavior you go further than just evaluating it as bad. You also hate them being that way. You keep getting mad that they are that way. Correct?

J: Yes, I cannot stand how they treat me, especially my husband.

T: When you say, "I cannot stand it" you are really saying, "I don't accept how reality is—I want to change reality."

J: Why should it have to be this way?

T: Ideally it does not have to be that way, but it is according to you. That's reality, you say. You then go on to think, "That's reality and it should be different. He should not treat me this way."

J: He shouldn't. [More insistence.]

T: But he does—that's the point. That's reality, but then you fight against reality.

J: [Visibly angry.] So what should I do? Think he treats me great when he doesn't?

T: Let's pretend that you hate white walls and want the wall to be green. You are free to prefer it that way and that causes no problem. You cause yourself a problem when you insist that the white wall be a different color. You cause yourself distress when you preoccupy yourself with the white wall and feel gloomy about having to see this white wall every time you enter the room. That is when you start hating the wall. At this point you are not accepting the reality that the wall is white and that's that.

You tell me your husband has been depriving you and neglecting you for years. If that is the case, that is reality. Can you accept him as your white wall, that this is him, or who he is?

J: [Speaking with anger.] No. Why should I have to put up with it?

T: That's a whole other issue you are talking about now. That involves behavior: to surrender to his ways or not surrender and try to change him. You don't have to surrender to his ways. You can try to change him, by learning how to be assertive. I would be happy to work with you to learn how to change others' behavior. But when I talk about acceptance, I am not talking about surrendering, which again is a behavioral matter. I am talking about what you do internally with your emotions and thoughts. That is a matter of acceptance.

J: What do you mean?

T: Internally, you condemn him when he treats you poorly. You think about his behavior indefinitely and brood about how he treats you. You punish him in your fantasies and criticize him mentally. When you do this you become more and more upset. This is what you do internally. I am not talking for the moment about what you can do behaviorally. I am talking about how to achieve peace of mind regarding your family's treatment of you. This is all about adjusting to reality and accepting it.

J: I don't want this type of marriage. I wish my kids treated me differently.

T: Yes, you can wish that and that is fine. Problems only arise when you *insist* that it be different. Then, at that point, you are not accepting reality. This is what you do inside yourself and that is what we are talking about.

J: But I don't like how my family treats me. You tell me to accept it, but it's not right how they act toward me. I don't deserve it.

T: What you are talking about now is approval. You are free to disapprove of negative behavior. No one is saying you can't. The only issue is how accurate are your evaluations of their behavior? If they are not accurate, then you will have more pain and suffering. But approval is not the same thing as acceptance. Approval is a rating, an evaluation, while acceptance is coming to terms with what is. It is learning to adjust to reality. A lack of acceptance of reality is the main thing that will cause you to suffer.

J: [Eyes filling with tears and looking dejected.] But I don't like my reality.

T: I see your tears, and you have a right to feel sad. You don't have the kind of marriage you want. Your sons don't treat you the way you dreamed of while you were raising them. A special kind of sadness needs to be felt here, and that is mourning. You have suffered major losses, and you need to mourn those losses. Mourning the loss is appropriate, and that is what I want you to do between now and next session. You will feel that loss from having disappointing relationships many times in future weeks, and it is appropriate to take some time on different occasions to feel the loss from your relationships. [This part of the dialogue leads June into mourning training, explained below.]

After educating a patient about the difference between acceptance, approval, and surrender, a strategy has to be formed regarding each. She has two options:

1. accept, disapprove of others' behavior, and surrender to actual condition (not trying to change reality via behavioral interventions)
2. accept, disapprove of others' behavior, and assume a nonsurrender strategy (trying to change others' behavior)

June decides on the first choice. The therapist reiterates, though, acceptance will still leave her in some degree of psychological pain because others are continuing to act in unpleasant, undesirable ways. This is what she has to accept. When she does this her intense pain will become moderate.

Up to this point, acceptance training involves cognitive restructuring, to alter someone's expectations and perception of the situation so that it is realistic. What makes acceptance training into a coping skill? It becomes a skill when someone can summon mental procedures to change his/her thinking about reality whenever s/he slips into hating or rejecting reality. Hence, *acceptance training is used when there is positional slippage post-therapy.* That is, acceptance training is able to deliver a state of mind upon demand when someone knows that his/her thinking is incorrect and unrealistic but has *problems sustaining or preserving rational, realistic thinking.*

Two techniques can be used to facilitate an accepting mental state. The first is *self-instruction training,* to be used when there is rejection of reality or difficulty receiving it into one's life willingly.

Handout 7.1: Self-instructions to Accept Others' Behavior

I don't have to like others' behavior—I just have to accept it.

Others may not please me, but I need to accept their behavior as what it is.

I don't have to surrender to others' behavior because I am free to work to change it.

I do have to accept others' behavior as a reflection of their values. I don't have to approve of their values—just accept them.

Others are separate from me, with their own ways of doing things.

I may not like how others act, but I cannot control another person; they will act as they choose to act.

Getting angry at them when they disappoint me does not help the situation. Getting angry only means I am not accepting the fact that this is their behavior—that is reality.

The second technique is *imagery,* to be used jointly with self-talk. For example:

1. The patient comes to a fork in the road. On one side is an arid wasteland; on the other side is a gate, and behind the gate is a rich, beautiful meadow. If she opens the gate, this symbolizes the act of acceptance which gains her a better life, while the wasteland symbolizes the futility of fighting against reality.
2. The patient sees a stormy sea with giant waves on a very windy day. Then, all of a sudden, the sea becomes pacific and flat, with a gentle breeze blowing by. The stormy sea symbolizes lack of acceptance with its accompanying consternation, while the calm waters symbolize how someone can feel once acceptance occurs.

These two techniques are used in conjunction with self-monitoring. First, the therapist needs to collect indicators of rejection of reality. The dominant one is psychological pain. To reveal the efficacy of therapy, a homework assignment can be given to monitor the pain level and rate it on a scale from 0 to 5 (with 5 being extreme pain). Then, after using imagery and self-instruction, the patient rates how much pain is felt. (For example, a rating of 5/2 means that someone feels extreme pain initially but it is lowered to a moderate level with self-instruction.)

In summary, acceptance training proceeds in the following way:

1. Secure the patient's thinking.
2. Declare what is and is not reality. The therapist can either declare what it is or collaborate with the patient to ascertain what it is.
3. Assess how much the patient is willing to receive reality into his/her life *and* acquiesce to it. A rejection score can be obtained, which is how much someone is willing to coexist and live with a given state of affairs.
4. If rejection of reality is high, dialogue with the patient to gain the recognition that something is reality to facilitate willingness to live with the facts as how they are in actuality.
5. Clarify confusion about difference between acceptance, approval, and surrender. Form an intrapersonal-interpersonal strategy regarding each (e.g., accept, disapprove, don't surrender).
6. Use self-instruction and imagery to develop capacity to accept a painful reality.

As an adjunct to acceptance training, patients often need to be taught *evaluative judgment training,* to make more accurate, realistic assessments when disapproval ratings are extreme (awful, terrible). First, the therapist discusses the relationship between inaccurate, extreme approval ratings and psychological pain (generally, the more of the former the more of the latter). Second, gradients of awful are presented, from mildly or faintly awful (which is redefined as an undesirable action) to severely awful (defined as catastrophic). Examples of each level are given (severely awful is murder of the patient, while faintly awful is a spouse ignoring the patient). Then the patient is asked which level of awful s/he has in different situations in her life. To gain practice assigning an accurate rating, the therapist can present various situations to the patient and she rates how bad they are on the awfulness continuum. This technique (see Wessler & Wessler, 1980) allows June to gain objectivity about what really constitutes "awful."

Mourning Training

Accompanying acceptance training is *mourning training.* In order to accept reality, people have to come to terms with their losses. This entails mourning. However, mourning can be a bottomless pit for people such as June, who slip into it and continue to feel bad about their lot in life. Hence, many patients need skill in how to mourn.

While mourning sounds like it is just a normal, spontaneous human emotion, it does require some skill to do it well. Mourning requires the use of the intellect to guide emotional expression. When mourning, people need to shift back and forth between having an objective understanding of their situation (their loss) and feeling the loss.

June has many losses due to her painful relationships with her husband and children. She is asked to arrange periods during the day where she formally mourns these losses, such as the loss of her dreams that her husband, sons, and friends will become the people she wants them to be. She feels the pain from the loss but then speaks to herself, using the ideas from acceptance training, to guide her emotions and give herself an objective understanding of the loss. She then rotates back to feeling the loss, followed again by intellectual understanding of her problem.

The therapist should demonstrate how mourning training operates, regarding the rotating between feeling and thinking about a loss. The therapist becomes the patient and speak as her. Here the therapist speaks as June: "I feel so much pain and sadness because my husband treats me like I don't exist. I feel so angry with him [feeling the loss]. But what can I expect from a white wall but whiteness [rotating to intellect]. What can I expect from a self-absorbed person but overinvolvement in his own life [acceptance of reality]. This is him. I do feel the loss from not having the marriage I desire [rotating back to feelings]. My losses hurt. But how long do I want to immerse myself in the pain? Do I want to shift my focus onto other matters and reduce the pain [perceptual shifting] [rotating back to intellect]?"

A *bailout procedure* often needs to be included if patients cannot escape from the feeling mode when experiencing a loss and sink into a depression. Have the patient, in the office, practice *psychological distancing,* where she sees herself becoming depressed and then instructs herself to resume an intellectual persperctive (patient talking to self: "Pull out; don't sink down. Assume an intellectual stance").

Perceptual Shifting

One of the basic reasons people stay in pain and suffer is because they focus on what is causing them pain. As simple as it sounds, the solution is to not think about the pain by shifting to another Gestalt, where a new foreground image reorders emotional and bodily activity. This is accomplished by preoccupying the mind with another image, fantasy, scene, or issue—to deliberately shift attention to something else. The emotions and body immediately respond to a new foreground image. Once the foreground image changes, the patient's response to the situation changes as well. Perceptual shifting is not only a subskill of psychological pain management but a component of a rational, adaptive coping response.

First, the therapist needs to assess the patient's willingness to embrace perceptual shifting techniques. If there is resistance or noncompliance with using the techniques below, then the patient's cognition needs to be examined and disputed. Once that is addressed, the techniques in handout 7.2 can be taught.

For homework, June is asked to continue self-monitoring how well she is able to lessen her pain by using perceptual shifting. Again, she does both before and after ratings, noting how she feels after using the above techniques.

Forgiveness Training

June is now beginning to make progress by using acceptance, perceptual shifting, and mourning her losses. However, she still has significant psychological pain. Hence other coping skills are needed. Her husband and sons continue to disappoint her, causing her to feel angry. June has a problem letting go of her anger, so a companion skill to acceptance needs to be taught—*forgiveness training*. This is an ability to abandon anger more easily and quickly. This skill is crucial for overcoming her revenge coping skill.

At the beginning of forgiveness training, the therapist needs to assess what the patient does to prolong angry feelings. That will detail the executive and operational beliefs. Next, the therapist secures an idea about how willing the patient is to surrender anger and forgive. If there is unwillingness to embrace forgiveness training, then cognition restructuring is used to dispute patient thinking supporting resistance. Once there is willingness, the patient is cautioned that she does not have to feel forgiving naturally but can facilitate a forgiving feeling by mechanically practicing the exercises below.

There is an education phase where the techniques are taught. Finally, self-monitoring is used to assess how well the techniques work.

Circumstantial Search

This is a response substitution strategy, seeking to implant alternative intellectual responses to replace the inveterate tendency to blame, endlessly review the misdeed, and mentally castigate the offender. This is a *subskill of both blame training and forgiveness training*. Circumstantial search teaches patients to seek extenuating circumstances to account for another

Handout 7.2: Techniques for Shifting Perception

1. Sensory Diversion

   If you are with someone who upsets you, or if you are thinking about an upsetting topic, select a sense and stay in that sense. If the sense is vision, use your eyes to trace along the edges of that person's face and body and the objects around that person. If any thoughts about that person come to mind as this is being done, move away from that thought and refocus on lines surrounding the objects. Continue to focus on lines as you are with that person. Make eye contact only fleetingly, so you remain focused on objects on or surrounding the person (e.g., their eyebrows, chin, and chair). If the selected sense is hearing, clear the mind and just listen to sounds in the room as musical notes. Do not try to identify what the sounds are—just hear them as a note from a scale or a sound from an instrument (i.e., the furnace "instrument").

2. Attention Diversion

   When upset, refocus attention onto other matters or perform a mental activity. Examples: (1) measure the distance between objects in one's old room as a child; (2) count backward from 100 by sevens.

3. Somatization

   Refocus on bodily sensations instead of what is upsetting, i.e. focus on sensations in the right toe, then the arch of the foot, then the heal, etc.

4. Imagery Manipulation Through Fantasy
   Goal-Directed Fantasy

   A detailed fantasy can be created to absorb attention so there is less chance to focus on painful stimuli. Example: Create a detailed fantasy where you are driving to the beach, then walking onto the beach, then getting into the water, then playing in the water.

5. Imaginative Transformation of Context

   Keep the psychological or physical pain but transform the circumstances surrounding it. Example: When you are upset with a family member, transfer the situation to the workplace, imagining that the family member is a coworker. Imagine that person is doing the same things that upset you at home, but now in the workplace you try to act differently because you have to tolerate that coworker.

person's supposed misbehavior. This counters the tendency to seek simplistic, unicausal explanations for the misdeed. It forces the patient to search for complex, multicausal explanations for someone else's actions.

A circumstantial search essentially operates as a reattribution technique. It reapportions blame among internal and external factors. It generally shifts blame away from an internal explanation (that someone could act better but chooses not to) to an external cause. A second option is to shift blame from one singular, internal cause (e.g., greed) to several internal factors. By broadening understanding, blame is less concentrated. At the same time, finding external causes for the misdeed forges empathy and compassion.

To aid the search for extenuating circumstances, handout 7.3 is designed to stimulate thinking about other causal factors. The patient is asked to review the handout each time she becomes angry, to facilitate pardoning of other's misdeeds.

Once the patient becomes familiar with the questions in the handout, have him/her apportion blame, from 0 to 100, with 100 being total blame and responsibility, using handout 7.4.

Blame training allows June to gain more understanding of why her husband and sons act as they do. It dilutes her anger and softens her bitterness. It corrects unrealistic thinking.

Transforming Imagery

Imagery is another useful technique to facilitate forgiveness. Below are examples:

1. Fantasize that your anger is an ice cube or Popsicle melting in the hot sun of charity. See the word *forgiveness* printed on the sun.
2. Imagine yourself as a famous lawyer presenting the wrongdoer's case to the jury of one—yourself. Give the extenuating circumstances for why the wrongdoer should be pardoned.

Positive Substitution

This technique is based on social psychology's consistency theory. There are two types of consistency theories that are presented here. One involves affect-cognitive consistency (Rosenberg, 1960). It occurs when people try to make their cognition consistent with their affect. For example, when June feels negative toward her husband, she simultaneously changes her thinking about him so that she also thinks negatively about him. Anger is then justified by conjuring up negative thoughts about the transgressor, to support the negative feelings.

Handout 7.3: Finding Extenuating Circumstances

You are having a difficult time forgiving ____________________ (name). Consider the following.

1. What events came before the situation or any past issues (i.e., old arguments) that could have influenced __________'s behavior that upset you?
2. What was happening when the misdeed occurred? How much did external conditions influence ____________'s behavior?
3. Did someone else's behavior in that situation influence ____________'s behavior? How much did your behavior influence________________?
4. What needs, hopes, interests, or expectations did __________ have in that situation? Did ________________have any unmet needs in that situation? How much did ____________'s unmet needs influence his/her behavior?
5. What were ____________'s goals in that situation? Did ________________ accomplish his/her goals? Is the behavior that ________________did that hurt you part of trying to realize his/her goal or satisfy a need?
6. What role do you play in keeping ____________________from satisfying his/her needs?
7. Is there some reason or motive ________________had that accounted for the misdeed, besides the one you believe he/she had?
8. Does ______________ have a psychological problem? How much of _____________'s behavior can be attributed to that problem? How much is the problem to blame for the misdeed?
9. Is there someone in ________________'s past that causes him/her to act as s/he does, such as parents, boss, or ex-spouses? If so, they are an external cause for his/her behavior. How did they shape his/her behavior?
10. Are you angry at ______________ because s/he does not meet your standards for proper behavior? If so, does ___________ know your standards? Does ____________ accept your standards, or reject them?
11. Does _________________ have another set of standards that guide his/her behavior? Does ________________ act on his/her standards and not on yours? Are your standards for _________________ realistic, given his/her values, temperament, and personality?

Handout 7.4: Who's to Blame?

When you became angry with __________________, estimate how much each factor below contributed to the misdeed that troubles you.

External Factors

1. Old issues or problems in the relationship__________
2. Present external conditions that contributed to the misdeed ___________
3. Your behavior __________

Internal Factors

4. __________________not getting his/her needs met.
5. __________________'s psychological problems__________
6. Other people from the past influencing __________________to act as he/she does __________
7. __________________'s deeply engrained personality traits and psychological problems ______

To treat this problem using consistency theory, affect can be altered, which in turn changes the beliefs about the transgressor. The techniques below act to stimulate positive sentiments to create inconsistency with negative beliefs about the wrongdoer. Patients are asked to:

1. Make a list of positive thoughts about the wrongdoer, especially how s/he has contributed to your life. Review the list when angry.
2. Write a life history with that person, recording the best moments together at different ages. When feeling upset, review the history. Remember the scenes as vividly as possible.
3. Keep a group of photographs of the wrongdoer that evoke positive sentiments when seen. When feeling upset, look at these pictures. For best effect, remember the positive moments in the photographs.
4. Make a list of the wrongdoer's positive traits and think about them when upset.

Another consistency theory is cognitive dissonance (Festinger, 1957). The theory maintains that people strive to be consistent between their behavior and their cognition. If there is inconsistency, a state of imbalance is introduced that feels uncomfortable. To reduce the imbalance, people will change either their cognition or their behavior to achieve consistency between them.

Using this theory, the patient can be urged to mechanically do something positive with the wrongdoer, even though negative feelings exist. This creates dissonance that is reduced by changing the negative opinion about that person.

As an offshoot of this idea, have the unforgiving person do a project with the wrongdoer. Cooperative interdependence often creates a positive feeling. This causes inconsistency with the negative thought. To reduce dissonance, the patient may change those negative thoughts.

Self-instruction Training

Self-instruction training is another approach for facilitating forgiveness. Below is a self-dialogue with instructions and responses about what to say to oneself to renounce anger and to overlook the misdeed:

Handout 7.5: Self-talk to Facilitate Forgiveness

Preparing to face the wrongdoer after s/he has done something wrong:

I have to face him/her, but I am still angry. How upset am I?

Remember to self-monitor. Watch my feelings.

I want to act cold but I don't have to—I have choice.

Think of the extenuating circumstances for my anger. Is s/he entirely to blame for the misdeed?

Think about the good things s/he has done for me in the past.

Focus on positives. Remember the good times together. Don't step into rejection. I can control my rejection—it is not automatic.

Accept him/her as s/he is.

Put aside the anger. Don't hold on to resentments.

Take a few deep breaths. Tighten and relax the muscles. Get the anger out of the body.

I care about the person. Show it. Do acts of kindness.

Redistribute the blame. Don't concentrate all the blame on that person.

I am mad, but I don't have to blame. Blaming only causes problems.

I have to put aside the anger sooner or later—why not sooner?

Handout 7.5: Self-talk to Facilitate Forgiveness, *Continued*

Dealing with the wrongdoer while s/he is doing something wrong:

I'm getting mad. Stay on top of the anger. Don't let the anger control me. Self-monitor: how upset am I presently?

Tighten and relax the muscles.

Look for other reasons for his behavior. Resist the single explanation of badness.

Don't focus on the problem. Remember how I want to be later when the anger is gone.

Focus on my love for that person.

Stay calm. Don't explode or implode.

Dealing with oneself after the wrongdoer has left:

I do not have to continue feeling resentful. Let it go.

How upset am I? Self-monitor.

Get relaxed. Get the anger out of the body.

I have to face him/her soon—don't be cold.

Don't reject. Renounce the anger. Don't carry-on.

Do some act of kindness. Restart the relationship.

Treating Insistence

This section is included to show how CCT treats insistence and brooding. Insistence is not conceived of as resistance but as a *coping skills excess.* The therapist needs to form a semantic differential between positive insistence and excessive insistence. The former develops determination and persistence while the latter leads to unwavering demandingness and rigidity. Therapists need to discuss when insistence is useful and when it is counterproductive. The intent is to preserve the positive form of insistence as a useful coping skill, and contextualize it for an appropriate setting. Show how it can have benefit in different settings (work or home).

Behind positive or excessive insistence is absolutistic thinking. CCT does not consider absolutistic thinking a problem when it benefits the patient, when it is part of positive insistence. The issue is not absolutistic thinking but the excessive use of it, and the unwillingness to drop it when it is reasonable to do so.

One way to treat excessive insistence is by cognitive restructuring of absolutistic thinking. June has several absolutes, including "If I do for others they should do what I want" and "My loved ones should have my values and ways of doing things." However, disputing insistent thinking may only yield modest benefits, primarily because of rigid, entrenched thinking. Cognitive restructurists would continue to chip away at this way of thinking, along with homework assignments such as Rational Emotive Imagery (Wessler & Wessler, 1980).

However, CCT believes that continued disputation of the same beliefs may have limited benefit with some patients. CCT will certainly use cognitive restructuring, but when change is not forthcoming, other techniques are tried, such as (1) experiencing the consequences from using a negative coping skill, (2) forcing the taking of responsibility, and (3) prescribing the use of the negative coping skill (excessive insistence). Each technique is presented in the dialogue below.

T: You continue to insist on others treating you differently. Imagine your husband or sons are not doing what you want and you continue to insist on them treating you the way you want to be treated. Replay a scene where this occurs. How do you feel in your body when you think about that?

J: I feel tense in my chest and jaw. I feel stirred up, as you call it.

T: Focus on that. Notice how it feels when you insist on them being different. Stay with that feeling for a moment. Feel the unpleasantness from insisting on them being different. [June looks distraught and tense.] Now here's the big question: Is this how you want to be? [The therapist forces the patient to take responsibility for the consequences of being excessively insistent.]

J: I don't want to get upset, but sometimes I cannot keep myself from getting mad.

T: Insistence is a habit. It's a way to cope with disappointment and anger. When someone doesn't give you what you want you mentally argue with that person to give you what you want. This is how you cope when you don't get your way. But it is only a habit and you can change that.

J: [getting angry] But I think if I stop insisting that my husband or sons be different I am letting them off the hook, like they do not owe me anything. But they do owe me better treatment.

T: You are right. They do owe you more than what you get, they should be more giving but the fact is they are not delivering what you want. You have a choice; you can make yourself upset and suffer, or practice pain management, practice acceptance of what is, and overlook the disappointment. If you focus on the disappointment and brood about it, you are choosing to suffer. I just want you to take responsibility for this. It's your choice.

J: I cannot drop my thinking because it is not right how they act toward me.

T: Whenever you fall into insistence, take responsibility for that and the consequences of doing it, which means you will suffer even more.

J: I really don't want to suffer, but I just wish it were different.

T: That's fine. You are free to prefer it being different, to wish it was different. You only get into trouble when you steadfastly insist that it be different. If you so choose, continue to insist that they treat you differently [the therapist prescribes the negative coping response]. Focus on how much they disappoint you. Become preoccupied with their sins against you. Then, experience how this feels. Feel your distress. When you are upset enough, perhaps you will be more willing to change your thinking.

In this dialogue, a crucial difference with REBT needs to be noted (Ellis & MacLaren, 1998). REBT would argue that June's absolutistic thinking is the major cause of her problem ("My family *should* do more for me."). REBT would dispute this, saying that different treatment by her family is only desireable but not something that they should do. CCT would argue that her "shoulding," her tendency to tenaciously stick with a demand placed upon her family members and friends, is not the major cause of her problem. Instead, it is how she handles her absolutistic thinking, or how she "plays it out." She engages in agonistic arguments with herself and family, broods, engages in excessive insistence, and cannot squelch her focusing on this problem. That is what causes her pathology. Also, she does not cope very well with the consequences of that type of thinking. She becomes angry and then becomes involved with revenge tactics, mentally and passive-aggressively. Hence, June's irrational, maladaptive coping response is the problem, not absolutistic thinking alone. Many nonpathological people engage in absolutistic thinking about the errant deeds of family members but they do not develop long-term problems. Absolutistic thinking will cause short-term difficulties and people like June are advised to change it. However, absolutistic thinking can be managed if the other components of the irrational maladaptive coping responses are not present.

Transition Point

June's treatment has now advanced to the point that she is much better able to coexist with the significant others in her life. Her pain has diminished substantially. By practicing the skills in pain management, she feels angry much less of the time. Yet her family and friends continue to perform actions that she rejects. She is less depressed but still dependent on her loved ones. At this point, the therapist attempts to move June in another direction to learn a new coping skill.

He gives her three options: (1) continue to remain dependent on her family and friends to be supportive of her, (2) change their behavior by learning how to be assertive, or (3) become more independent of family and friends. Independence is defined as not centering her life around loved ones, not leaning on them for support, getting more support from herself, and pursuing other interests. If she only practices pain management, she will continue to feel pain regularly, but the pain will be mild to moderate and not as intense as it was at the onset of treatment. She will still have losses when others do not deliver the goods, but the losses won't bother her that much. However, if she pursues greater independence, June will not care as much. She declares that she is not a fighter, so she rejects assertiveness training. She selects independence training instead.

☐ Strategy Two: Independence Training

Beck and colleagues (1990) would agree with her decision for independence, maintaining that "the goal of therapy with DPD would be `autonomy'" (p. 293). *Independence training is presented as a skill,* not just a pursuit or goal. It includes the following subskills: (1) value clarification, (2) entitlement training, (3) imperviousness training, (4) self-support training, and (5) training to be affectively pacific.

As an aside, even though June has decided not to practice assertiveness training, she will nevertheless learn many of the subskills of this coping response. All of the skills discussed in this section are necessary for and subskills of an assertiveness training program. The only subskill that needs to be added to an assertiveness program is communication training. Hence, practice of independence training lays the groundwork for an easy transition into assertiveness training. Conversely, patients who learn assertiveness acquire the subskills necessary for independent living.

Value Clarification

Millon (1996) refers to patients with DPD as "interpersonally imbalanced" because they are heavily weighted in the direction of attending to others' needs first and not their own. They emphasize other-actualization rather than self-actualization. A dependent personality hesitates to promote one's own values if they are in conflict with the caregivers' values. Because of this, there is typically a lack of awareness of what matters to the individual, because fulfilling others' priorities is more important. In addition, there is a tendency toward low novelty seeking, because persons with DPD only satisfy themselves in ways approved of by the caregivers. Dependent personalities are stunted in how they can satisfy themselves.

The first step in treating this problem is *value clarification.* It places a primary emphasis on the self. Two key questions are asked: (1) "What do you really want for yourself, or what is your interest and desire?" (2) "What is important to you?" The first question involves the skill of *self-awareness.* The second question requires the skill of *prioritizing,* by ranking the importance of personal interests and needs.

Value clarification can be done in different ways. First, the therapist secures the patient's values. Then the therapist discusses or rates the chance of realizing those values. Next, consequential thinking is used to assess what will happen if the patient pursues values against his/her best interests. Finally, the therapist seeks to increase patient motivation to pursue positive values. This can be accomplished by encouraging and supporting new behaviors. In addition, the therapist can prescribe a behavior that the patient is already pursuing but does that action to excess (Therapist: "Do for your husband. Make sure he is totally happy all of the time. Only when he is happy should you think about yourself."). This is a way to make the point that there is too much weighting on certain values and not enough on others.

One way to perform value clarification is by keeping a three-column list, which increases awareness of motivation for goal attainment. The first column contains the general interests of the person that can be pursued that day. The second column is the priority placed on that interest (ranked on a continuum from high to low). The third column notes whether the interest has been accomplished. A fourth column can be added to cite the reason for not satisfying an interest.

Another option is to increase awareness of the influence of other people on goal attainment. A three-column entry is used here too. The first column lists the general interest and its value to the individual. The second column contains the belief about the primary care provider's rank for that interest. The third column indicates whether the interest has been pursued or dropped. If the care provider (e.g., husband, son) has a low rank for an activity and the dependent person ranks it highly but does not pursue it, then the care provider's influence becomes obvious. This will help the patient discover how much s/he allows others to co-opt choices or compromise individual pursuits.

Value clarification should not just stay an intellectual exercise. The patient also needs to feel his/her valued interests in the body and in his/

her emotions. Fantasy can be used to imagine what life would be like when a valued interest is achieved. The experience in doing so is then highlighted. The non-pursual of personal values also has to be felt and experienced to produce change.

Entitlement Training

After the patient identifies high-ranking interests, s/he needs motivation to tenaciously pursue personal interests. *Entitlement training* stimulates that motivation by *concretizing a sense of right.* It is concerned with the issue of freedom, which is a cognitive-affective construct. There is a belief that the self is free to follow personal pursuits, accompanied by a feeling of empowerment to follow them. The components of entitlement thinking include: (1) a claim to pursue or possess something, (2) a view of self as deserving, (3) an assertion of a right to make this claim, and (4) an expectation or demand for one's just due.

Included in entitlement thinking is absolutistic thinking. Because of that, patients need to be careful when they engage in entitlement thinking because it can lead to *excessive* demandingness. That can result in vulnerability to symptomatology. Because of that it has a bad name in mental health. A semantic differential needs to be made for the patient, to distinguish healthy entitlement thinking from an unhealty form. In actuality entitlement thinking only becomes an aspect of pathology when the assertion of a particular right is unrealistic and incorrect, so it is not in accordance with fact, tradition, or reason. A second problem arises when the demand to pursue a right is accompanied by imperative, absolutistic thinking, that something not only should occur but *must* occur. A third problem is when entitlement thinking is combined with other activities such as brooding, castigation of others who frustrate goal attainment, and agonistic arguments. In this case the demand to pursue a right is coupled with a preoccupation with unsatisfied rights, damning of others, along with an inner argument against anyone frustrating the pursuance of a right. If these three problems are avoided, then entitlement thinking becomes a vital means for achieving motivation, personal growth, individuation, and self-expression.

When entitlement thinking is first presented to a patient with DPD, there is usually resistance. Often there is uncertainty about one's rights in general. A discussion about the rights of people in general is helpful at this point. Second, there is frequently a fear of making an improper assertion of rights. A person with DPD is very careful about not being "pushy" because s/he is conditioned to shun power. June presumes that she will be rejected, which is not always the case. Generalizations such as this have to be confronted. There may also be a fear of rejection or abandonment if "I assert my rights and become independent." A patient with DPD is anxiously attached, to use Bowlby's term (1982), living with constant anxiety over losing the support from the attachment figure. Loss of support is considered catastrophic.

Catastrophic thinking often prevents patients from engaging in entitlement thinking. Consequently, there is a need for *decatastrophizing training*. This involves four subskills.

1. *Objectivity* is needed to assume a dispassionate stance about the catastrophic event. Psychological distancing is a microskill of objectivity. The patient can become someone else dispassionately viewing his/her situation. The spectator role encourages objectivity. Next, someone else presents the argument for why something is catastrophic, and the patient hears the argument like a jury.
2. An *evidence search* is conducted. Data are gathered to test whether the feared consequence will actually occur ("How likely is it that this will happen?").
3. If the patient still believes that the consequence may happen and maintains that it will be awful or catastrophic, then *diminution training* is needed, to reduce the significance of the feared consequence. The evidence that is gathered is scrutinized to determine if the consequence will be so bad ("What is so terrible if x occurs?"). The patient's belief is challenged to reduce her level of perceived severity that something terrible will occur. See chapter 9 for a fuller discussion of this subskill.
4. If the patient continues to think the consequence will be very bad, *problem solving* can be used to find alternative solutions to resolve that problem. The feared behavior is identified, and solutions are generated to cope with that difficulty. The best solution is selected along with a plan for executing it (means-end thinking).
5. A support skill of *relaxation* is also helpful to quell autonomic arousal from catastrophic thinking.

There are two techniques for developing entitlement thinking. One is to find a role model that the patient can pattern herself after, similar to the patient yet possessing the qualities that are desired or demanded for change. In June's case, the role model needs to possess limit setting ability, assertiveness, and be independent. The need is to learn from one's opposite. In the case of a person with DPD, the opposite of her is a narcissistic personality. For June, this is her husband and sons. June is asked what she can learn from them and to discover how they operate. While she does not want to be like them in total, she can gain by incorporating their strong sense of entitlement and use it to attain her needs. At home, she practices being her husband, feeling entitled to do as she pleases.

Entitlement thinking needs to become an inveterate response so that the patient immediately, automatically feels entitled to act a certain way. To facilitate this, the following homework assignments are typically given. When the patient wants to perform an action, she follows that thought with the question "Am I entitled to do this and is this my right?" The purpose is to stimulate an inner debate about rights. If the right is confirmed, then the patient says to herself repeatedly as she engages in various actions, "I want to do this and I am entitled to do this. I should be able to do this." This cements a link between desire, urge, intention, and the assertion of right. A general right may not be irrational or inappropriate, but can be in a specific situation. Where and how a right is played out is the crucial issue regarding entitlement thinking. Even for the smallest of actions, the patient is encouraged to assert her right, such as "I want to lie down now and that is my right," "I want to brush my teeth now and that is my right," "I choose to eat now and that is my right." The intention is to make entitlement thinking an active mind-set.

Imperviousness Training

As Joan continues her training in value clarification and entitlement training, she notices mental interference with these pursuits. Someone with DPD habitually notices others' needs and directives first, which is an other-orientation. That way of operating has to be resisted if independence is to be attained. This is the task of *imperviousness training*.

A person with DPD spends his/her life noticing any breaks in rapport with the primary care providers. Loss of support and disapproval stir anxiety and are viewed as catastrophic. In general, someone with DPD is hypersensitive to disapproval and overly receptive to the opinions and suggestions of the primary care provider, who is able to penetrate and affect the patient with relative ease, stunting or detouring independent action. Mindlessly, the patient abandons his/her own agenda and pursues the agenda of the other.

To counter the other-orientation, the patient is taught to *become impenetrable* when desired, *selectively indifferent when need be in order to nurture and sustain autonomy.* Imperviousness supports independence in several regards. It keeps the individual focused on his/her own values and agenda. Second, others' criticisms, aspersions, or rejections are given less concern and weight. Finally, it helps to resist the urge for confluence with the primary care provider.

Imperviousness training is a twofold process involving *self-tuning* and *rejection tolerance*. Together, they facilitate *self-containment*—a singular unit indifferent to the environment. (Of note: imperviousness training can be taken too far, as in the case of narcissistic personalities. In that case it becomes a coping skills excess. Because persons with DPD are imbalanced in the direction of doing for others, imperviousness training only helps to correct the imbalance. If done in an appropriate amount, it will not lead to self-absorption and insensitivity.)

Self-tuning

Self-tuning extends the work of previous subskills. After value clarification clarifies the patient's interests, entitlement thinking stirs an assertion and motivation to pursue that interest. To sustain this effort, the patient with DPD needs to remain focused on his/her own interests, ideas, and needs. In essence, the self acts as a tuner or a receiver by tuning out others' frequencies or signals while tuning in to oneself; others' agendas are tuned out. Self-tuning sustains the focus on what has personal value.

To use terms from Gestalt (Polster & Polster, 1973), the patient keeps a steady figure-ground formation while pushing other figure-ground formations into the background. Other gestalts (such as another person's needs) may push to become foreground, but self-tuning restrains them from dominating attention.

In the induction phase, the therapist will in all likelihood encounter resistance to self-tuning, because persons with DPD have trained themselves to tune in to other people first and foremost. DPD will cause an immediate fear that self-tuning will inevitably lead to selfishness and self-absorption. To lower resistance, a positive and negative category can be created: *selective imperviousness* versus total indifference. The former becomes the desired skill. It is practiced in specific situations to minimize being hurt by others and to pursue one's own objectives. The therapist needs to emphasize that selective imperviousness does not exclude sensitivity to others, a primary concern of patients with DPD. Joan is told that she can operate like a radio and tune in to others when appropriate and then tune them out periodically to follow a personal interest. This contrasts to total indifference, which is defined as a way of life practiced by people who view others as inconsequential.

Several subskills and techniques are used to achieve self-tuning.

1. Self-tuning involves extensive *self-monitoring* and *self-evaluation.* Joan is told to stay aware in order to notice if she changes focus

from personal interests to follow others' priorities. Self-evaluation is used to assess how well she practices self-tuning and if she perseveres in following a personal agenda. An hourly schedule is kept of daily activities and is reviewed to determine if she pursued her desire. On the schedule Joan writes down what she wants to do in the first column, and in the second column whether she did what she desired for herself.

2. Guilt can arise while self-tuning in to a personal pursuit. Promote *entitlement thinking* at this point to overcome resistance to self-tuning: "I am entitled to do this activity and it is my right."
3. Have the patient tune in to the flip side of guilt—resentment. There is often resentment about having to surrender a valued interest to please others. Have the patient verbalize and experience that resentment, which can motivate self-determination.
4. Imagery can be used to solidify self-tuning. The patient can imagine herself in a soundproof room unable to hear the complaints of others. As she stays in this room, she says to herself, "Their complaints are their problem and not mine."
5. Altering physical activity is another way to gain self-tuning. June walks in a soft, tentative way. The therapist had her change to a "power walk," where she walks with a definite thud when she put her foot down. She pushes out her chest and raises her chin as she walks, to get in touch with her power. When she sits down she assumes her "power position," arching her back and keeping her chin up and chest out. In this posture or walk she is to bullishly stay focused on her own agenda and not waver to consider another's agenda.

For June, self-tuning meant several things. She began to place much more weight on work and career advancement, setting a goal to get promoted, which she had formerly devalued. She asked for more assignments to gain approval from her boss. This forced her to be away from home some evenings a week. Her husband objected to this, but she ignored his objections. She focused on her need to make new friends at work and went out socially with them, which she had not done previously. Finally, she decided to take adult education courses at the local community college to develop new job skills to make more money and not remain so financially dependent on her husband. Her husband had rejected all of these interests in the past, but *she stayed tuned to her own agenda*.

Rejection Tolerance

Joan's husband and sons greeted her strivings for independence with skepticism initially. Later, they grew concerned because she was not as readily available to them as they preferred. Her husband liked her "in her place," always ready to furnish him with services. To stifle her independence, he and his sons would become critical and withhold support by suspending communication, smiles, or emotional pats on the back. Their purpose was to use rejection to stifle or extinguish her independent strivings.

To maintain her independent course, a crucial skill is needed: *rejection tolerance.* It involves remaining indifferent to or unaffected by others' disapproval or one's own self-criticism while pursuing independence.

The first step in rejection tolerance is to identify and dispute the beliefs about rejection. These beliefs are:

1. "Rejection of my actions means total loss of support and guidance, and that would be awful."
2. "If I am rejected, I will have to face a cold, dangerous world by myself, and I cannot bear that."
3. "If I am rejected, I will remain isolated and alone, and that would be awful."
4. "If I am rejected or have to function independently without others' support and guidance, I will fall apart or disintegrate."

Each of these beliefs is unrealistic and causes anxiety and dread. Cognitive restructuring is initiated to dispute these ideas. Two companion cognitive skills are helpful to aid restructuring. One is *diminution training,* to reduce the significance of the rejection. This involves the following steps:

1. The badness of rejection is rated in a given situation.
2. The argument supporting the awfulness of a rejection is heard. The patient has to prove that the rejection will be terrible.
3. The patient then impugns the charge that rejection will be so bad ("Can I not go on if I am rejected? Yes, I certainly can.").
4. The case is then presented to a mental jury to decide if rejection will be so significant. If rejection is deemed not so bad then it is diminished.

A second helpful subskill is *evaluative judgment training,* to learn how to make accurate ratings. First, the patient rank-orders so-called terrible events as rejection and then places them on a continuum (e.g., "Is it truly awful or terrible if rejection occurs? What would be more terrible than that?").

While cognitive restructuring is helpful, patients may admit that their thinking is incorrect (that rejection by a care provider is not awful) but nevertheless slip back into dreading rejection. When faced with disapproval, habitual, automatic, overlearned thinking can return. This is due to positional slippage. In that case, there is a need for a self-dialogue to recondition the mechanical response to rejection. The following is a set of self-statements to "inoculate" the patient against the virulent or hurtful nature of rejection.

Handout 7.6: Self-statements for Rejection Tolerance

Preparing for a situation where I may be rejected:

S/he may not like what I am about to do. Is that so bad?

Where is it written I have to do things his/her way?

I can get by if s/he withdraws approval.

I have a good mind and can figure things out by myself.

Just relax and don't get upset if s/he gets mad. Take a few deep breaths. Don't panic.

Facing rejection when it happens:

Rejection hurts, but I can live with it. It's not the end of the world. I can tolerate this pain.

I want his/her approval, but I also want to do things my way. Focus on my priorities. What's most important?

Don't cave in. Remain independent. I am entitled to do things my way.

I can learn to tolerate rejection. It will get better over time.

I can get approval from others even if s/he dislikes what I am doing. There are other people besides him/her in this world.

What to say if I'm starting to get depressed:

The rejection is becoming overwhelming. I am sinking into depression. I don't want this.

Become objective. Examine my thinking. Get the facts.

I can tolerate being alone. It's not the end of the world.

The pain will end at some point. Just hang in there. I can tolerate the discomfort of rejection.

Once the automatic response regarding rejection is managed, the next step is to stay impervious to other's disapproval. One technique for accomplishing this is imagery. Joan is given fantasies (see below) that she uses to stay impervious to others. In these scenes she visualizes herself remaining loyal to her own interests and staying calm when others disapprove or reject her chosen course.

- You are a duck and someone else's words slip off you like water running off your back. You continue swimming in the water, unaffected by others.
- You are a Teflon pan and someone else's words slip out of the pan without sticking to you. You remain clean, untouched by others.
- You are holding a magical umbrella and someone else's criticisms are raindrops. The umbrella is keeping you dry so their comments cannot affect you. They run off the umbrella.
- You are a radio receiver and you do not want to listen to others' input. Turn the knob to another station, thus ending their ability to reach you.

There may be a problem with lingering concerns about rejection. *Perceptual shifting* is then utilized as a support skill to stop lingering, residual beliefs about disapproval. When a person with DPD thinks of others disapproving of his/her course of action, tuning them out is recommended. This can be done by thought stopping or shifting to another idea (e.g., a favorite TV show). Either prevents the belief about others' disapproval gaining "playing time" in the mind.

Self-support Training

Along with rejection tolerance, there is a need to supplement the loss of support from others with self-support. Quite often a person with DPD resists entitlement thinking because of low self-esteem and a poor self-image. This is because of habitual downgrading of abilities and minimization of achievements while magnifying failures and defects (Beck et al., 1990). This causes self-confidence to remain shaky. Lacking self-confidence, ambition remains modest and striving is limited. A person with DPD assumes that s/he is incapable of achieving more. By not attempting more, a poor self-image stays intact, continuing to limit independent action that can challenge the basic inadequate view of self. Without an adequate level of self-esteem, the patient does not feel entitled to assert his/her rights.

Cognitive restructuring is one way to treat this problem, by challenging the view of self as inadequate. Another option is to build a coping skill—*self-support*—that can indirectly dispute the negative self-image. Self-support is defined as an ability to encourage oneself, reassure oneself, raise one's spirits when feeling low, advocate for oneself, supply evidence of one's capacity for attainment, and in general aid one's own cause. It bolsters self-confidence, which is needed to increase willingness to attempt new behavior and to assert one's rights. It corrects the tendency to overlook and minimize self-accomplishment. It supplements loss of support from the primary caregivers, who often withdraw guidance and support when the pateint becomes more independent. For this reason it customarily accompanies the inculcation of entitlement thinking.

In presenting the concept of self-support to the patient, it is presented as a skill, as an ability that can be learned. This skill is best learned from self-confident people. The patient is asked to think of self-supportive people and to identify how they think and act. Curiosity is stimulated about how self-confident people operate, maintain enthusiasm, and sustain effort when defeated or when facing adversity.

The first step in self-support training engages the patient in a general discussion about the definition of support. What constitutes good support? Two, an assessment is made about how the patient lends support to him/herself and when s/he does not. The third step is educating the patient about how to be self-supporting. Three key behaviors form the basic ingredients of a self-support program:

1. *Noting or paying heed to one's achievements in general.* This means monitoring of self-accomplishment. To facilitate this, a mastery rating schedule (Beck et al., 1979) is recommended, whereby the patient writes down the tasks for a given time period (e.g., each hour of the day) and then monitors if the tasks are accomplished. If they are, then the patient compliments him/herself.
2. *Highlighting or focusing on the positive components of performance.* This is a special type of self-evaluation, whereby the patient is trained to give more weight to the positive aspects of performance, while deliberately minimizing or paying less heed to negative or disappointing endeavors. This acts to correct the tendency to minimize victories and maximize defeats. In addition, evidence is gathered that the self can satisfactorily perform needed tasks.
3. *Reinforcing successful aspects of the performance.* Self-praise needs to be steady and profuse.

These three behaviors parallel Rehm's (1977) theory of self-control, which includes self-monitoring, self-evaluation, and self-reinforcement. The basic difference is in the quality of the self-evaluation and self-praise. A self-support program seeks to turn the patient into a personal booster, a ready-made source for approval, encouragement, and self-reassurance. The intention is to make a big to-do about oneself when an accomplishment occurs, instead of quietly moving on after a success—the pattern of a DPD.

To become a self-booster, other activities are promoted:

- Learning to celebrate one's victories, such as by going out to dinner after attaining a goal.
- Announcing to others an accomplishment by using "healthy" bragging.
- Giving oneself a gift or reward for a victory.
- Noting an accomplishment by deliberately thinking about it several times a day, such as by arranging for self-praise sessions in which a list of accomplishments are reviewed.

Train the patient to normalize self-support as a continuing, basic component of regular activities. Self-support sessions are scheduled, such as at the end of the day, when time is taken to note one's achievements. The patient needs to plan his/her activities for the day and then decide in advance what type of self-support is desired for those activities. A three-column table can reinforce this action, with the colums listing (1) activity, (2) type of self-support desired for it, and (3) whether self-support was given. The following self-evaluation form is commonly used as homework regarding the above tasks, to be filled out hourly.

Self-evaluation to Build Self-Support

1. Did I notice the positive activities done this hour? ______
2. Did I give more weight to the positives than the negatives? _____
3. Did I praise myself for doing the good things? _____
4. Did I stop myself from highlighting the negatives? _____

Address beliefs that curtail self-support. This means changing the habitual self-dialogue regarding errors and low attainment. Patients are taught to remain self-confident and minimize the focus on mistakes. This means learning to quickly reorganize the internal dialogue after making an error, so disappointments do not dominate and self-criticism is avoided. Below is a self-dialogue to replace the tendency to maximize miscues. The self-dialogue below seeks to encourage perseverance, raise spirits following an error, develop a positive attitude, and change the perception of mistakes.

Handout 7.7: Self-dialogue for Self-support

Preparing for a difficult task:

Why can't I do this? Where is my evidence I cannot be successful?

Don't limit myself. Work at it and see what happens.

Stay with it until the end—don't give up in the middle.

Think of my abilities and not my failings.

Statements when goals are not attained:

I made a mistake—so what? It's not the end of the world.

Don't drop the effort. Stay with it.

Learn from my mistakes. Mistakes teach. They're not bad.

Don't put myself down. Be fair.

I don't have to be the best. Where is it written I have to be the best?

Relax. Don't get tense.

Enjoy the challenge. Challenges are fun.

Training to be Affectively Pacific

A final skill involves an ability to stay calm internally when others object to and counterattack the growing independence of the patient with DPD. This means being *affectively pacific.* A pacific response is important to reduce others' rancor about changing the traditional relationship. It is part of a mollifying strategy: by remaining calm, the patient can gradually allay others' anger.

One way to accomplish this is to utilize a skill people with DPD already possess. Someone with DPD is characteristically warm, tender, caring, appeasing, and noncompetitive (Millon, 1996). S/he avoids social tension and interpersonal conflicts by remaining calm while others rage. Yet s/he may not be aware of how s/he does this. The therapy task is to learn someone's method of being affectively pacific.

From this inquiry, June realizes that she naturally employs several skills that allows her to be affectively pacific. One, she suppresses muscular movement and slows her breathing, which helps her contain her emotions. Two, she uses a form of perceptual shifting, by making other objects in the room foreground instead of attending to others' angry words. Three, she talks to herself while others are upset, telling herself to not get upset and just let them rattle on. The therapist encourages her to continue using these techniques when her family is angry with her.

Conclusion to Treatment

June's decision to become more independent led her to make a *quiet revolution,* which fit her personality. She persisted in following her personal priorities, which gave her much more personal satisfaction. Ironically, her husband paid more attention to her when she needed him less. He never did become the man she wanted him to become, but he did give her more attention, so the marriage improved enough to satisfy her. With the aid of acceptance training, she also developed tolerance for marital disappointments. She dropped insistence that he change. The major change occurred in her communication with him. Once she became more independent, she felt more able to become bold and assertive with him. She gradually learned communication skills, which she used with him and her sons, coworkers, and friends. Knowing how to express her anger, she stopped using her revenge coping skill. She did not need her husband and sons nearly as much because she pursued her own interests, even against their objections. Acceptance training allowed her to live with their neglect of her. It was no longer so painful. Moreover, she was able to drop her anger and forgive them more quickly. She stopped brooding about their lack of support, partly because she gave herself her own support. Overall, she became much calmer and much less conflicted. Her depression ceased as she found alternative sources of satisfaction.

In summary, June got what she wanted from therapy. She did not want to leave an unpleasant, disappointing situation so she learned how to stay in her situation with a minimum of pain. Is that the best situation for her? No, but that is what she wanted. The purpose of therapy is to help patients get what they want—as long as they understand the drawbacks of their decision.

June was treated in a "mid-term" therapy format. She was seen initially weekly and then biweekly over a course of six months. Follow-up visits were arranged afterward on a monthly basis for three months to monitor and support the changes she had made.

Summary

A dysthymic, dependent personality disorder is presented. Initially, she rejects changing the behavior of those who frustrate her. Taking her resistance and schemas into consideration, the therapist recommends two general skills: psychological pain management and independence training. The following table summarizes the subskills and microskills that constitutes these general abilities.

I. Psychological pain management training
   A. General subskills used to build this ability
      1. Self-monitoring and self-evaluation
      2. Relaxation training
   B. Acceptance training
   C. Constructive mourning
   D. Perceptual shifting by learning
      1. Sensory diversion
      2. Attention diversion
      3. Somatization
      4. Imagery manipulation
   E. Forgiveness training by learning
      1. Circumstantial search
      2. Redistributing blame
      3. Transformational imagery
      4. Positive substitution
II. Independence training
   A. Value clarification
   B. Entitlement thinking by learning
      1. Evidence search
      2. Decatastrophizing
   C. Imperviousness training by learning
      1. Self-tuning
      2. Rejection tolerance
         a. Objectivity training
         b. Anti-imperative thinking
         c. Making accurate ratings
   D. Self-support training
      1. Achievement focus
      2. Self-boosting
   E. Training to be affectively pacific

8

CHAPTER

Treatment of Major Depressive Disorder

This chapter demonstrates how CCT would treat major depressive disorder. It also shows how it would work with someone who has a depressive personality disorder or a perfectionistic personality.

There are various theories of depression, but one of the most popular is the characterological predisposition hypothesis. In this theory, personality factors are primary and depression is a secondary feature of the pathology. Elements of the personality result in vulnerability to psychosocial stressors, leading to depression. In the case study in this chapter, personality functioning receives major attention because it so strongly influences prognosis and responsiveness to treatment.

In CBT, absolutistic thinking and awfulizing are viewed as a major cause of this disorder. The case study demonstrates that these two irrational, unrealistic ways of thinking do not have to result in pathology, providing the coping skills set is changed and augmented. In fact, the treatment goal is to preserve and continue absolutistic thinking, but new ways are found to accomplish its mission. In addition, the case illustrates how virulent schemas can be altered or neutralized by reorganizing and supplementing the skills set. The chapter demonstrates that once the coping response changes, absolutistic thinking and schemas can remain in effect but no longer exert a pernicious effect. A dialogue is included to show how CCT uses process. The chapter shows that a patient can select an irrational treatment goal but still progress and feel better with the addition of key coping skills. A comparison is also given about how cognitive restructuring and CCT would address the presenting problems of major depressive disorder. The chapter presents a different way of treating an irrational maladaptive coping skill than was done in chapter 7. Correcting skill deficits is a major focus.

Case Study: Joe

Joe has had a problem with recurring, severe major depression since high school. He is a special-education teacher in a public school, working with children with learning disabilities and emotional problems. The year he was treated for depression was particularly difficulty for him. He was assigned an even more disorderly group of students than normal, and the class had not achieved even close to the high expectations that he usually has for his students. He was filled with guilt and remorse because he held himself totally responsible for his students' lack of achievement. The fact that they had significant problems did not alter his thinking about who was to blame. Over time he had grown increasingly depressed; finally, after enduring enough pain, he tried to commit suicide by ingestion of sleeping pills. Panicked by what he had done, he called a friend and was admitted to a psychiatric hospital. This was his second suicide attempt and second hospitalization. Upon his release he entered therapy for the fourth time in his life. Antidepressant medications have not benefited him in the past.

Joe is single and thirty-eight years old. He was married once and has a child, a son, from that marriage. He sees him regularly and is a devoted parent. The marriage ended because Joe made it a lower priority than his work, son, and golf, in that order. Dating relationships with women do not last long because he makes them a lower priority as well.

In almost every endeavor Joe pursues, he strives to be the best. This is done to overcome a basic feeling of inferiority since childhood. He is the consummate achiever and has been this way throughout his life. Meeting his high standards is considered vital, and he places strong demands on himself to do so. Golf, his only hobby, is pursued zealously, with high performance expectations for every shot. Similarly, he demands that he be the perfect parent, always saying and doing the right thing. His job as a teacher, though, receives his most ardent attention; he gives himself completely to it, intent on making the best lesson plans, having the best teaching style, and having the best students possible. His ways of being, though, are not odd in Joe's circle of friends. They are quite similar to him: hard-driving, success-oriented workaholics.

With such high standards for himself, he is doomed to disappointment. He is most vulnerable when his students do not progress. When they have a poor year, he does too. While he is regarded as a very good teacher, golfer, and parent, he nevertheless rates himself poorly when he fails to meet his high standards. At those times, he thinks of himself as awful—a total, utter failure. He disparages and denigrates himself strongly and feels completely worthless and highly inadequate. He broods and castigates himself for not attaining his goals. He endlessly reviews what he has done wrong and squelches other pursuits that can ease his sadness. In summary, Joe has an irrational, maladaptive coping skill, which is the major reason for his depression.

When severely depressed, he avoids social contact, stays withdrawn, and does not date. Generally, he is pessimistic, but when depressed this escalates into a gloomy, despairing, fatalistic way of looking at the world. He stays heavy-hearted and hopeless. He feels sad, irritable, gloomy, morose and is vegetative. He has poor sleep, lack of appetite, and low libido. Out of caring for his students, he rallies in school, is pleasant, and does not appear depressed. Once home, he collapses and sinks into a joyless, dark world. There is little energy left for fun. His existence is basically ascetic. Thinking that he deserves little, because he has not attained his high standards, he gives himself little.

His father is also a perfectionist, and both parents set high standards for him as a child. When he did not meet them, though, they became critical and he became disconsolate. He became severely depressed for the first time in high school, when he could not attain the high grades he desperately wanted to attend an elite college. This pattern of depression following disappointment about lack of achievement has repeated several times during his adult life.

Identifying Present Coping Responses

As therapy begins, the therapist wants to learn how Joe functions, and he wants the patient to understand this as well. To facilitate this, CCT initiates a process inquiry. The following dialogue is included to reveal how CCT utilizes process to identify coping responses and instrumental functioning (the use of self or others to attain goals).

Therapist (T): I hear all the problems you are having with your students, how so many of them are multiproblem kids with major conduct problems. I hear from you that don't get the support you need from their parents and administration to help change them. Yet this has not altered your standards for yourself or your goals for this school year. You keep your standards high—no matter the circumstances.

Joe (J): That's right. I still have to deliver the goods. These kids cannot read, and they will fail in life unless they can.

T: How do you get yourself to deliver the goods, higher reading scores, good classroom conduct, et cetera?

J: Well, I work harder.

T: You tell yourself to work harder?

J: Yes, I bear down.

T: You bear down on yourself. How do you bear down? How do you get yourself to work harder? [The therapist converts Joe's comments into a process, so he can realize what he is doing to himself.]

J: All I know is when I am not getting the results I want from my kids, I think of myself as inept and that I'm never going to reach my teaching goals by the end of the year.

T: So you create scary stories to motivate yourself. What do you do when you don't reach your goals?

J: I get really down on myself. These kids will sink in middle school if they cannot read. If I cannot help them, they're in trouble.

T: So you rate yourself in a very negative, severe way if you and your kids don't reach your goals. You make a dire prediction about what will happen if you don't succeed. Do these tactics work?

J: Well, all I know is that I feel pretty low now. I guess they don't work that well.

T: How do you keep motivating yourself when you get depressed.

J: I really get upset with myself. I give up, but I can't stand being that way.

T: You tell yourself very bad things about yourself if you don't succeed. That how you motivate yourself? [Joe shakes his head in agreement.] What do you do when you don't push forward because of your depression?

J: I rant and rave with myself to get going, to stop sitting around in a funk when I come home from school and to get busy.

T: You become very severe with yourself—a tough taskmaster, a real tyrant. You get angry with yourself. You issue orders in strong terms. Do these tactics work? [The therapist focuses on the pragmatic use of Joe's coping response, if it works or doesn't. He stays focused on the process to reveal instrumental functioning and does not work with content.]

J: I guess not.

T: How do you issue orders?

J: That's when I call myself names, like loser, fool, incompetent.

T: You sum up your net worth as a loser.

J: I am a loser if I don't deliver what's expected. I am not getting my kids to achieve.

T: So the totality of yourself at that point in time is equal to a loser. All of who you are is reduced to being a loser.

J: That's how I think at that time.

T: Does that get the response that you want?

J: No, I get more depressed.

T: So you try a critical approach that does not work. Do you stay with that approach or try another one.

J: I just continue to bear down on myself. I continue to call myself names.

T: So you do more and more of the same thing. I hear what you do when things are not going the way you want. What do you do when things are going well? [The therapist now switches the focus from solutions that do not work to those that do work.]

J: Well, I am happy then.

T: So you tell yourself that you are happy with yourself. [Again, the therapist converts a static emotion—happiness—into a process.]

J: Well, I am pleased with how things are going.

T: You tell yourself that you are pleased with what you are doing. So you become more supportive and nurturing with yourself. However, when you don't accomplish your goals you abandon that approach and become negative and hypercritical with yourself.

The process inquiry reveals absolutistic thinking, demandingness, awfulizing, a tendency for reductionistic thinking, extensive overuse of evaluative judgments (termed hypercriticalness), especially ones that are severe and highly negative, and underuse of sensory-based, descriptive judgments. With this and other information, the therapist is ready to make a diagnosis.

Diagnostic Considerations

Joe has a double depression. When not severely depressed, he has dysthymia, a mild depression that he has had since high school, intermixed with fleeting periods of mild contentment. Generally, Joe presents with the same qualities that Akiskal (1983) has called a depressive temperament. Someone with this temperament is:

1. Quiet, introverted, passive, and nonassertive
2. Gloomy, pessimistic, serious, incapable of fun
3. Self-critical, self-reproaching, self-derogatory
4. Hard to please himself and hypercritical
5. Conscientious, responsible, and self-disciplined
6. Brooding and given to worry
7. Preoccupied with feelings of inadequacy and shortcomings

These qualities are present outside of major depressive episodes but often lead to a characterologically-based depression, as in the case of Joe. Millon (1996) would describe him as having a depressive personality disorder, because he displays a worthless self-image, self-denigration, low self-esteem, a view of himself as defenseless (mostly against himself), an ascetic way of living, and pessimism.

However, the category of depressive personality is controversial. The American Psychiatric Association chose to include it only in the appendix of DSM-IV for further study. It was excluded from DSM-III and DSM-IIIR because it was subsumed under dysthymia. Others disagree, though, and maintain that there is a depressive personality (Klein & Miller, 1997; Millon, 1996; Kernberg, 1984; Akiskal, 1983).

Further, perfectionism is not a personality disorder in the DSM-IV. The closest to it would be obsessive-compulsive personality disorder, which would make Joe someone with a depressive-obsessive-compulsive mixed personality disorder. The qualities Joe shares with obsessive-compulsive personality include being overly conscientious and inflexible about values, preoccupation with rules, excessive devotion to work and an exclusion of pleasure-seeking activities, rigidity, stubbornness, and of course perfectionism. On the other hand, Joe shows significant differences with this category, especially Millon's description of it (1996), so this diagnosis is not a perfect fit.

Cognitive Assessment

Joe has two schemas, as described by Young (1999), that are typical of a depressive personality. Each will be described below along with the derivative basic assumptions (BA) and automatic thoughts (AT).

1. *Unrelenting standards/hypercriticalness schema.* This template for handling achievement situations includes a belief that one must strive to meet high standards of behavior and performance, along with hypercriticalness of self when this is not accomplished. Rigid rules for self predominate, leading to a feeling of pressure.

BA: I am worthless and a nobody when I don't meet my standards.
AT: Bear down, don't give up. Don't be a screw-up. That's intolerable.

2. *Defectiveness schema.* This is a template for handling inadequacy when it occurs. There is a primary belief that one is defective, bad, and inferior. This results in hypersensitivity to criticism, but also self-rejection and self-blame when goals are not attained. The consequence is a feeling of shame about supposed self-flaws.

BA: I will be exposed as who I am—a defective person—if I don't achieve.
AT: I am shameful when I fail.

The combined result of these two schemas is an overvigilance to meet standards, which has curtailed Joe's spontaneity, self-expression, and pleasure seeking as both a child and an adult.

The schemas form his policy beliefs, which are absolutistic beliefs about how he should act: "Non-achievement is awful and should not occur," and "Mistakes are intolerable and must be avoided."

Treatment Plan

Initially, the therapist decides to use cognitive restructuring to change Joe's irrational, unrealistic absolutistic thinking (that he must be a high achiever and must meet preconceived standards, regardless of the conditions or situational parameters) and extreme, severe ratings of himself (not meeting standards is terrible, awful). Being somewhat of a conformist and wanting to please the therapist, Joe dutifully tries to restructure his thinking. Previously in therapy he chose the same goal: to stop being an overachiever and perfectionist. Using cognitive restructuring on those occasions, Joe changes his thinking for a while but slips back into old cognitive habits, demanding high standards and becoming hypercritical when they are not accomplished.

Joe intellectually agrees that his critical evaluation of himself is severe and extreme when he does not meet his standards. He admits that his self-criticism and self-image are unrealistic, and that he is not worthless or as bad as he thinks he is when he does not attain his goal. Yet, when he is faced with not meeting his standards, habitual, destructive cognitive habits reemerge.

Joe tries to convince himself that not gaining his goals or meeting his standards is not a must but a strong desire. However, this is not what he believes. He maintains that operating at peak level—meeting standards—is a must for him. To him it is vital and feels vital. Meeting his goals is an unrelenting activity. He continues to insiste on being a high achiever and setting high standards for himself and his students. He continues to self-denigrate, self-blame, and be hypercritical in a habitual, almost mechanical way, when his efforts do not meet with success. The ingrained nature of his thinking is resistant to cognitive restructuring.

In part, the reason for this is rigid schemas that continue to influence his thinking, feelings, and behavior, and inveterate, highly engrained cognitive distortions and habits; in particular, the tendency to rate, evaluate, and assign blame. Young (1999) maintains that rigid thinking, as in Joe's case, is one of the major limitations on cognitive restructuring, and rigid thinking is most common among personality disorders. Because of rigid schemas, Joe has positional slippage, where he reverts back to assume irrational thinking after a while.

Cognitive restructuring would treat his insistence by continuing to hammer away at irrational, unrealistic thinking until there is more durable change. The problem is, *Joe is resistant to changing his thinking and insists on remaining a perfectionist. He loves being a high achiever* and relishes life when he can accomplish "great things," such as helping his learning-disabled students achieve at a higher level or the times when his golf game is "running perfectly." These are his peak life moments, he professes, when he feels most alive. He maintains that only when he is close to meeting his lofty goals does his life have meaning. Essentially, Joe not only prefers being an absolutistic thinker, he insists on it. High achievement is not a desire but a must—for both himself and his students. In essence, he prefers to think irrationally. At that point, the therapist realizes that he has been working to accomplish the goals of cognitive restructuring (to overcome absolutistic thinking and to think rationally) and not the patient's goals for himself.

On the other hand, Joe also is tired of how he despises himself and feels contemptuous of himself when he does not meet his own standards. He does not like feeling worthless, hopeless, and defenseless in the face of his hypercritical, castigating ego ideal. He is depressed about being depressed so much of the time. He is ambivalent—he does not want to make a change in his life goals but he also realized that his life goals of overachievement and perfectionism cause him to have recurring problems.

The therapist offers a compromise and moves treatment in a new direction: "Joe, there are perfectionists who are depressed and miserable and there are ones who aren't. Would you be interested in becoming the best perfectionist you can become, but one who doesn't slip into depression? Would you like to be a well-adjusted high achieving perfectionist?" *The treatment goal now shifts to one that maintains Joe's absolutistic thinking and his policy beliefs but minimizes their negative consequences. It maintains the schema of unrelenting standards but reduces its pejorative consequences. The focus is now on changing the template for handling inadequate job performance and not meeting standards.* The focus is on altering executive beliefs while preserving his irrational policy belief. Joe readily welcomes this, because this is what he has wanted all along.

However, the therapist points out the dangers in maintaining his absolutistic thinking. By converting a desire for achievement into a must, Joe *will remain vulnerable to depression* because his anger and disappointment will be more intense at times when he does not meet his standards. Pleasing himself will be more difficult, and he may fall into brooding. He will be more liable to use self-reproach. He will have many more moments of feeling frustrated and disgruntled.

Yet the therapist concedes that if Joe learns the skills recommended in therapy, he can minimize his pain and vulnerability. Joe is most willing to move forward at this point, because this plan preserves a basic component of his personality that he relishes—his rabid perfectionism.

Two general coping skills are presented to Joe and he agrees to work on them. One is perfectionism training, to learn how to modify the perfectionistic part-of-self to avoid depression but yet preserve its basic mission to meet high standards of operation. The second skill is healthy narcissism, to address what is lacking in the depressive personality: self-support, self-enhancement, and self-appreciation.

☐ Strategy One: Perfectionism Training

Joe has overlearned behaviors. When he does not meet his standards, he mindlessly, immediately becomes self-critical and self-derogatory. He slips into self-blaming in a harsh, mean-spirited way. He stays preoccupied with his shortcomings. To correct this automatic, inveterate response pattern, *a substitute, mechanical pattern is recommended* to take its place. It is consists of the following skills: (1) acceptance training, (2) effective mourning, (3) processing training, (4) evaluative judgment training, (5) blame training, (6) inadequacy tolerance, (7) perceptual shifting, (8) self-nurturance training, (9) value clarification, and (10) disappointment tolerance training. Together, this skills package accomplishes *two aims* at the same time. One, it helps Joe reach his goal of *being "a better perfectionist."* Two, it *changes the traits and tendencies of his depressive temperament* that previously has laid the foundation for recurring major depressive episodes.

Acceptance Training

In the last chapter, acceptance training dealt with admitting reality into the patient's life, by changing beliefs and sustaining realistic ones about her situation. In this chapter, acceptance training is used in a different way: to accept realistic goals and realistic plans to attain those goals. Beginning any task, people have to decide what their goal is. *Acceptance training* is an important skill when making a goal selection. It shapes the goal that is selected, which ultimately influences satisfaction with self.

A major reason for the negativity that depressive personalities and perfectionists exhibit is their *selection of unrealistic, unattainable goals*. Their standards for performance are tied to goals that cannot be directly influenced by the individual, and this ultimately sets them up for failure and heartache. When their goals are not attained, they sink into fatalistic thinking and feel frustrated, hopeless, pessimistic, and defeated. This is accompanied by self-derision and self-denigration. However, the tendency toward hypercriticalness could be avoided in the first place if realistic, attainable goals were selected. This increases the chance for success, and with success come self-satisfaction, hope, and optimism.

Once a realistic, attainable goal is set, perfectionists can strive to accomplish their goals perfectly. Their standards for performance can still be rigorous, demanding, and exacting but capable of being realized. They can continue to drive themselves as hard as they want, providing that does not contribute to lack of success. They can set high standards for performance and have a chance to achieve those standards, providing the goal is realistic.

There are three components of goal-setting. The first is *choosing means-focused or process-oriented goals.* For perfectionists, this entails *seeking perfection of the means to the end, instead of seeking a perfect end-stage.* There is much more control over the former than the latter and consequently much less chance of disappointment and failure. Examples of means-focused goals for a perfectionist include being "perfectly motivated" (giving one's best effort), having perfect skill performance, or knowing the exact information necessary to perform a task. These goals, while being very high and demanding, are attainable and influenced by one's own efforts. These goals are compared to Joe's goals of having a class behave up to the standards of the school administration, or reaching a high performance score in reading. These goals are end-state or outcome focused goals, which are much harder to reach and mostly beyond his own efforts. They are affected by many other factors beyond his individual input.

To illustrate further, Joe wants his learning-disabled students to read at grade level by the end of the term. That is an end-state goal that is mostly beyond his control. It is influenced by numerous external factors, such as the involvement of parents and the motivation of the students. If he demands that the class meet that goal, he will be vulnerable. Instead, he would be advised to focus on goals related to the means, such as having the best lesson plans, alternative teaching methods, or a winning manner of relating to his students. They are within his control and he will have much more opportunity to realize those goals perfectly. Joe is an avid golfer. He can seek perfect form for hitting the ball. That is a means-focused goal and within his control. But if his goal is to shoot in the sixties, then he is vulnerable to disappointment because there are many factors external to the golfer that can interfere with goal attainment. Shooting in the sixties is an outcome-focused goal that offers much less opportunity to achieve perfection.

The second component of goal-setting is accepting what goals cannot be achieved. That entails *willingly receiving that reality into one's life,* and in time being favorably disposed toward that reality. The goals that cannot be achieved are end-focused goals because they are beyond one's point of influence. Acceptance means a person is living with his limitations, living with what one cannot have or achieve. In summary, goal-setting is knowing where one is potent and where one is impotent or ineffectual, and accepting that willingly.

To form means-focused goals and to accept what goals cannot be achieved, CCT inculcates another skill: *area thinking.* It involves identifying what the individual can affect or influence by using information, skills, and techniques that he knows. It involves learning skills or techniques or acquiring information that can achieve a goal. This is all part of one's area, so to speak. Anything within one's area can be worked to the fullest. This means giving an all-out effort to learn appropriate information, to use that information wisely, or be as skillful as possible. However, at some point a person lacks power and control to make the situation completely go the way he wants. At that point, he encounters what is beyond his area, where other people are in control and in charge. What is within the other person's area? They can accept or reject Joe's input, or stay non-compliant to his assignments. The second component of area thinking is accepting that fact, to realize what is within and what is outside one's area. Again, this means accepting one's limitations.

To develop area thinking, detailed discussion needs to occur with patients about what is and what is not within their area. Role responsibilities have to be identified and broken down to differentiate between the two. For example, the assigning of homework is within Joe's territory. If students do not do their homework, that is outside his area. Directing them to do it is within his area. If they ignore his warnings, that is outside his area of influence. Telling parents what they can do to help with homework is within his area. Gaining their cooperation is outside his area. Only they can give cooperation. He can only influence it by his words. Choosing his words wisely is within his area.

To form an accepting response, the following self-evaluation form is used, where each day is broken into time periods and evaluated.

Self-evaluation for Acceptance

1. Did I have realistic goals for myself during this time period? _____
2. Did I accomplish my goals? _____
3. Did I accept the fact that I cannot always accomplish my goals? _____
4. During this time period, did I accept what I can change or what is within my area? _____
5. Did I work my area to the fullest and best way possible? _____
6. Was I content with myself when I did this? _____

A third facet of goal setting is selecting what reality a person will surrender to and what reality a person will fight to change, which is a nonsurrender strategy. Specifically, Joe does not have to surrender to the fact that he or others will not meet his standards. He can struggle on to meet his standards or press others to meet them. That will cause some degree of tension, stress, and anxiety, but as long as he has acceptance of reality and realistic goals he will have tolerable tension, stress, and anxiety.

In summary, goal-setting training involves the following steps: (1) select means-focused goals, (2) accept the fact that end-focused goals are not as easily attainable or may not be realized, (3) identify what the individual can do to achieve a goal (area thinking), (4) accept what is outside of one's area of influence, and (5) select when a goal will no longer be pursued (a surrender strategy) or will be pursued further (a nonsurrender strategy).

A final component of *acceptance training* in regard to perfectionists involves receiving reality willingly into one's life and bearing up to it (see the discussion in chapter 7). Specifically, Joe has to accept certain facts: life is a series of defeats and victories. Not all performances or skills are done perfectly. Life is a state of more or less becoming who one wants to be. Time needs to be spent with the depressive personality and perfectionist discussing these matters in order to develop a proper philosophy for relating to life, especially when performance does not meet standards.

Use of Historical Material

CCT seeks to identify major life coping strategies when appropriate. They are coping strategies practiced over significant portions of a patient's life. The issue of not meeting standards and goals lies at the heart of Joe's depression. His basic feeling of inferiority has spawned a life coping strategy to be a rescuer, a Don Quixote figure. As an impractical idealist, he is bent on righting the wrongs done to others (e.g., overcoming educational handicaps in his students). Hating to feel inferior, he copes by struggling to be as significant, consequential, and potent as possible, to make the Herculean effort and attain the unattainable or what is beyond his area of influence.

The cognitive coping therapist performs six steps regarding the major life coping strategy. (1) Help the patient realize why that strategy was selected in the first place. In Joe's case, it is because of his feeling of inferiority. He overcame his inferiority by becoming a heroic figure. (2) Have the patient experience the early-life feeling(s) that spawned the coping strategy. In Joe's case, he experiences his inferiority, the mainspring for his drive to rescue others. (3) Discuss the genesis of that feeling. Some early-life scenes are discussed where Joe felt inferior. Encourage experiencing those scenes. (4) Educate how others, especially parents, that feeling caused. (5) Emphasize how the patient copes with dominant negative life feelings. In the case of Joe, he copes by becoming a knight in shining armor to other people. (6) Re-live the moments of decision when the major life coping strategy is selected.

The purpose for using this technique is to increase self-awareness—on a deep emotional level—about the mainspring for his actions and the cause for his decision making. Joe, like other rigid thinkers, needs to understand not just intellectually but emotionally why he has his musts, why achievement *feels* so vital. He needs to know why, deep down, he has such entrenched thinking. It is one thing to grasp the reason intellectually for the existence of a cognitive set, as can be gained in psychodynamic treatment, but it is another matter to grasp the reason emotionally. It is one thing to understand what is one's thinking, as can be gained in cognitive restructuring, but another matter to understand emotionally why that irrational, unrealistic thinking persists. Joe has to experience the cause of his driving life force. He needs a deep level awareness that can pierce his inner being, and that is supplied by the experimental technique of changing major life coping strategies.

With enhanced self-awareness and experiential learning, Joe is better able to choose, on an intellectual level, how he wants to live his life. He can change the major life coping strategy, or preserve it but practice it in a healthier manner. He chooses the latter, preferring to stay a rescuer to others. Many times CCT will try to help patients succeed in their life plans if at all possible, providing this does not cause addtional problems.

Hence, the therapist, in the discussion of acceptance, discusses what a "good" knight in shining armor can and cannot do realistically and the need to receive that reality willingly. The therapist discusses *how to be a successful rescuer,* by selecting realistic goals, working his area, and knowing when to stop tilting at windmills.

Acquiring Resiliency Training

The therapist emphasizes that if Joe seeks perfectionism, he has to be resilient after defeat because the next challenge for perfection appears quickly. Joe's problem is that one defeat decimates him so he is not ready for the next challenge.

The need for resiliency training in a perfectionist is then discussed with Joe. Resilience is acquired by three key factors:

1. Working through the sadness from not succeeding. This entails effective mourning.
2. Selecting the right path to succeed, which necessitates processing training.
3. Not becoming immersed in self-criticism after a defeat because that only deflates the effort. This entails evaluation training. Each of these skills is covered below, to help Joe acquire the ability to be resilient.

Mourning Training

A companion skill to acceptance is *effective mourning*. As part of life, there are disappointments that result in a feeling of loss and sadness. Cognitive restructuring only identifies those feelings, and that is not enough. Taking time in treatment to feel the loss is important. CBT has had problems recognizing this fact. CCT encourages mourning when there is a loss. Grieving a loss facilitates acceptance. It helps people to accept an undesirable, unpalatable fact. It washes away the regret and dislike that something unwanted has occurred.

Frustrated perfectionists and depressive personalities are especially encouraged to engage in mourning, to feel the loss from not meeting standards. Part of why Joe becomes depressed is because he does not take the time to emotionally work though the losses from his disappointments about not achieving his goals. After a while the accumulation of sad moments eventuates in depression.

However, if there is difficulty being able to mourn in general, or being able to mourn effectively, then CCT will train this ability. The teaching of effective mourning is a response substitution strategy to replace the inveterate, immediate tendency to self-denigrate and be hypercritical following a disappointment. Instead, the patient needs to take time to mourn.

Effective mourning features a combination of feeling the loss, focusing on the pain, and then intellectually understanding why it has happened. In an oscillating fashion, the patient rotates from affect to thinking and back to experiencing the affect. (See discussion in chapter 7.)

Cognitive restructuring may be needed to mourn effectively. If there are irrational, unrealistic ideas that intensify the pain from the loss ("This disappointment should not have happened to me"), they have to be disputed. There is also the intellectual tendency to rewrite history: "If I would have done that, then the loss would not have occurred." This is the endless round of what-if thinking that increases the feeling of regret and keeps the loss fresh while history is reviewed as part of an agonistic self-argument.

Prospective and Retrospective Processing

Once realistic, attainable goals are established, perfectionists have to know how to achieve their goals. Once a standard is not met, depressive personalities have to train themselves to focus on what went wrong while avoiding self-evaluation, self-denigration, and self-castigation. They have to know what to do next and what not to do next in order to accomplish their goal. This is all part of *processing training. Processing* details and describes what has occurred or what will occur in a given sequence, either in the past or future, respectively. It is a key component for becoming an adept, less frustrated perfectionist.

After a disappointment or when not achieving a goal, the first step is to gather extensive information via sensory-based descriptive judgments on how oneself and others functioned in the near or distant past ("I did x when he did y"). This is termed *retrospective processing.* The information that is gathered about what went wrong is used to modify or correct behavior.

If need be, *objectivity* training is taught, where patients observe events and give sensory-based feedback to oneself. Stress to the patient that definitions or assumptions about the meaning of the situation are deemphasized in favor of empirical observations. Some patients need practice in training themselves to stay in an observing mode. The *continuum of awareness* can facilitate objectivity. It is a Gestalt technique (Polster & Polster, 1973), in which a person proceeds through the day saying to him/herself, "Now I am aware of . . ." At the same time that processing training is taught, a companion skill is also required, *evaluative restraint.* It inhibits and sidetracks the immediate habit of editorializing about and passing judgments on behavior and assigning a value to outcomes, events, and people (e.g., "This situation is terrible," "I stink"). Evaluative restraint has to occur immediately after not meeting a standard to short-circuit evaluation and hypercriticalness.

An education phase is often needed to facilitate evaluative restraint. Educate the patient about differences between evaluative judgments and descriptive judgments. For instance, the statement "I did well in that" is assumed to be a description, but it is actually a rating. It also does not illuminate the process, which description judgments do. Second, educate the patient about the difference between sensory-based descriptions and assumptions. Finally, educate the patient about the difference between sensory-based judgments and meanings about the event. The former is facts being put into words, while the latter is a probability judgment about the definition of the situation.

Following retrospective processing is *prospective processing.* It is conducted to plan the steps leading to goal attainment, which is also termed *means-end thinking.* A microskill of prospective processing is *alternative solution thinking,* which considers several options before making a decision about which course to take.

A support skill is often needed to maintain processing. Often depressive personalities become stuck at the point of disappointment about not meeting a standard. An *extrication strategy* is needed to pull out of affective activity: specifically becoming mired in depression. Self-instructions can be formulated to help patients manage negative feelings: "Don't feel—observe, gather data. Move on. Accept not meeting the goal. Live with it."

Processing training is a response substitution strategy, to replace the tendency toward criticalness and self-denigration observed in depressive personalities. CCT seeks to *build the habit of turning to processing after not meeting a standard instead of being self-reproaching or self-castigating.* Stress to the patient that time spent in intropunitive behavior and criticalness interferes with goal attainment and eventually results in depression.

Below is an example of processing in action.

Situation: Joe's class misbehaves while in the library.
Retrospective processing: When did they start to misbehave? What events were occurring at that time? How did they act? Who did what?
Prospective processing: How can I avoid misbehavior next Tuesday when they visit the library again? What steps need to be taken?

In summary, the steps in processing training include: (1) Evaluative restraint; (2) Retrospective processing; (3) Prospective processing; and (4) Extrication from negative affect. There are many times, though, when evaluative judgments need to be made. Hence, skill is needed in making evaluative judgments, and this is covered next.

Evaluation Judgment Training

One of the salient qualities of the depressive temperament is the tendency toward hypercriticalness (Akiskal, 1997). It is a key reason for depressogenic thinking and the negative, self-referential thinking that is at the heart of depression (Sacco and Beck, 1985). Motivating the patient to inhibit its use is an important treatment task.

CCT can deal with hypercriticalness and evaluation in two different ways. First, it can label these behaviors coping skills that are used in the wrong context. In this regard, they become a contextualization error. The procedure for dealing with a contextualization error is to perfrom a contextual search. Discuss the contexts where the skill in question (criticalness) has benefit. For instance, when someone gives a halfhearted, uncaring, blasé, unmotivated effort, criticalness may be used to motivate a more spirited, caring performance. Likewise, evaluation has utility when there is a need to appraise behavior, attribute blame, or establish an action's worth. The patient is then told to continue being critical and evaluative—but only in the appropriate context.

Another approach is to assess if a person actually needs a particular skill. The use for a particular skill—in this case hypercriticalness—is identified. Hypercriticalness is useful for a person who is lacking in motivation and caring and needs a "good kick in the rear" to get going. The qualities of the person the skill is intended for is then identified. In regard to Joe, the discussion quickly reveals that criticalness is unnecessary for a person such as him. He is already overly motivated, serious, and caring about role performance. Hence, the contextual search reveals a lack of match between person and skill.

A third way to deal with hypercriticalness and self-evaluation is by performing an incentive analysis. Identify the pros and cons of those behaviors, or what is gained or lost by being hypercritical to attain Joe's goals. The dangers of evaluative thinking are noted. For example, evaluative judgments can lure someone into reductionistic thinking, where someone equates his or her goodness to the rating (nonachievement equals inadequacy as a human being).

A fourth treatment is *contextual sorting*. The skills for Joe's life situations are then rank-ordered in terms of which is the best way to manage situations. Criticalness and evaluation receive a lower ranking compared to skills such as processing and self-support.

Similarly, the harsher forms of self-evaluation—self-reproach and self-denigration—are also discussed as a contextualization ereror. CCT wants the patient to understand the very limited number of contexts where they are appropriate and advisable. For instance, if Joe shows an utter disregard for being successful or is highly neglectful, then these responses may be warranted. However, Joe is certainly not like that, so he does not meet the criteria for using them.

There is an alternative way to treat the evaluative, critical tendency besides viewing it as a contextualization error. Discuss it as a coping skills excess. The point is again made that these two behaviors are skills and that all skills should be preserved but used only in an appropriate amount. The patient is then asked if he is using them judiciously, in the appropriate amount. Obviously, in the case of depressive personalities, they are used to excess and need to be curtailed greatly. The last treatment for hypercriticalness is to rehabilitate the critical, evaluative tendency. The therapist examines how the patient actually employs these skills when they are used. When Joe becomes critical, he is too vehement, speaks with venom, is derogatory, or at a minimum is too negative. He is then coached in how to speak to himself or others to avoid being scathing and injurious.

RET would want to drastically reduce self-evaluation (Wessler & Wessler, 1980). While CCT agrees with this approach in general, it doubts if it can be accomplished with highly rigid patients who habitually, routinely self-evaluate themselves. Instead, CCT works to make self-evaluation more adaptive and less pejorative of an activity. This is because perfectionistic, depressive personality is attached to criticalness and evaluation as responses, and they are an essential part of his personality functioning. Conceptualizing them as a coping skill excess or contextualization error does not put the depressive personality on the defensive, while at the same time it enlists his cooperation in correcting their usage. Because criticalness is such a major feature of depressive personality functioning, CCT does not want to disparage it directly. That may be taken as an attack on the depressive personality's essential nature.

To help the patient inhibit this tendency, though, a *reframing technique* is used. The content of the criticism (the harsh, devaluing comments) is declared unhealthy, but the intention behind the comment (wanting to improve performance and be the best possible person at something) is labeled as positive. The goal is to preserve the intention but alter the means to achieve it.

To help the depressive know how, where, when, and how much to be critical, the handout below is utilized.

Handout 8.1: Learning to Self-evaluate

1. Identify the situation where you feel bad.
2. Identify the thoughts you have about that situation.
3. Appraise your belief if it is an evaluation. If so, what is your evaluation of the event? How do you rate yourself in that context?
4. Ratings occur on a graded continuum, from mild to harsh. There are other values that can be given to an action or object. What are other ratings that you could have used instead of the one you selected?
5. What is your criterion for the rating you selected? For instance, if you label the situation as "awful" or "terrible," what are you basing that on? What is your criterion for "awful"? What actions are you comparing the awful behavior to?
6. If the rating is severely negative (i.e. "awful," "horrible"), then justify it by providing a rationale for making such an extreme rating.
7. Examine other behaviors that could have been committed in that context and rate them as well. Then compare the behavior in question to those other actions, if the former is as bad as the latter.
8. Dispute the severe evaluation. Ask yourself, "Why is this situation or action so bad? What's worse?"
9. Evaluate the pros and cons of the situation. Identify the positive aspects of the situation in comparison to the negatives. What is gained as well as lost when that behavior is performed? All actions are a double-edged sword, where you gain and lose whenever something occurs. When you consider the good that can come from that negative situation, does that change your negative rating? Is it still warranted?
10. If the rating is incorrect, make a new evaluation that is less severe and negative. Substitute the realistic, rational evaluation and assess how you feel using a milder rating.

Blame Training

Joe's unrelenting standards schema causes him to cast blame habitually and mindlessly, especially in a self-derogatory, self-castigating manner. He (like other depressive personalities) spends an inordinate amount of time assigning blame. The result is a recurring or persistent feeling of guilt, inadequacy, and worthlessness. His belief about who is to blame is influenced by his defectiveness schema, which automatically makes him concentrate on himself as the sole reason for troubles, poor results, or not meeting a standard, while ignoring the role of other factors.

Cognitive restructuring is one way to challenge assertions of blame ("Is it true that you are totally responsible for this problem?"). Statements of blame are labeled unrealistic, erroneous thinking and are disputed. However, because blaming is an overlearned behavior in depressive personalities, they easily slip back into attributing sole blame to themselves. Because of that, *blame training* is initiated to supplement cognitive restructuring, to help the patient become more adept at assigning responsibility. Blame training is presented as a skill to overcome omnipresent remorse, guilt, and shame. It reshapes the blame tendency, so it is not used to denigrate or castigate the self.

To induct the patient into using blame training, CCT wants the depressive to experience the emotions that lead to the blame response. The therapist acknowledges the cause of why Joe blames himself so brutally—his overwhelming sadness and rage at himself for not succeeding and making mistakes. An attempt is made to have the patient experience that sadness and rage, to connect the depression to his feeling of impotency about committing errors or not reaching a standard. Next, the therapist links the depression to the blaming tendency as one contributing factor for it. Finally, if there is a need to blame, the patient is asked if he would like to know how to do it correctly, so that it is not self-injurious. The goal is *to become an adept blamer.*

Once a contract is made to correct the blaming tendency, the patient is first educated about the many external and internal factors that can influence behavior. This is done to develop intellectual ability in conducting a *circumstantial search* (see chapter 7 for discussion in section on forgiveness training). He is given handouts (7.3 and 7.4) that will guide the search for extenuating circumstances and the assignment of blame. Second, to gain practice being an objective, fair blamer, a list of past disappointing situations is examined to analyze who or what should have received blame in those cases. Present problems in Joe's life are also examined regarding who or what is to blame in those cases. The focus is on achieving unbiased, accurate blaming. In addition, blaming has to be combined with self-nurturance and self-support training (discussed below) because it can hurt self-esteem.

The final step is to know when to defer or suspend blaming altogether. While Joe blames freely and excessively, there are many situations (if not most) when blaming is unneeded. One can adopt the viewpoint that "shit happens," as the saying goes, and is part of life. To know when blaming is helpful and fits the context, criteria need to be discussed about when blaming has utility and is appropriate. Joe is asked to categorize situations in his life where blaming is advisable, such as to improve performance or to stop someone from erring in the future. Afterward, contextual sorting is utilized to rank order blaming in comparison to other coping responses for specific situations. Contextual sorting places blaming as a less important way to improve performance.

When teaching blame training to depressive personalities, a support skill is needed—*emotional disengagement*. This is because depressive personalities assign blame accompanied by intense negative feelings, which actually fuels the self-castigation urge. They have to be educated that blame can be ascribed without being negative—without emotional investment in hurting. *Blaming is presented as a cognitive activity only, a cerebral, analytic activity bereft of emotion.* If blaming or criticalness is attached to a negative emotion, brooding can result. To avoid this, *objectivity training* is first required, to pull away from one's emotional position and assume a cerebral stance. *Psychological distancing* is a helpful microskill to achieve objectivity. The behavior in question is viewed as if it were occurring onstage. The patient imagines him/herself sitting in the audience viewing the action as a dispassionate critic. When assessing who is to blame, *self-awareness* is needed to monitor emotional involvement. The presence of negative labels ("I messed up") or scurrilous self-accusations will clue the patient that negative emotion is present. In that case, the blaming statement will need to be challenged for emotional bias.

Once depressive personalities become adept at assigning blame or being critical in an analytic and nonemotional way, the problem of brooding can be avoided. *The tendency to awfulize does not have to be so problematic if it is only a pedantic, intellectual activity bereft of emotion.* In that case the rating of "awful" does not intensify negative feeling the way it usually does.

The self-evaluation form below will help inculcate these points.

Self-evaluation for Assigning Blame

1. What is my reason for blaming in this situation? ____________
2. Can I defer blaming in this situation? Is it necessary? _________
3. If I assign blame, did I do it in a nonemotional way? ________
4. Was I tactful when I assigned blame? Yes ___ No ___
5. Did I say something supportive and nurturing afterward, to balance the blaming statement? _________
6. What other factors or people can receive some of the blame in this situation beside myself? How much blame am I assigning to myself? _________

Self-nurturance Training

Anger turned inward has long been noted as one of the dominant reasons for depression. It is one of the factors fueling self-denigration and the hypercriticalness tendency. Both actions are a means to punish oneself. Abraham (1911) referred to this as retroflexed anger, where depression results from the inward turning of aggression. The critical love object, angry at the child for not meeting his/her standards, is internalized and incorporated into the self. The child then turns the anger onto him/herself and becomes the target of aggression.

Two issues are involved in retroflexed anger. One is anger as a result of irrational, unrealistic thinking. In that case, cognitive restructuring is helpful to challenge negative thinking that stimulates it. However, the patient may agree that his/her negative thinking about him/herself is unrealistic but nevertheless continues to slip back into being self-derogatory, impatient, and quick to find fault. In this regard, *anger is operating as an action tendency—a habit*—to attack with hostility. In this case, cognitive activity does not occur prior to the response. The anger at self is part of a knee-jerk, mindless reaction, and a general way of relating to self and others. Disputing and challenging thinking may not stop the automatic negative action tendency. A response substitution strategy is required to supplement cognitive restructuring, and that response is *self-nurturance.*

To make the switch, the therapist first needs to discuss the limitations of hypercriticalness as a coping skill in comparison to self-nurturance. An incentive analysis is initiated for this purpose: what do you gain and lose by each response? In the case of Joe, the analysis is conducted to help him decide which response will help him achieve his goal of perfection and which will sidetrack it. He quickly realizes that the result of being self-denigrating is a loss of motivation, a dispirited performance, and eventually depression. Another approach is to have patients critique their parents' style of relating when the patient was a child. Patients can reexperience how they felt when a parent related in a critical or nurturing way.

Once there is willingness to try self-nurturance, the therapist needs to educate the patient about how to be self-nurturing. *Communication training* is needed at this point to instruct the patient in the mechanics of delivering nurturing messages (e.g., "I like how I do this," "I did a fine job on this"). Non-nurturing people often lack knowledge of actual words to use. Another approach is to distinguish critical from nurturing messages. Transactional analysis (TA) discusses two ways a person can relate when acting like a parent figure: a critical parent and a nurturing parent (James and Jongeward, 1973). Each is explained to the patient, regarding how each state relates to oneself and others. Examples of how each would give feedback are given. Then vignettes containing a problem are presented and the patient has the task of saying how each parent state would give feedback.

A third way to inculcate self-nurturance is to use the empty chair technique from Gestalt therapy (Polster & Polster, 1973) and have the patient enact each parent state in the first person. Before doing this, the therapist elicits problem situations from the patient's past. Next, the patient becomes the critical and then the nurturing parent and gives feedback to him/herself in that respective role concerning past problems. Finally, the roles are reversed and the patient becomes him/herself and talks to the critical and nurturing parent in the empty chair, giving each parent state feedback on how it feels to be talked to in that manner.

To solidify the habit of self-nurturance, Joe is given the task of becoming a nurturing parent to himself. A diary is kept of problem situations and what is said to himself in those situations. The diary is then reviewed in session to assess his nurturing style. When he is uncertain of what to say to himself in difficult situations, the therapist coaches him in how to be self-nurturing.

Value Clarification

As a perfectionist, Joe is personally unbalanced, heavily involved in activities that feature achievement and performance expectations, and only slightly involved with frivolous, pleasure-seeking activities where performance is not an issue. Joe prefers being achievement-focused, or at least the perfectionistic part of himself wants it that way. To be fully functioning, though, he needs to empower other facets of his personality that have been eclipsed. Then he can decide how much of the time he wants to operate as a perfectionist vis-à-vis other roles. A *value clarification skill* is required for this task.

The therapist raises the point that there are other parts-of-self with their own inherent values that are underrepresented when he makes life decisions. Joe is first asked to identify those other parts-of-self that have been suppressed, such as his hedonistic, artistic, playful, spiritual, or romantic parts. Second, he is asked to become one of those parts—in the first person—and describe what that part wants or likes, and how that part feels being suppressed. Third, Joe rank-orders a variety of other pursuits in comparison to achievement-oriented activities, to realize how he has deemphasized other ways of operating. Fourth, to give a voice and power to other parts-of-self, Joe is then asked to consider performing an achievement-oriented activity, but from the perspective of another part-of-self. For instance, he can let the playful part-of-self teach some classes, instead of his serious, somber, perfectionistic self, and then judge the results. Finally, Joe is asked if there is anything he could learn from another part-of-self (e.g., his playful part when it acts as a teacher). For example, an option is to let another part-of-self make out Joe's weekly schedule and then follow that schedule to judge if this improves the quality of his life. The key is altering behavior and then deciding what is valued *after* trying out a different way of being.

When presenting the idea of empowering other parts-of-self to Joe, the therapist is careful to preserve his goal—meeting his standards—but to do so by assuming other ways of being. The therapist emphasizes that other parts-of-self may be more effective for achieving perfection, even better than Joe's overly serious, harsh, critical way of functioning. In addition, the therapist asks Joe to consider when he does not want to operate in an achievement role, if he wants to expand the time as a nonachiever.

Disappointment Tolerance Training

The final component of perfectionism training is tolerating not being perfect when that occurs. This is an ability to bear the disappointments from imperfection, and living with not meeting standards. To accomplish this, depressive personalities and perfectionists need *disappointment tolerance training.*

The first step in developing this skill is acceptance training. The patient has to choose to accept the prevailing reality, which is not wanted but has to be admitted into one's life. Specifically, there are the inadvertent errors that comes with learning a task. The intention is to accept mistakes as a part of life, and to choose to tolerate degrees of inadequacy. The second step is to learn how past disappointing situations was tolerated. This is a solutions-oriented approach (Selekman, 1999), where the patient becomes a role model for himself. Third, there is a physical component to tolerance training: bearing negative bodily states that accompany negative emotions, such as muscular tension and increased blood pressure. *Relaxation training* is then needed to ease the concomitant physical tension. Fourth, the patient has to learn how to shift away from focusing on disappointment. This involves the skill of *perceptual shifting*, a perceptual skill to deliberately shift the negative foreground image into the background so that it has less influence on the emotions. As simple as it sounds, it is easier to tolerate a negative situation when not focusing on it. Finally, there is a need for *frustration tolerance training*, to cope with the pain entailed in disappointment. In some cases this is due to low frustration tolerance (Dryden and Ellis, 1986), an inability to cope with difficulty, or absolutistic thinking, where someone sets a standard for his/her life that it should not be so frustrating, and if it is, then that is considered awful. Those who engage in absolutistic thinking do not want to bear the frustration and discomfort of not getting what they want. Self-instruction training is used to build frustration tolerance.

Self-talk for Tolerating Disappointment

Preparing for situation that will be frustrating:
I can cope with this even if it is unpleasant.
Think of situations where I have coped in the past.
I was able to manage negative states before, so I can do it again.
Discomfort is not the worst thing that can happen to me.

Coping when feeling frustrated:
This discomfort I feel now comes with life and has to be tolerated.
Accept it. Don't reject unpleasant feelings.
Don't be so upset. Relax. Don't be uptight. Take a few deep breaths.

Disappointment tolerance training is combined with effective mourning. It, along with acceptance, provides the intellectual side of mourning.

Self-pity Rescue

A second factor that increases intolerance is self-pity. Underneath it is resentment that is fueled by absolutistic thinking, which places a demand on oneself or life to be a certain way. When that does not occur, there is intolerance of the situation that takes the form of self-pity. To treat self-pity, *self-pity rescue* can be used as a drill to halt the slide down into regret and misery. This is a cognitive-affective drill to treat an inveterate tendency to engage in brooding, regret, and bitter review of the situation that can degenerate into sniveling pouting.

One reason for self-pity is an inability to cope with loss; for perfectionists, loss comes from not meeting standards. In part, self-pity is sorrow or grief. *Effective mourning* can help with that. First, there is a need to feel the regret about having a less favored situation. There is a need to feel the sadness that accompanies disappointment and loss. There is a need to experience the body's tension and heaviness while feeling sorrow. Then, at the point where the patient is about to slip into self-pity, self-instruction training is utilized to question oneself and offer instructions on how to manage emotions.

Self-talk to Avoid Self-pity

Do I want to be this way?

Do I gain anything by feeling miserable about not getting what I want?

Don't condemn myself for whatever mistakes I made. Accept them.

How much should I condemn others? What is the benefit in that?

Not getting what I want is part of life and has to be tolerated.

Accept a defeat or disappointment into my life. It exists. It is real. Live with it. I don't want it but it is a fact.

Self-support training (see chapter 7) can then be used as a substitute response for self-pity. There is a positive aspect to self-pity. It is a form of compassion and empathy for oneself for suffering a misfortune (not meeting a standard or making a mistake). It is a way of giving oneself condolence. This positive aspect should be preserved, but skill is needed to offer caring self-support. The patient has to be taught to focus on positive aspects of performance and be a self-booster.

To facilitate escape from self-pity, imagery can also be used. For example, Joe sees himself rising from the mire, mud, and dirty waters of regret and excessive self-pity and emerging into the pure, fresh air, clean and light, as he achieves tolerance of disappointment.

In summary, Joe insists on being a perfectionist, which means he prefers to keep his absolutistic thinking intact about performance. In addition, he exhibits rigid thinking where he is unwilling to alter his schema that perpetuates his perfectionism. Given his imprudent choice, the therapist works with him to make his decision less injurious. He inculcates many of the facets of a rational adaptive coping skill, including acceptance, tolerance, perceptual shifting, and problem solving. The skills that are presented simultaneously address some of the basic problems of depressive personality disorder, including the tendency toward hypercriticalness, guilt, negative thinking, dwelling persistently on negative matters (the agonistic activity), and brooding. Therapy has given him response alternative to inveterate cognitive tendencies that he previously did not have.

☐ Strategy Two: Narcissim Training

We will now move on to discuss one basic, glaring deficit of depressive personalities: the lack of healthy narcissism. Depressive personalities have a depletion of what may be called "narcissistic supply," which is a motivation for self-caring, self-enhancement, and self-support. They have inveterate tendencies that damage this basic drive. They are inattentive to habits that can build self-esteem. Asceticism predominates and permeates activities to give less rather than more to oneself.

Cognitive restructuring can implant beliefs necessary for healthy narcissism. It can change thinking that damages it. However, a change of thinking may not necessarily inculcate and nurture the habits that can build healthy self-love. A direct focus on skill building is required for that. To introduce this issue, Joe is asked to identify new skills he needs to posses. The therapist asks the following rhetorical questions to stimulate Joe's thinking.

- "Given your tendency to be hypercritical, what skill do you need to have so you don't end up feeling bad about yourself?"
- "Given your negative, pessimistic viewpoint, what skill do you need to have so you don't end up feeling hopeless about your future?"
- "You live for the moment when you meet your standards and then you feel satisfied and good about yourself. But, that feeling is fleeting. Would you like to find a way to prolong the feeling of satisfaction with yourself?

These questions lead to a consideration of what role model possesses those skills. The therapist asks, "What kind of person could you emulate who could make you a complete person?" The therapist proposes just such a person—the narcissistic personality. (Again, this is presented to the patient as "I know someone who possesses skills that would be very useful to you.") CCT differentiates between a healthy form of narcissism, which contributes to self-confidence and high self-esteem, and an unhealthy form of self-love found in the narcissistic personality disorder. The goal of CCT is to give the depressive personality some of the beneficial qualities of healthy narcissistic functioning, or the worthwhile components of the narcissistic personality.

Narcissists possess several beneficial skills: (1) an ability to savor life's pleasures and seek pleasure (hedonism training), (2) an ability to appreciate themselves, (3) an ability to offer themselves support and encouragement in various ways, (4) an ability to reassure themselves to maintain self-confidence, and (5) an ability to remain optimistic. Each of these skills will now be discussed.

Hedonism Training

Narcissists place a priority on finding pleasurable activities for themselves. They have a zest for living because they think they are entitled to feel good. Oppositely, the persistent gloominess of depressive personalities has long stood out as one of the dominant features of the disorder (Schneider, 1923; Kahn, 1931). The gloom becomes an overly serious attitude toward life, an involvement in brooding, and an inability to throw negative things off. The consequence is a lack of interest in the environment associated with an inability to enjoy food, sex, or hobbies (Jacobson, 1971; Klein & Miller, 1997). The anhedonia that typifies depression presents itself as disinterest in the frivolous and a diminution of the basic drive for pleasure seeking. To overcome this problem, CCT recommends *hedonism training.*

Both cognitive therapy (Beck et al., 1979) and behavioral therapy (Hoberman & Lewinsohn, 1985) address this need. They emphasize daily scheduling of pleasurable activities that are meaningful and gratifying. The activities are graded on a continuum for level of pleasure. This increases awareness about the capacity of activities to yield pleasure and satisfaction, something depressives ignore.

While pleasure scheduling is certainly useful for breaking the depressive out of his/her disengaged stupor, it does not address the *problem of an inability to enjoy pleasure.* There are many people—not just depressives—who have this problem. They lack the capacity to cultivate, deepen, and savor pleasant pursuits. Without this capacity, the pleasurable activity is either not pursued because it does not offer enough reward or is pursued but the pleasure is meager and fleeting. To overcome this problem, CCT teaches depressives *savoring training,* something that narcissists do effortlessly. It needs to become a subskill of pleasure scheduling.

Savoring Training

Hedonism training involves the ability to savor. Savoring is predominately a perceptual-affective skill. Here are the steps for developing this ability:

1. While an activity is being performed, the person activates a dominant sense that makes contact with the object. The lead sense is actively, not passively, involved. If the activity is eating, the food is tasted and not just mindlessly chewed. If the activity is viewing, the object is looked at carefully and not just seen passively. If the activity is hearing, the sound is listened to intently and not just heard passively. Gestalt (Polster & Polster, 1973) terms the activated sense a "contact function," because the sense makes contact with the outside world. CCT recommends teaching contact functioning to depressive personalities.
2. Attention is then used to sustain and prolong the sensory-based

activity. If eating, attention remains focused on the food that is foreground, while everything else is pushed into the background. Maintaining the gestalt is the primary goal.

3. Awareness is used to notice nuances and differences in the quality of the object. If the person is eating, attention is used to detect differences in taste, texture, and consistency. If the person is looking at someone, vision is used to notice differences in the object, color, and shading.

4. As attention is sustained, this will have an effect on the person. The goal is to experience making contact with the object. At this point the focus shifts to the emotions and physical sensations affected by the savoring activity. The intent is to enhance the experience by remaining exquisitely tuned in to one's feeling while making contact with the object.

5. As savoring continues, the patient oscillates back and forth between experiencing the effect from the activity and making contact with the object via the dominant sense.

In presenting this skill to patients, modeling can be helpful. The patient is asked if s/he knows someone who is competent and has high achievement but also takes the time to enjoy life.

Depressives are unable to savor in part because of the action tendency of disengagement (Barlow, 1988). CCT views *disengagement as a sequencing error,* where the depressive first psychologically or physically withdraws before discovering if it is necessary to do so. Instead, depressives are encouraged to first stay in the situation and experience objects and other people and then decide if it is best to disengage. If disengagement is chosen, the depressive needs to justify this behavior and not just do it automatically.

Once the ability to savor is developed, the next step in hedonism training is to learn to enjoy the facets of one's life. Savoring can be scheduled prospectively. The upcoming day's events can be viewed in advance and whatever is pleasant can be fantasized and then savored—prior to the event. Then, as the actual activity occurs, the person is better prepared to savor it. Depressive personalities need to be ready to savor.

Further, sharpened *awareness* is needed to track pleasure as it occurs. Depressives overlook small gradients of pleasure when it is happening. For example, when Joe is teaching, a student with dyslexia reads a paragraph well. To savor this moment, Joe needs to listen carefully to the fluent reading and then notice his satisfaction from hearing it. He tunes in to the experience of helping and instructing. This prolongs the pleasure so that it can be savored. The self-evaluation form below helps to solidify experiences such as this, and it is to be completed at specific intervals throughout the day.

Self-evaluation to Encourage Savoring

1. What was pleasurable during this time period? ___________
2. How pleasurable was the activity, from 0 to 5? _____
3. Did I focus in on the activity and sustain contact with it? ______
4. By how much was I able to increase my own pleasure by savoring?_____ % more

Self-appreciation Training

Self-appreication is another basic ability of healthy narcissists. It is an antidote for the hypercriticalness tendency that lowers self-esteem and self-respect. Healthy narcissists hold themselves in esteem and feel pleasure just for being themselves. (This becomes a problem only when self-appreciation becomes a coping skills excess, resulting in vanity, haughty behavior, and arrogance, as in the case of narcissistic personality disorders.)

CCT conceptualizes self-esteem as not just a static rating placed on oneself at a given moment in time, equating the total complexity of a person to a set value. RET has discussed the dangers of this way of thinking because it is reductionistic (Wessler & Wessler, 1980). Instead, *CCT conceives of self-esteem as a verb—the act of self-esteeming*. This is a two-part, cognitive-affective activity: accurately measuring an accomplishment according to some criterion, and admiring or taking pleasure in that accomplishment. Admiration and taking pleasure are considered skills because they involve the tasks of noting or attending to a given quality (a perceptual ability) and then savoring it. Self-appreciation addresses one of the basic problems of depressive personalities, inadequacy preoccupation, which is a cognitive-perceptual dysfunction. Depressives have to learn to admire themselves whenever a task is performed well, regardless of outcome.

This involves several steps. First, a *mastery rating schedule* (Beck et al., 1979) is conducted, where tasks in consecutive time periods of the day are evaluated regarding how well they are performed. Next, *attention narrowing* is used to give sustained attention to the accomplishment. Depressive personalities use this skill to dwell on negatives, while CCT trains the patient to focus on positive aspects of task performance. Third, *self-support* is used to schedule time to take pleasure in task fulfillment, praise efforts, and celebrate accomplishments. Fourth, *savoring* is used to increase and prolong the pleasure from the accomplishment. CCT stresses that the last three skills need to be included when assigning the mastery rating schedule. This is all noted on the evaluation below.

Self-appreciation Evaluation

1. What did I accomplish in this time period? ________________
2. Did I stop and appreciate the achievement? _______
3. Did I feel better after doing this? Yes____ No ____
4. How much pleasure did I feel from doing this, from 0 to 5? _______

Self-support Training

Closely correlated to self-appreciation training is *self-support.* (See chapter 7 for a fuller discussion.) In this regard too, narcissists are a role model. They offer maximal support to themselves in general, but especially when there is an error, lack of achievement, and inability to meet the standard. They enhance themselves when they do not look good to solidify self-esteem when it is falling. This is an important activity for perfectionists and depressive personalities.

Self-support is presented to patients as a skill because it structures the perceptual field and organizes cognition to present a positive view of the patient, his/her work, relationships, and the future. It is a way to overcome the disparaging view of self that depressive personalities and perfectionists create. Narcissists model positive ways to support themselves. They are listed on the handout below that is given to patients.

Handout 8.2: Ways to Be Self-supporting

1. Be familiar with past positive traits and accomplishments. Prepare a mental list of them to be recalled when there is a lack of accomplishment, to ease disappointment in self.
2. Be ready to provide a reason for why there is a lack of success. Don't absorb all the blame if there are other factors or reasons to account for a lack of accomplishment.
3. Highlight positive elements of performance while paying less heed to negative elements. You may point out problems with how you acted, but don't dwell on them. If there is an error or defeat, notice what you did that was good in that situation.
4. Take prudent and cautious liberties with the facts by embellishing personal accomplishment or contributions. Exaggerate your accomplishments a bit and realize how significant they are. There is no problem doing this as long as you don't carry it to extremes.
5. Praise yourself often and repeatedly. Review your activities during a given time period and be sure to admire your efforts and accomplishments.

(As an aside, the depressive personality is complimented because he has skills that a narcissist can use, such as self-reproach, review of errors, and acceptance of responsibility for error.)

A self-evaluation form (see below) will help sustain self-support during the week, to be filled out throughout the day.

Self-evaluation for Self-support

1. Did I use some of the ideas from the self-support handout during this time period? ______
2. What self-support tactics did I use during this time period?
3. How much was I able to raise my self-esteem and feel better by using self-support tactics? _________%

Self-assurance Training

The depressive personality's tendency for self-denigration takes its toll, resulting in a lack of self-confidence over time. Entering a new and challenging situation, there is a lack of trust in oneself, and a feeling of anxiety and insecurity. This is what causes the sense of defenselessness. Challenges quickly produce a feeling of intimidation.

Depressive personalities can learn from narcissists how to note their accomplishments and be aware of their abilities. Because of this, the latter group has little self-doubt, remains sure of themselves, and stays calm in the face of a challenge (Millon, 1996). (Problems arise only when narcissists carry this skill to excess and glorify themselves, thus becoming immodest and cocksure.) While *self-assurance* is generally an inveterate response for narcissists, depressive personalities often need training to become that way. One way to acquire self-assurance is by increasing awareness of personal abilities. A performance diary is helpful in this regard. Handout 8.3 instructs the patient in how to gain self-assurance.

A historical review is one way to build self-assurance. The depressive can write a "slanted" biography of his/her life and list the positive accomplishments. That will become the "potency moment," to be remembered when feeling insecure. Because depressives underestimate and minimize their accomplishments, feedback from others on past accomplishments will be needed. Flash cards can also be used, listing present and past accomplishments. Because the cards are small they can be kept on the person and reviewed before beginning a task to boost self-confidence. The patient can list potency moments to be recalled when confidence is needed, such as before starting work or before facing the boss. S/he can perform a

Handout 8.3: Your Performance Diary

1. Keep a diary of activities performed during the week. Record even insignificant activities, because if that is the task at hand, then credit should be received for doing it well.
2. Highlight your role in leading to the success of whatever project is performed during that time period, no matter how small it is. For example, if you engage in self-care (e.g., brushing your teeth, showering), is this activity done well? Note it and enjoy your work.
3. Get feedback from others on how your activity leads to success and record it in the diary.
4. Read the diary often and feel the sense of accomplishment from contributing to the success of a project. Consider your prowess and intelligence and enjoy them.

potency drill, in which s/he mentally combs through past or present victories or accomplishments. *Anchoring* (King et al., 1983) can be combined with this. It is useful for quickly acquiring self-assurance. Past moments of potency are remembered, and at that moment the person touches a particular spot on his body (e.g., a particular knuckle). When the person wants to feel self-assured, s/he touches that spot, which refires the memories from past situations.

Optimism Training

Pessimism is one form of negative thinking that is most commonly observed in depressive personalities. The gloomy, dire, bleak predictions for the future become an enormous weight to carry, leading to a defeatist attitude. It is a major cause of suicidal ideation and gesture because it leads to a feeling of hopelessness and fatalism.

In a way, pessimism is a type of coping skill. Depressive personalities assume the worst will happen. By doing so they avoid the roller-coaster ride of life, where spirits rise but sooner or later fall as well. This happens to everyone, but depressives do not want to feel the pain of disappointment, so they opt out of the quagmire by becoming a pessimist: no hope means no dashed hope. Disengagement becomes a pain avoidance strategy. In a perverse way, pessimism allows the depressive personality to be carefree—indifferent to the world because there is no longer any concern about disappointment. Such individuals pay a price, though, by having to endure a dour, dark mood.

Oppositely, narcissists are optimists. They have a buoyant mood, act nonchalantly, are not perturbed by minor defeats, and remain mentally tranquil because they believe only good things will occur. Why? They believe (in many cases naively) that their abilities will lead to success. Because they are optimists, their temperament is insouciant: carefree and indifferent to the vagaries, problems, and indefiniteness of life (Millon, 1996). Again, depressives are informed about how narcissists operate, so that they have a comparative model.

Optimism is a cognitive-perceptual ability. First, an expectation (a prediction) is made that the consequences of a situation will be favorable, that good will triumph over evil, and one's circumstances will improve. Even when the facts in the situation do not support the expectation, optimists dwell upon whatever is hopeful in a situation. This is a perceptual ability to stay fixed on positive factors and keep them in the foreground.

Both cognition and perception are used in *optimism training*. A specific type of thinking ability is inculcated that CCT presents to patients as "*bright-side thinking*." As the name implies, the useful and beneficial aspects of a defeat, mishap, or disappointment are sought, noted, and given more attention than negative factors. To train bright-side thinking, patients are given scenarios containing a problem and have to search for the upside. They imagine what good can come from a problematic, troublesome situation.

A special type of *consequential thinking* is inculcated, to train oneself to imagine short- and long-term positive consequences that can arise from a defeat or disappointment. The patient imagines a problem and then brainstorms about all the good things that can arise in future situations by virtue of that problem. In the case of Joe, he is given the task of engaging in optimistic fantasies. He is to make a list of problems that happen daily, but then think of the positive aspects of those problems. For example, one of Joe's students is being oppositional. Instead of immediately slipping into pessimism, Joe is to imagine the good aspects of oppositional behavior, such as developing perseverance and drive. Using fantasy, he imagines how these qualities will help that student in the future, such as in a job situation. *Thought stopping* is also used to mentally remove negative factors that interfere with or compete for attention.

Optimism—self-created illusion—does not have to be harmful when used properly. The therapist has to contextualize illusion and identify its benefits. This will allow the depressive to believe that undesirable situations can improve even while there is substantial and contradictory evidence that it will not. This will inspire hope that can allow him/her to push on.

In presenting optimism training to depressives, the therapist can raise this question: is optimism or pessimism a better way to live, and which will lead to a more satisfying existence? Reveal the link between pessimism and depression as well as the link between optimism and resilience, motivation, and enhanced performance.

☐ Use of Cognitive Restructuring Versus CCT

In the treatment of depressive personalities, cognitive restructuring (CR) and CCT have their own methods of altering some of the basic facets of the disorder. As a way to review the ideas presented in this chapter, this section will present how CR and CCT deal with some of the basic problems of the disorder.

Self-image of Worthlessness; Belief in Personal Inadequacy

CR can dispute unrealistic beliefs, such as "I must achieve up to the level of my standards and not err, or else I am worthless." CR can dispute reductionistic thinking where the total worth of a person is equated to an act of low performance. In addition, CR can challenge a self-rating of being awful or terrible if a standard is not attained. By changing these beliefs, self-image indirectly improves.

In CCT, narcissism training is used to boost self-image directly. Patients are trained in how to esteem themselves. Evaluative judgment training is used to alter the tendency to give extreme, negative self-ratings that increase feeling of inadequacy. Blame training is used to alter erroneous attributions that cause the patient to consider him/herself at fault for everything. Indirectly, processing training and self-nurturance training improve self-image as well, by improving performance that decreases the negative view of self.

Feeling Dispirited, Hopeless, Discouraged, or Defenseless Against Life Forces

CR is used to attack certaintistic, negative thinking that the self and others are awful and that the future will be terrible. Schema of defectiveness challenged directly as unrealistic.

CCT changes these feelings by inculcating components of a rational, adaptive coping skill. The tendency to be hypercritical that leads to a sense of defenselessness is diminished by such skills as processing and evaluative judgment training, acceptance training, and blame training. Narcissism training adds to the overall positive feeling about oneself. By adding skills that make the person more potent, the schema of defectiveness is indirectly challenged.

Cognitive Style of Pessimism

CR is used to refute unrealistic negative beliefs about the meaning of a situation and erroneous predictions by seeking evidence to support contentions.

CCT addresses this problem through optimism training.

Melancholy, Gloomy, Brooding Mood

CR disputes the self-denigrating, self-reproaching thoughts that lead to these feelings. It challenges beliefs that are maladaptive and nonutilitarian (therapist: "If you think of yourself in such a negative way, how is that useful?"). It focuses on cognitive distortions as they appear.

CCT replaces the self-denigrating tendency with healthy narcissism and self-nurturance. It limits hypercriticalness by using processing in its place. It teaches how to accurately evaluate and replace extreme, severe self-ratings that cause a dour, downcast mood.

Lack of Joy, Inability to Seek Pleasure

CR would challenge thinking that diminishes the overall feeling of joy. It discusses the maladaptive thinking that only a somber, serious, hard-driving push will attain life goals.

CCT inculcates the coping skill of savoring to build an ability to enjoy life and seek pleasure. Healthy narcissism makes the patient more joyful overall.

Persistent Feelings of Guilt and Remorse

CR would challenge erroneous, unrealistic meanings about oneself and irrational expectations for self that lead to guilt.

CCT would shift thinking from focusing on disappointment to focusing on how to resolve the problem. This is accomplished by processing training and problem solving. Extreme evaluations that also lead to guilt are altered by evaluation judgment training and blame training.

Conclusion to Treatment

Overall, Joe has made substantial progress. He continues to have absolutistic thinking that he and others must meet his high standards, not make mistakes, and achieve at a high level. His schema of unrelenting standards remains in effect, which is what he wanted. However, the template for relating to himself when standards are not met has changed considerably due to the implanting of new coping skills. The tendency toward hypercriticalness has been reduced significantly. While he makes far fewer extreme negative ratings about himself, due to evaluative judgment training, at times he does slip back into awfulizing. However, this causes little problem because it remains an intellectual exercise only. He does not engage in self-denigration following a defeat because he quickly refocuses on processing what went wrong. Evaluative thinking has decreased considerably, but when it occurs it is accurate and realistic. This is because he has learned how to make sensory-based descriptive judgments that provide accurate data for the evaluation. He begins problem solving in place of getting stuck in self-pity about being disappointed with his performance. His tolerance of imperfection is much better. Because his goals are realistic, and because he only focuses on his area or the means to the end, he has the opportunity to succeed as a perfectionist. If he is not successful, he is better able to accept not being perfect. This greatly limits the amount of time spent brooding over defeat, and that limits the agonistic activity of endlessly reviewing self-perceived failures.

Hence, not changing his absolutistic thinking is causing little damage. His periods spent brooding are short-lived, and his feelings of depression from not meeting absolutistic thinking are fleeting and mild. Knowing how to effectively mourn the lack of achievement allows him to ventilate his feelings. The squelching of other activities is corrected in part by perceptual shifting and value clarification, which has identified other ways that Joe can achieve his goal of perfection. Value clarification has also expanded his interest base to pursue nonperformance activities such as dating. Finally, learning to be self-nurturing has helped to halt self-castigation. He has realized that if he wants to be perfect, his means of achieving it are counterproductive; self-castigation is seen as sabotaging himself.

In addition, Joe has learned skills that counterbalance maladaptive ways of operating. These skills work to build a healthy narcissism. He is better able to take pride in his achievements and savor them, support himself when he does not succeed, and feel self-assured and self-confident even when he incurs a defeat. He is able to see the bright side to defeats and focuses on the positive much more than in the past.

The net consequence is a change in his thinking that he is a defective person. This schema has been changed indirectly by the combined effect of learning new coping skills and not using old skills to excess (namely, evaluative judgments and blaming).

In conclusion, Joe's perfectionism is no longer resulting in pathology. He has succeeded in becoming a *"well-adjusted perfectionist."* Not changing his absolutistic thinking has resulted only in minor, short-lived disturbance, which he can tolerate quite well. Ventures into awfulizing cause minimal problems. His expectations for himself are still high, extreme, and rigid. The benefit from treatment is that *his irrational thinking regarding perfection no longer injures him to any great extent.* The focus in this case has not been on making the patient rational but rather on making him successful and more adaptive by improving the utility of his skills.

Joe is really not different from so many of his peers. CCT believes that the modern economy has produced a world of Joes: hard-driving, success-oriented individuals with high, unyielding standards for themselves. They come to treatment not to change their basic life philosophy, goals, and standards but because they do not want to be penalized so much by their pathology and irrational thinking. While CCT would have preferred that Joe change his thinking, in particular his absolutistic thinking about perfectionism, it chose to help the patient accomplish *his goals* instead. After all, mental health is a service-oriented profession.

☐ Summary

The therapist chooses to work with Joe's desire to become a better perfectionist. His schemas of unrelenting standards and defectiveness are not directly challenged, but the negative consequences from thinking that way are greatly reduced by learning new skills: perfectionism and narcissism training. In addition, the therapist preserves the patient's present skills (criticalness, tendency toward blaming) but makes them work more effectively. Thus, the skills approach is able to reduce the duration and intensity of depression. Below is a summary of the skills used for perfectionism and depressive personality disorder.

A. Perfectionism training
   1. Acceptance training
      a. Selecting realistic, means-focused goals
      b. Area thinking
   2. Effective mourning
   3. Prospective and retrospective processing training
      a. Sensory-based descriptive judgment training
      b. Evaluative restraint

        c. Problem solving
    4. Blame training
        a. Circumstantial search
        b. Emotional disengagement
    5. Self-nurturance training
    6. Value clarification
    7. Disappointment/tolerance training
        a. Relaxation training
        b. Perceptual shifting
        c. Frustration tolerance
        d. Self-pity rescue
B. Narcissism training
    1. Savoring training
    2. Self-appreciation training
    3. Self-support training
    4. Self-assuredness training
    5. Optimism training

9

CHAPTER

Treatment of Generalized Anxiety Disorder

In today's treatment of anxiety disorders, coping skills therapy is used extensively, more so than in the treatment of other disorders. Yet the range or variety of skills is limited and mostly focuses on anxiety reduction. Outcome studies support the use of this skills-based intervention (see Barlow, 1988 for a fuller discussion of this). Given the success of a modest coping skills approach, CCT presents a more comprehensive care program. This chapter specifically focuses on generalized anxiety disorder (GAD) and presents a conceptualization of what causes this disorder. When therapists use a skills approach with GAD, it is predominately dealt with as a coping skills deficit. This chapter presents a different way to view GAD, as a coping skills excess. The chapter presents an anxiety management program that integrates the coping responses of a GAD with new skills not previously discussed. The chapter shows how a schema does not have to be disputed directly to be altered and lose its toxic effect.

Case Study: Roger

Roger is a thirty-one-year-old, single college graduate who has never been married. He owns his own home and lives there with friends who rent space from him. He began a new, well-paying job as an accountant six months prior to treatment. He dates often and has several friends. On the surface, his life appears to be going well.

Yet he has severe, daily anxiety, describing himself as restless and a "bundle of nerves" from feeling keyed up and on the edge most of the time. He is irritable and tense, and he has problems sleeping and difficulty concentrating. He presents with a variety of autonomic-type symptoms including heart palpitations, chronic muscle fatigue and tightness, urinary frequency, nausea, diarrhea, dry mouth, and sweating.

His presenting problem is work-related. He is anxious that he is not learning the required tasks at work quickly enough and will be fired. While there is no evidence that his superiors are disenchanted with him, he stays preoccupied about this matter. He is apprehensive that a coworker will become his boss's favorite and be promoted over him, although there is little evidence to support this as well. He examines conversations with his boss over and over, trying to determine if his boss disapproves of him.

Roger has many worries outside of work as well. He wants to evict a housemate but worries inordinately about his disapproval. One of Roger's main worries concerns his relationship with the opposite sex. Roger will date for just a few months and then break up when the woman seeks more involvement and commitment. He does not know why this scares him as much as it does. He is the only single, unattached adult child in the family. Friends and family ask him why he is not settling down. This causes him to worry that "there must be something wrong with me." He has had panic attacks, but the last one was a year prior to treatment. He is quite worried, though, that his recent anxiety will trigger another one, to the point of being in panic over having a panic attack.

Often Roger is anxious and has no idea why. In other cases the reported cue for his anxiety is global, nonspecific, and vague (e.g., "just going into work" or getting more involved with a woman.) In general, one worry replaces another worry as his temporary primary focus; any issue can become the worry du jour. Specific problems quickly escalate into the worst-case scenario. He worries that bad colds will become the harbinger of the breakdown of his immune system. A busy friend is seen as someone rejecting him.

Roger has had this problem with catastrophizing since childhood. His parents considered him a "little old man" even in elementary school because he was always worrying about something. He stayed anxious about grades, pleasing teachers, being approved of by friends, or making sports teams. Yet he generally has done quite well in what he pursues.

To not worry and to avoid disappointment, he plays it safe by taking few chances and avoiding risk. He hesitates to take on new assignments or accounts at work, goes to the same restaurants, and vacations in the same place each year.

While Roger has a distant relationship with his father, he is very close to his mother, whom he describes as overprotective, smothering, and excessively involved in his life. Throughout childhood and even now as an adult she uses withdrawal of approval and involvement with her to control his behavior. The long-term result is a general need for approval from others.

There is a biological basis for his problem with anxiety. His mother is also a worrier, and a few family members have been treated for anxiety or panic attacks. Both parents are also poor role models in how to manage anxiety. They fret, become irritable, and stay preoccupied with an issue, just like he does.

Diagnostic Considerations

Roger has generalized anxiety disorder (GAD). This is defined by worrying about two or more life circumstances that occur on more days than not. The perceived threats to his well-being are not based on reality. The same level of worrying can occur about a minor or a major matter. There is hypersensitivity to any threat, no matter how small. Roger presents with the basic features of anxiety disorders in general: muscle tension, autonomic hyperactivity, vigilance and scanning for threat, and apprehensive expectation (Barlow, 1988). However, to reiterate Barlow's point (1988), GAD is not a residual category containing the features of other anxiety disorders, but a separate entity due to the presence of chronic, pathological worrying (apprehensive expectation). Pathological worrying is defined as excessive, unrealistic ideation accompanied by apprehension. This ideation intrudes into consciousness, is reviewed over and over, is difficult to control, interferes with and impairs functioning, and causes distress. At the same time, a specific concern can be welcome and is voluntarily reviewed for utilitarian reasons, such as to resolve a problem, form a plan, or to assess a situation.

Roger also has had a problem with panic disorder. However, his panic attacks are only one of many worries he has, instead of being the dominant concern, as in the case of panic attack patients. The more severe clinical disorder has been GAD. The panic attacks have occurred after a prolonged period of chronic, intense anxiety, so addressing the latter may avoid the former.

Cognitive Assessment

Roger has cognition that limits and impairs his autonomy and ability to function independently and perform successfully. At the heart of his pathology is a *vulnerability to harm schema,* which Young (1999) describes as a belief that catastrophe can occur at any time and that danger lurks everywhere, but the self will be unable to prevent it. Life forces external to oneself are presumed to be too strong and too overwhelming to manage. This creates an exaggerated fear about life. The schema leads Roger to make a basic assumption that life is unsafe and that he will be rendered helpless in the face of threat, unable to prevent problems and mayhem. A secondary assumption follows that he will have a life of difficulty, trouble, and pain.

Roger has another schema that this author describes as a *self-lacking schema.* This is a belief that the self is capable in many respects but not quite up to the challenge at hand or lacking in some key quality. There is a nonspecific but definite view of self as unable to grab the brass ring or put it all together in the end. This leads to a basic assumption that the self will inevitably fail in matters of achievement. The self-lacking schema differs from Young's defectiveness schema (1999), which views the self in a far more condemning way, as basically inferior, bad, and defective.

These two above schemas also result in a basic assumption that approval from others is vital and must occur in order to succeed, minimize vulnerability, and avoid catastrophe. This leads to overconcern about approbation and hypersensitivity to possible rejection. Self-esteem is dependent on others' evaluation of him.

Yet Roger is similar to others with GAD in that the facts do not support this self-image. While he thinks of himself as lacking, Roger has been an achiever in school and in his professional career. He has pride in his work and knows that he is talented in his job. He has his share of dates, and generally women like him. Unconsciously, though, there is routine uneasiness about himself and persistent self-doubts that his life skills are not quite up to the challenge before him. Hence, he has opposing views of himself as inadequate and adequate. The slightest hint of rejection from others or even lukewarm lack of acceptance can trigger his vulnerability and self-lacking schemas, causing him to question and not trust himself. The positive self-image and self-esteem build from solid accomplishments and natural endowment can quickly crumble, especially when others do not approve of him; fact-based thinking gives way to schema-based thinking.

Another schema complicates his relationship with women: *closeness is dangerous.* He has a belief that involvement and intimacy threaten his well-being and will be painful in the end. This emanates from the smothering, overprotective relationship he has had with his mother. While he likes involvement with the opposite sex, he also fears it. He can go only so far before anxiety becomes too intense. He then must choose between greater involvement or withdrawal from the relationship. He selects the latter in order to reduce anxiety and to feel more comfortable.

The schemas lead to the following policy belief that is at the heart of GAD: "Above all else, *I must stay safe from danger, reduce risk, and avoid threats to well-being.*" This absolutistic belief sets in motion executive beliefs that are typical of GAD in general. The executive beliefs form an overall *avoidance strategy* that operates mostly on a mental level. Like others with GAD, he faces his perceived threat, but *his mind stays focused on how to reduce, eliminate, or get away from danger instead of coexisting with it and learning about it.* In some situations such as dating, Roger is also behaviorally avoidant.

In seeking to determine which has the most deleterious impact—the absolutistic policy belief or the executive beliefs—CCT maintains it is the latter. The policy belief does create the driven nature found in GAD, whereby rational, reasonable needs that most people have (to avoid risk and danger as much as possible) are transformed into an urgent, dire, vital need. However, CCT maintains that *the executive beliefs form the structure of GAD. They account for the symptomatology and the chronic, pervasive, and persistent nature of this disorder.*

While the policy belief demands safety, freedom from vulnerabiity, and avoidance of danger, the executive beliefs select how this will be accomplished. They cue the action tendency of vigilantly scanning for danger and the effort to avoid danger in particular circumstances. If a threat is identified, then the executive beliefs demand *continued attending* to it until it is no longer a problem. The threat is reviewed again and again to impress upon the self that a danger is present and must be managed. It is as if a red warning light inside the brain signaling danger ahead, is stuck and cannot be turned off. The executive beliefs demand and search for a full understanding of the breadth and total ramifications of a threat, creating a trail of suppositions to discover the furthest possible deleterious impact. This is what leads to *catastrophic thinking.* The executive beliefs influence the operating beliefs to engage in a series of what-if questions about any and all negative consequences, to fully understand the worst case scenario. A solution to the danger is sought as part of *elaborate precautionary planning.* The chosen plan of action is reviewed repeatedly to find any fault with it; for instance, if the preparations are adequate, if all contingencies have been planned for, or if the plan can be improved somehow. This is what leads to the ruminative nature of GAD. It is part of a *redundancy strategy*—endless, repeated pondering, planning, reviewing, and problem solving—that is the basic facet of the condition and is what causes so much distress and symptomatology. The executive beliefs demand it in its design to satisfy the policy belief.

Ironically, the executive beliefs demand worrying to avoid greater worries. There is a presumption that greater risk of harm will ensue down the road, which will only cause greater worries unless a danger is reviewed in the present. The belief is: be anxious now instead of being anxious later. This is the "superstitious element of worrying" (Deffenbacher and Suinn, 1987, p. 338), that worrying now can avoid future worries.

This presupposition is reinforced intermittently, which is why someone with GAD believes so strongly in their way of operating. By engaging in constant planning and staying on guard, the patient is able to cope with danger but pays a heavy price for this management solution. The executive beliefs lay the groundwork for a lack of extinction of the anxiety pattern. Calling for sustained, vigilant scanning for danger, the patient stays at risk and worries more. The core fear of being in danger is never extinguished because the premise for resolution—hypervigilance—does not succeed in creating a feeling of safety.

The policy belief also contributes to a continuance of anxiety. Because it calls for safety and risk reduction as the ultimate goal, the focus is on avoidance of danger. This is not realistic nor adaptive because danger is part of life. Instead, the *policy belief needs to shift from "safety from threat" to "tolerance of threat and risk,"* a more realistic goal.

Coping Skill Assessment

The policy belief calls for avoidance of danger. The job of the executive beliefs is to carry out this policy. In the patient with GAD, a set of coping skills has been developed for this purpose. At the beginning of therapy, these skills are identified. They are a potent collection of skills.

Prior to entering a situation, the cognitive ability of *forethought* is exercised. Preparations are made about how to manage problems, and prior planning is conducted about how to act in a given situation.

Aiding forethought are problem-solving skills. One is *consequential thinking*. Anxious people consider both short- and long-term consequences in minute detail. They assiduously search for all possible consequences of a problem or action. Along with this is a *planning capacity,* especially an ability to plan for every contingency and every consequence.

They have a *capacity for review* of their planning and problem solving to prevent hasty decision making. This includes a capacity to *persevere* and *persist* in thinking about a problem to ameliorate or resolve it. This is part of the redundancy strategy—repeating previous thinking to find some error in thought or something that has been missed.

This is supported by a well-developed *threat identification ability* that can search and scan for danger or challenge to well-being.

Supporting this ability is a *motivational skill*. Anxious people are steadfast and *vigilant* about remaining watchful for difficulties or threats.

There is an *attention-narrowing skill* that permits the person to concentrate solely on a perceived threat. The anxious person has an ability to stay preoccupied with a threat even when other matters compete for attention and may divert the focus elsewhere.

Upon entering a situation, anxious people have an *impulse-control function* that prevents rash, risky behavior. They do not proceed further until reassured that the danger has lapsed.

If a threat to well-being is identified, the individual with GAD has a capacity for *quick activation and mobilization* to confront danger. This can take the form of fight (facing the danger) or flight (avoidance).

Treatment Planning

Because this list of skills is efficacious, CCT has no intention of abandoning them. No attempt is made to suppress their use even though they lead to GAD. Instead, the treatment task is to continue to use them but in the proper sequence, proper context, and proper amount. Individual therapy is initiated with Roger. Five strategies are selected: (1) anxiety reduction, (2) worry management, (3) threat reduction, (4) anxiety tolerance, and (5) threat management. There are several coping skills deficits and new skills are taught and inculcated to address those deficits. They are blended with skills the GAD already possesses to form a more potent, less tormented individual.

In regard to the vulnerability to harm schema, CCT does not directly dispute it as in cognitive restructuring. Instead, it indirectly disputes the schema by teaching new skills that modify the schema and reduce its virulent effect. These skills alter the perception of vulnerability as inevitable and unavoidable. The skills can create a new perception that even if vulnerability exists it can be dealt with, so there is less anxiety about presumed threats. The intention is to demonstrate to Roger that he is capable of coping with danger, and that he is not nearly as vulnerable as he presumes.

First, he learns how to reduce the number and size of the dangers he believes exist in his life. Second, he learns how to manage the threats that do exist. Third, he learns how to reduce and tolerate the anxiety that arises from those threats. He does this by learning new skills in combination with his present skills, and knowing how to use his skills more appropriately, so that they do not result in symptomatology. In regard to the self-lacking schema, CCT provides skills and readapts his old skills to change the schema's injurious effects. For his "closeness-is-dangerous" schema, therapy provides him with a new policy and executive beliefs that change and eliminate the harmful effects of his thinking.

In regard to the policy and executive beliefs of a GAD, CCT puts much more emphasis on the latter than the former. CCT attempts to change the template for dealing with danger by changing the executive beliefs. The policy belief is dealt with by promoting a competing policy belief and by inculcating new skills that lessen the need for an avoidance strategy.

Strategy One: Anxiety Reduction

With GAD, the patient's method of coping, his solution for life's dangers, has become the primary problem. Cognitive-behavioral therapy and behavioral therapy have mostly focused on anxiety reduction, in part because this is what patients want the most when they come for therapy. Patients are overwhelmed by their own coping responses, which they believe in and turn to daily. Their minds will not turn off, and their bodies are too tense and overly aroused to live a pleasant life. Because of this, patients with GAD seek amelioration: to "dial down" how they operate. Hence, the initial treatment strategy is symptom relief and symptom management. The techniques recommended in this section follow the basic CBT format for anxiety management: self-monitoring, relaxation, self-instruction, and thought control.

The anxiety reduction strategy is also implemented to address a secondary problem: the anxiety about becoming anxious. Roger, like most individuals with GAD, is apprehensive that he cannot reduce his own anxiety level. He erroneously believes that his anxiety has a life of its own and is therefore beyond his control. This accounts for the feeling of victimization and powerlessness that can result in a state of learned helplessness, which may eventually lead to depression (Seligman, 1975). Anxiety reduction techniques are taught to create self-confidence that the patient can achieve self-control and self-efficacy—the latter being a belief that the patient can make the situation go the way s/he wants, that the consequences or outcome of a situation is under personal control or can be influenced by the individual (Bandura, 1977, 1982).

Self-monitoring

Anxiety can present itself in two ways: as appraisal-mediated fear and as unmediated sensitivity to external or internal cues. In the latter case, there is a lack of awareness of the source of anxiety and the presenting cue. The conditions for the acquisition of information about a threat are stored without awareness. The emotional experiences that result in anxiety are removed from consciousness (Hamilton, 1982). Encountering a similar condition or experience at a later point in time arouses anxiety without understanding of the cue effect. The anxiety response can also be conditioned independently of conscious awareness, which makes the person vulnerable to anxiety in particular circumstances (Rachman, 1981; Zajonc, 1980).

Because of this, a cognitive restructuring approach is not possible until knowledge of the activating event is secured. Skill in appraising threat cannot be inculcated without specific knowledge of the threat itself. Therefore, knowledge of cues is the first step in altering the feeling of being out of control and powerless over the internal state. This knowledge is obtained by *self-monitoring*. It illuminates the connection between activating event and response, as well as the role of thinking in mediating between the two. It reveals how emotion varies in relation to people and place. It demonstrates the degree of effectiveness of anxiety reduction techniques by providing evidence of progress in treatment, which is important for refuting the vulnerability schema. This instills hope while helping to overcome the conditioned pessimism about the future. Finally, it informs the self that it can influence the outcome of a situation, which develops a sense of self-efficacy. A lack of self-efficacy is one of the major reasons for the anxiety response (Barlow, 1988).

From a practical standpoint, self-monitoring is crucial because a patient with GAD cannot utilize anxiety reduction techniques unless s/he knows how and when anxiety occurs. Because anxiety is omnipresent, a patient takes it for granted until it reaches a severe level, when it becomes poignant and obvious. The patient is habituated to being tense and aroused and is not aware of lower levels of anxiety that result in an uncomfortable existence. Self-monitoring is the first step in breaking the automatic stimulus-response chain.

As a prelude to self-monitoring, CCT focuses on *increasing general awareness* of anxious experiences, to make them as vivid as possible. The Gestalt technique of the continuum of awareness is used to facilitate this. Throughout the day, as the patient enters situations, he continues to say to him/herself, "Now I am aware of . . . " When anxiety is experienced, the patient is asked to stop and feel what it is like to be apprehensive. This identifies bodily indicators of arousal and tension (e.g., tight shoulders, a creased brow). A second Gestalt technique, identification, is able to sharpen awareness further while also facilitating ownership of bodily reactions. The patient becomes the anxious part of his/her body and describes in the first person how it feels to be that way (e.g., "I am my clenched jaw; I am jutting and tight"). The intention is to intimately learn about the vicissitudes of the experience, on a physical and affective level (Naranjo, 1980).

Once the patient is fully aware of the anxiety experience, recording it is crucial because memories can be forgotten or data can be distorted and ignored. Each hour the patient can document the highest level of anxiety experienced in that time period, from none to high anxiety. High levels of anxiety can then be recorded on a three-column table. One column lists the time of day. The second column describes the situation in which anxiety occurred. The third describes the anxiety experience on physical and emotional levels along with an anxiety rating.

Time period	Situation	Experience and rating
8 to 9 A.M.	Talking to boss	Breathing fast, sweating, anxious (8)

Once more aware of the activating event for the response, a second table can be initiated that adds a fourth column for recording the mediating belief between stimulus and response (Beck & Emery, 1985; Beck et al., 1979).

To learn the effectiveness of therapy, the total number of severe anxiety experiences (with a level of 4 or more) can be added and placed on a graph each week. Another option is an anxiety graph. The subjective units of discomfort (from 0 to 100) are kept on one axis and the time is kept on another in one-hour time intervals (Beck and Emery, 1985). Or the number of anxiety episodes is kept on one axis and the days of the week are on another (Craske et al., 1992).

Once self-monitoring reveals the link between anxiety and cue conditions, treatment can proceed onto anxiety and threat reduction and threat management. Three methods of anxiety reduction are proposed: (1) relaxation training to lower autonomic arousal and reduce anxiety, (2) self-instruction training, and (3) perceptual shifting to erase anxiogenic thinking.

Relaxation Training

Relaxation training is a staple of anxiety treatment, used for lowering sympathetic arousal and adjusting the level of activation. An example of a relaxation technique is the widely used Jacobsonian method of progressive muscle relaxation, where the patient proceeds through the muscles of the body and tightens and relaxes them (Jacobson, 1939, 1972). Another example is autogenic training, which uses relaxation-inducing self-statements and images. The protocol for relaxation is as follows. A patient imagines the anxiety-provoking scene and when anxious, s/he utilizes a relaxation method. This helps produce habituation to the stimulus. Once the patient is adept in relaxation, training shifts to graded practice sessions and scheduling of activities that allows him/her to practice relaxation in the actual anxiety-provoking situation. Finally, a self-assurance score is compiled, measuring how assured the patient is based on how much s/he can relax when feeling stressed (see "Self-Assurance, Tolerance, and Anxiety," below).

Relaxation is a part of many treatment programs. For instance, anxiety management training by Suinn (1976) uses muscle relaxation, deep breathing, relaxation imagery, and relaxation without muscle tension. Anxiety-arousing scenes are presented to the patient, and his/her task is to relax using one of these methods, thus creating a deconditioning effect. The next step is using relaxation during exposure to real-life threats. The model developed by Craske et al. (1992) also features relaxation therapy. Stress inoculation training (Meichenbaum, 1977) similarly uses relaxation cued by self-talk.

Self-instruction Training

As patients become aware of cues for anxiety, they are trained to notice their self-talk about those cues. Threat-driven self-talk or threatening imagery is identified. The goal at this point is to replace anxiogenic self-dialogue and imagery with consciously produced self-instructions that ameliorate autonomic arousal.

Meichenbaum (1977) has developed a cognitive program known as *stress inoculation training* that provides this. It cues the following activities:

1. Preparation for confronting the threat: "I am about to deal with him. Just stay calm and don't attack."
2. Inhibition to terminate unneeded preparation and planning: "Stop worrying; don't go over the plan again."
3. Productive behavior when confronting the threat: "Use 'I' statements and don't use 'you' statements."
4. Reinforcement of rational, adaptive coping responses: "Good job of relaxing."
5. Reassuring oneself that management of cues is possible: "I can manage myself in difficult situations. I was not overwhelmed."
6. Realistic self-statements to replace pessimistic or catastrophic thinking: "If I get fired, there is no reason I will end up living with Mom again. I can find another job. I have skills."

Self-statements are prepared for stages of confrontation: prior to confronting the stressor, the initial moment of confrontation, when aroused or overwhelmed by stress, and after the confrontation is over. Homework is assigned to expose the patient to anxiety-provoking situations. See Meichenbaum (1977, 1985) for examples of self-dialogues for stress and for use with specific anxieties.

Perceptual Shifting Training

Affective and physiological responses reflect the immediate, present cognition; change of thinking changes emotional and bodily responses. Perceptual shifting is utilized for thought control. One way to do this is to halt anxiogenic cognition with *thought stopping* (Wolpe, 1973). Undesired worries are recalled, and when anxiety arises the patient shouts, "Stop," which disrupts the rumination. An alternative is to shift attention away from an upsetting belief to a value-neutral or pleasant foreground image. This is a *sensory distraction* technique. For example, when anxiety is noted, the patient visually trace lines around the threatening object or note physical sensations in various body parts. *Psychological distancing* is also helpful for shifting perception. To gain distance, a patient sees him/herself onstage in the anxiety-provoking scene and watches him/herself cope, even giving him/herself advice on how to cope.

While thought stopping has not been found to be helpful for GAD by itself (Deffenbacher and Suinn, 1987), it may be helpful as part of an overall cognitive-behavioral treatment program, as discussed in this chapter. This same warning can be applied to perceptual shifting techniques in general.

☐ Strategy Two: Worry Management Training

CCT considers worrying in a patient with GAD as a legitimate, important coping response that has been carried to excess, as compared to the nonanxious individual who uses it in a utilitarian and functional way. Deffenbacher and Suinn (1987) define worrying in GAD "as a uncontrollable cognitive-emotional-physiological *habit disorder* . . . many environmental circumstances trigger it, and it is therefore under poor stimulus control" (1987, p. 333).

However, if worrying can be scheduled and limited to a particular time and place, then this habit would not be so omnipresent or its effects so pernicious and unpleasant. This way only a specific moment in time can stimulate worry, bringing the habit under the control of the individual. In turn, scheduling produces a realization that this intrusive habit is really a matter of choice. Worry scheduling utilizes but also preempts the patient's coping skill of redundant planning and hypervigilance. In addition to being a stimulus control intervention (a behavioral technique), worry scheduling is also a pattern intervention technique commonly used by Erickson (O'Hanlon, 1987). Altering time, location, and the number of activities to be performed while worrying changes the pattern.

Barkovic and colleagues (1983) use a protocol where worry sessions are scheduled for a half-hour period at the same time and place daily. Any worries are postponed until the appointed time, when the patient worries intensely about the problem and then problem-solves to resolve the difficulty. CCT has modified this protocol in several regards, including worry exposure, time projection, the worry checklist, and the format for making it into an ordeal, along with giving the patient freedom to schedule his/her own worry sessions once s/he tires of this habit. These issues are discussed below.

Similar to Barkovic, an appointment is made to worry. A list of worries is placed on an agenda. All worrying in between sessions is to be tabled until the appointed time. However, different from Barkovic, the worrier is given permission to worry about a problem more or less often than once a day. At the start of therapy, there is often a desire to have more worry sessions, which CCT has no problem accommodating. With continued use of this protocol, a desire for fewer sessions often occurs. Allowing this gives worriers greater freedom to control their habit, which is the end goal. They still practice terminating or tabling worries to the next worry session. Further, they need practice in stretching out the time between sessions.

Another modification to the Barkovic procedure involves the content of the sessions. During the session, the following steps are to occur. First, the patient not only thinks about reality-based or psychological problems but also imagines them occurring like a movie. During the "worry movie" the worst-case scenario is imagined, carried to the catastrophic conclusion. The patient is to stay with the scene, feel the anxiety, and then rate it on a scale from 0 to 5, with 5 being high anxiety. This technique is called *worry exposure*, an implosion technique. Craske et al. (1992) maintain that lengthy exposure to a repeated thought or image results in reduced anxiety over time. This is termed habituation.

The next part of the worry session involves anxiety reduction techniques. A *relaxation exercise* is performed to lower autonomic arousal. Following this, *problem solving* is conducted to resolve the difficulty. While the patient is adept at consequential thinking, he may not be skilled in *alternative solution thinking,* so this ability may have to be trained. After selecting the best alternative, a plan is formulated. At the conclusion of problem solving, a time projection (A. Lazarus, 1968) is conducted to view the problem six months to a year into the future, after the worst-case scenario has occurred and a plan of action to resolve it has been implemented. The intention is to show the patient that distance from a difficulty reduces its significance.

At this point, a second anxiety management measurement is made and recorded. If there is still moderate or greater anxiety about an issue at the conclusion of the session, then that worry is rescheduled for the next day and continues to be scheduled daily until only mild anxiety is present. At that point, the worry can be rescheduled whenever the patient desires. An increase in anxiety at a later time about an issue places it back on the schedule. In addition, an appointment is made to verify how well a chosen plan is working regarding a particular threat. This entire procedure is then repeated for the next worry on the agenda.

The worry session is to last for a specific time period (which is generally fifteen to thirty minutes), and that is agreed upon between therapist and patient. If the patent runs out of ideas to worry about in a session and there is still time to worry, then s/he is to repeat a previous worry and the above protocol regarding it. The therapeutic intention in structuring the session this way is to make worry partly an ordeal. When the patient tires of the ordeal, s/he may surrender or limit this habit (Haley, 1984).

There are other rules regarding worry scheduling. First and foremost, the patient cannot worry about an issue, problem-solve how to resolve that worry, or alter a plan for dealing with it in-between sessions. If a worry surfaces, then self-instructions are used to terminate the worry ("Now is not the time to worry about this"). This places the intrusive worry under stimulus control. If new ideas about a worry or solutions to resolve it pop up in between sessions, then they should be written down and taken to the next worry session. This is to reassure worriers that no idea or solution will be forgotten. The end goal is to develop trust in oneself, because worriers need to feel safe that they are in good hands—their own. Perceptual shifting can be used to terminate a worry in between sessions if need be.

The following is a worry checklist that is to be completed for each worry on the agenda in each session. In part, the checklist is designed to *make the patient into the best worrier possible,* and to make him/her feel confident that s/he is proficient in worrying and problem solving to bolster self-assurance.

Worry Checklist

1. What is my present worry? ______
2. Did I imagine the worry in action as a movie? _______
3. How anxious do I feel when I do this, from 0 to 5? _____
4. Did I do a relaxation exercise? _______
5. Did I project into the future and think about how my problem will be six months to a year from now? ________
6. When I think about my worry, have I considered everything that is dangerous or troublesome about this issue, now and in the future?
7. Have I considered all possible alternative solutions for resolving this problem?__________
8. Have I considered all possible consequences that can arise from executing my plan of action? _________
9. Taking into consideration questions 6–8, do I feel content with the quality of my worrying? _________________
10. How anxious am I after relaxing and problem solving, from 0 to 5? ______

    Reschedule the worry if there is at least moderate anxiety.
11. Do I need to review my plan at the next worry session? ________

    How will thinking about my plan again help me? Will thinking about it again make me any safer or resolve the problem any better? __________
12. If I already have a plan in effect for dealing with this problem, is there anything wrong with my plan? _____ If yes, what should be modified? _______________________

As patients gain greater control over emotional and bodily responses, the focus of treatment shifts to changing cognition about the stimulus. Threat reduction is an attempt to alter the conception of the activating event.

☐ Strategy Three: Threat Reduction

Once self-monitoring and record keeping have identified the cues that stimulate anxiety, the focus shifts to dealing with the perceived threat. In one regard, GAD is a quantitative, not qualitative, problem. CCT agrees with the GAD perspective that this is a dangerous world. The vulnerability schema is correct in this regard. The main question is, *how dangerous is the world?* The patient with GAD sees many threats, big threats, and immediate threats. His/her world is involved with danger—everywhere. The threat reduction strategy seeks to produce a realization that the patient's basic belief is *not valid to the degree the s/he believes.* Danger does not lurk everywhere. Catastrophes do not occur as often as believed. The strategy works to *lower the number and magnitude of perceived threats.* (This strategy has to be tempered by the issue of socioeconomic class. The poor in the inner city do live in a far more dangerous world than the middle class in the suburbs. The strategies for the former will involve knowing how to cope with their menacing, ominous existence. However, even inner-city patients can have GAD if they stay preoccupied with threat and cannot adjust to their life.)

To reduce the number of threats in the patient's world, three skills are recommended: (1) activation management training, (2) no mind, no thing, and (3) diminution training.

Activation Management Training

Because anxious people live their lives activated to cope with danger, they need skill in managing the activation tendency (which is an increase in autonomic arousal and an activation of traditional GAD coping skills). A basic cognitive-physiological ability is required to create congruence between the level of challenge or the degree of threat and the level of physical activation. CCT refers to this as *activation management.* There are two underlying goals when using this coping skill: (a) form beliefs that realistically portray the degree of danger stimuli poses, and (b) adjust the response to the stimulus so it reflects that assessment.

There are three general levels of activation. CCT terms each level of activation a *risk readiness position* (RRP). The lowest level of activation is an *inert response,* where mind and body remain inactive, at rest, peaceful, and calm in a conflict-free state. It is appropriate for the following conditions: (1) there is an absence or only a mild level of challenge or threat, (2) the threat is so distant that activation is not necessary at that point in time, or (3) a threat is uncertain or amorphous. In the last case, knowledge about the threat needs to be accumulated, which means tolerating the supposed threat and experiencing it to learn more about it. While this occurs, a low level of activation is appropriate.

The next level of activation is an *alert stage.* Mild to moderate challenge or threat appears but is not an immediate danger. The *threat has to be lived with* on a daily basis because it is not causing an immediate problem that needs to be addressed. Only a moderate amount of guardedness is necessary. During this time the *threat needs to be experienced so its nature becomes known.* Planning and problem solving need to occur and skills need to be identified to be maximally prepared in case danger escalates. The mind stays watchful and responsive but not fully activated. The body remains inert but needs to be ready to act. In this case there is a low-level physical mobilization of self.

A third level of activation is when moderate to severe challenge or threat is identified and it is immediate enough to call for *active mobilization* on either a mental or physical level or both. Problem-solving plans are activated and skills are deployed to cope with the danger. At this stage, there is a need to be fully on guard physically and mentally.

Each of these levels is explained to the patient. To train the patient to correctly respond to a stimulus, situations in his/her life are discussed regarding which RRP would be appropriate for that context ("Your boss taps on your office door. Which RRP is appropriate at that time?").

To repeat, *the RRP has to accurately correspond to or match the level of challenge or danger that is present.* A cognitive ability is needed to comprehend the nature of an event and its influence on the individual. This is the skill of *risk determination,* which involves calculating the possibility of suffering harm in some way. Risk determination forms the meaning of the situation (e.g., dangerous, no big deal). When done skillfully, it is a realistic assessment of the activating event. The companion skill, *risk readiness,* forms the appropriate RRP for the level of perceived threat. This skill organizes the internal state and behavior. It is actually a response to the person's conclusion about risk and not a response to the actual event.

In activation management training, the GAD is being trained to do what the nonanxious person does naturally. However, people with GAD need skill development in both risk determination and risk readiness.

We will now examine the subskills necessary for risk determination and the misapplications or errors the GAD patient commits using each of those subskills. To overcome those errors, the patient needs to be trained in the skill of *self-questioning*. This is a self-administered form of cognitive restructuring that includes the following steps: (1) rate the degree of anxiety present in a given situation; (2) identify the beliefs concerning that issue; (3) assume an objective stance; (4) self-question one's beliefs; (5) rate the degree of anxiety present after questioning, and if anxiety is still present, continue self-questioning. In order to assume an objective stance, the patient is advised to pretend being someone else who is reviewing the data that self-questioning generates. In an empty chair format, the patient talks to himself as someone else and then answers back. To aid self-questioning efforts, handout 3.1 can be utilized for disputing descriptive judgments, and handout 3.2 can be utilized for disputing extreme negative value judgments (training in anti-awfulizing).

Risk Determination Training

Risk determination is a three fold process that requires three subskills to determine when there is danger, which is defined as anything that can harm well-being or endanger safety and security.

1. Threat Identification

This is a threefold ability. First is an ability to study events for their potential to cause harm, to look for signs of trouble, or to determine whether an event has problematic or dangerous aspects to it. The second ability is gathering data and characterizing the event. Accurate threat identification reduces the number of dangers or problems in a person's life. The third skill is estimating when the danger will become a real menace that needs to be actively addressed. Most certainly, anxious people possess each of these skills. However, they commit four basic errors in threat identification.

One, a patient with GAD has *a coping skill excess regarding threat identification.* He searches for danger in situations where this skill is unwanted or unneeded (e.g., during relaxation or when reflecting on other matters). To treat this, a patient with GAD is trained to ask, "Is threat identification needed for this context or time?" If not, then *perceptual shifting* can be used to shift attention to other matters and to deactivate threat identification.

Two, a patient with GAD cannot turn off threat identification and continues to mull a threat. To treat this, he has to force himself to move on to *problem solving.* After a plan of action is formed, then further worrying is extinguished, using worry management protocols.

Three, an anxious patient *searches for threats prematurely,* before knowing if danger is even present, before getting to know the stimulus. If a determination is made that danger is not present, threat identification cannot remain inactive and continues the search for danger. The patient has to be taught to stay in contact with a threat and experience it before making a determination about danger.

Four, there are sequencing errors. Roger, for example, becomes anxious and searches for danger in the beginning of a dating relationship, when he is first getting to know a woman. He cannot simply enjoy the new person in his life. Instead, he is trained to suspend threat identification until a real danger or problem emerges (i.e., if the woman becomes smothering or possessive like his mother), and then identify a threat to well-being.

A patient with GAD has *an incorrect characterization of danger far too often, resulting in more threats than actually exist.* One, the evidence for determining a threat is too scanty to support the designation of threat and the degree of activation present. For this problem, the patient has to be trained to scrutinize existing data and judge if more data have to be collected before a threat designation is made. Two, there is an inaccurate appraisal of danger. Something is not actually a menace or challenge, but the patient believes it is or will be in the future. The problem in this case is certaintistic thinking. To treat this problem, the anxious person has to self-question him/herself to assess the accuracy of his/her thinking. For example: "Why is this stimulus being labeled a threat? What about it is menacing? Do I know enough about this event to label it a threat? Have enough data been collected to characterize the stimuli?"

Beck and Emery (1985) list other self-questions to correct usage of threat identification: "Am I confusing the habit of seeing a threat with the fact that a threat actually exists (or at least exists to the degree I think it does)? Does my version of the facts correspond to reality? Am I thinking in all-or-nothing terms, that there is either a major problem or no problem at all? Have I considered gradients of risk in this situation? What makes this danger so awful as I believe it to be?" If a danger is identified in the data collection stage, *only then* does the patient consciously decide which RRP is appropriate.

A third error in threat identification is appraising danger as more probable than it actually is. The patient accurately appraises something as menacing, but there is a lack of evidence that it will come to pass. This is because there is difficulty forming accurate probability judgments or estimates about the degree of danger present in a given situation. To treat this problem, the following self-questions need to be posed: "If there is danger, is it imminent? How much time is left for planning and problem solving if this is a threat? Do I already possess the skills necessary to cope with this threat? If so, can I relax until the threat becomes more of a danger?"

Also, a patient with GAD needs help refining his/her ability to handicap the odds of danger materializing. A four-column table can help. The first column lists the worrisome thought and the second provides an estimate that the worry will eventually become a reality. The third column supplies the evidence to support this estimate, while the fourth column lists the second or revised estimate that the worry will eventually become a reality—taking into consideration evidence that has been gathered (Craske et al., 1992).

2. Severity of Threat Estimate

If a person or event is identified as a threat, then another skill is needed to estimate the threat's severity. This is a most important issue because the appraisal of any event shapes the emotional response (R. Lazarus, 1966; Beck et al., 1979).

The patient with GAD commits two basic errors regarding this issue. First, *problems are exaggerated,* so they appear more ominous and challenges appear bigger than they are in actuality. The danger is accurately identified as a potential problem but is given too much weight, assumes a greater magnitude, or is given too much credit as a menace. To treat this problem, *diminution training* is necessary (see below for details).

The second error is appraising an event or person accurately as a severe danger but *assuming that the danger will become problematic sooner than later.* The danger has to be dealt with at some point in time, but not as soon as the patient believes. To treat this problem, a timeline can be made listing activities that have to be conducted at various times regarding a threat. For instance, if a problem exists in the future, the time-line would include the components of the plan to resolve the threat and when they would be carried out. If the threat was not a problem at that point in time, the timeline would address how the threat would have to change in order to mobilize a more involved response and when that response would have to occur.

What is the effect both errors have on the individual? The patient becomes upset, activated, and mobilized much earlier than necessary. The risk readiness position is too intense, too prolonged, and occurs too frequently than is necessary and appropriate, given the level of challenge or degree of threat that is present. This causes the mind and body to be readied for a threat far too soon and stay fully activated and guarded far too long.

3. Risk Susceptibility Estimate

This is an ability to rate the degree of risk a threat poses to the individual and significant others. Regarding this issue, a patient with GAD commits two basic errors. First, the susceptibility to danger is exaggerated. A danger seems more devastating to the individual than it will be. Second, the self's capacity to manage a danger is underestimated. The danger is accurately understood but the ability to manage it is not. In this case the person lacks a sense of self-efficacy. He does not believe that he possesses the skills to reduce risk in a threatening situation. When this happens, the threat appears more ominous than it is. *Self-assurance training* is needed to ease concerns that skills may not be adequate for the job at hand. In part, this requires *objectivity training* to fairly judge abilities. Remembering times when similar threats were managed can facilitate objectivity. Getting feedback from others about one's capacities can also be helpful. Cognitive restructuring will be necessary to dispute inaccurate, unrealistic thinking about self-capacity.

Risk Readiness Training

Risk readiness training involves adopting the appropriate risk readiness position, so cognition, affect, and physiology are congruent to the level of threat. This involves adjusting the level of activation up or down, depending on the threat appraisal. The body gears up or down by tensing or relaxing, respectively. The mind is quieted and ceases to review the problem, plan, and problem-solve, or it is activated and plans, problem-solves, and deploys skills. Affect is diminished or intensified.

Patients with GAD have difficulty at each level of risk readiness. In the inert phase, the patient has difficulty stopping the vigilant scanning for threat. While the s/he has no problems readying mobilization to manage a threat, s/he does have a *problem resisting activation*. The patient spends inordinate time in forethought pondering threats that have not materialized. Concerns are converted to worries. For this specific problem, it is helpful to teach the patient a *perceptual shifting skill,* such as thought stopping and sensory diversion, along with worry management.

In the alert phase, once planning and problem solving have been completed, the patient has *difficulty simply being watchful for changes in threat status*. Instead, s/he *reviews plans ad infinitum and overprepares*. For example, Roger spends his time at work thinking how he will answer his boss if he is criticized. All he needs to do is stay alert to watch for changes in his boss' behavior that would indicate frustration with his job performance. He does not need to engage in repeated self-dialogues about how he will respond. For this problem, *worry management training* is needed.

In the mobilization phase, when confronting the threat, the GAD patient commonly overwhelms him/herself with *catastrophic thinking* and is far too anxious, thus hindering performance for threat management. When there is excessive autonomic arousal (activation out of proportion to the degree of danger that is present), *relaxation training* and *self-instruction training* can be used to lower the RRP. They will directly affect physiology and indirectly affect the emotional response (a calmer body leads to calmer emotions). This is a response substitution strategy, where relaxation replaces chronic vigilance. *Psychological distancing* is another way to lower the RRP. By diverting the senses to notice value-neutral or pleasant images (the patient's eye traces along parts of another person's body instead of making eye contact), a feeling of distance is achieved, which simultaneously relaxes the mind and body. Another distancing technique is to imagine seeing oneself be an anxious person. If anxiety is still high, then the next step is to imagine seeing oneself seeing oneself seeing oneself be an anxious person. This is a triple removal tactic. It forces the patient into a cerebral mode, operating away from his emotions.

However, the problem with all of the above methods is that they work after the fact, after the patient has become tense and aroused. To avoid tensing in the first place, *no mind, no thing* can be used.

No Mind, No Thing

CCT maintains that cognitive restructuring may not be enough, though, to suppress the anxious patient's habitual operation. In GAD the problem is due not just to erroneous thinking but to the action tendencies of hypervigilance and redundant planning. Physiological elevation is more due to these action tendencies than unrealistic, irrational thinking. Certainly the latter contributes to anxiety, but once a mind-set becomes ingrained, it occurs automatically—in an almost mindless fashion—because it is an overlearned response or because there is genetic predisposition. It is as if hypervigilance takes on a life of its own.

Barlow maintains that "allowing action tendencies associated with fear and anxiety to occur is countertherapeutic" (1988, p. 311). CCT would agree with this, but only in part. In the inert and alert phases, there is no reason to have a fully activated mind and body. In the inert phase, preventing the action tendency is one of the main goals of treatment for GAD. In the alert phase, action tendencies should be limited and controlled. (Only in the active mobilization phase are action tendencies useful, and then CCT would preserve them.)

The Zen technique of *wu-wei* offers help in this regard. It acts as a response control strategy by preempting GAD coping skills. It is a means for staying in the here and now, for becoming present-centered and not shifting into the future to look for negative consequences, or not shifting into the past to fret about past problems. *Wu* means "non" and *wei* means "action," making, doing, striving, or straining (Watts, 1965). In other words, *wu-wei* means suspending thinking, stopping the internal chatter, and erasing cognition from consciousness; hence, having *no-thing on the mind*. CCT uses the "no mind, no-thing" technique as a way to *temporarily quiet the mind,* to suspend the action tendency of hypervigilance and the redundant strategy of endless attending to a threat and overplanning. It develops a mental discipline when risk determination dictates a low level of mental activity.

Wu-wei is a dynamic state where everything is taken in but without any special effort. The mind does not search for threats. It does not worry about something unrelated to the here-and-now. Instead, on a cognitive level, there is calmness or "non-graspiness" of mind. Intellectual activity such as assigning meaning to a situation, deducing, problem solving, and reasoning is halted temporarily. Efforts to find the meaning of a situation are quelled. Attention is just on objects or an image in the perceptual field without finding any meaning for them. Vision is used to carefully view objects. Sounds are heard without trying to guess what they are; they are heard only as musical sounds.

Yet the mind is not a vacuum but uses the senses to attend to the world. Training modules have to be created to discipline the mind to suspend thinking and evaluation and to only be sensorily active. There is no purpose to anything at the moment of *wu-wei* except being with the world, like a baby taking in all that is around him/her. Watts (1965) describes this Zen experience as "profoundly inconsequential," and in that lies the power of *wu-wei* to circumvent the perceiving of danger. The anxious person is attached to his/her thoughts about danger (the thoughts are most consequential for the anxious person). With *wu-wei,* though, there are no attachments to a thought or object, just sensory activity without any conclusions about what is happening—just looking, hearing, and touching detached from significance to the individual. The result is an absence of self-dialogue, which is at the heart of worrying. To develop *wu-wei,* patients are told to schedule periods during the day to practice this technique.

From the standpoint of CCT, *wu-wei* is a perceptual shifting activity. Attention is diverted away from thoughts about danger to coming into contact with the event-in-view via the senses. For instance, Roger is worried that his boss will not like him or respect his work. When he sees his boss, anxious recollection and apprehensive expectation color his perception. The world is seen through the prism of insecurity. Instead, with *wu-wei,* Roger's mind-set is erased and supplanted by sensory information. His senses respond to whatever his boss brings to him at that moment in time. If his boss smiles, has a calm voice, and uses noncritical words, then this is what Roger sees and hears and responds to, not his own mind-set, which evaluates the interaction as threatening. Using *wu-wei,* Roger trains himself to have no thing on his mind (e.g., job promotions or possible disapproval from others is erased) and to stay in the here and now, watching, hearing sounds, and responding to whatever people bring to him. He is *not to make assumptions or inferences* about what people are saying. That puts something on his mind. In essence, Roger is told to *"lose his mind" by having no thing on his mind except for sensory-based data.*

When *wu-wei* is presented to patients, this term is usually not used. Instead, CCT tries to utilize the patient's interests. For example, if the patient is a pet owner, the terms *felinotherapy* or *canineotherapy* are used, to make people more like unassuming animals in touch with the world through their senses without reflecting on the proceeding events. If the patient is a parent, CCT suggests learning from newborns about how to deal with the world, by adopting the observing, nonjudgmental, nonanalytical mind of the baby.

Diminution Training

"Diminution training" is utilized to reduce the magnitude or size of a threat. In social-evaluative anxiety, others' estimates of the patient receive an inflated worth and are unduly emphasized. In fact, others' opinions and approval ratings become more important than the patient himself: bigger psychologically, bigger in value. *Diminution training is used to reduce the inflated size of another person or his/her significance.*

In part, diminution training is used to train a patient in restructuring his/her own cognition, to learn how to dispute his/her own irrational, unrealistic thinking. It is also used for positional slippage, whereby the gains from cognitive restructuring are lost once the patient is away from treatment. In therapy, a patient may agree that s/he magnifies a danger to unrealistic proportions, but faced with a real situation, s/he often slips back into thinking nonsensically. This is because overlearned, ingrained, or rigid thinking is difficult to erase. A skill is needed not just to examine one's own thinking but to disparage it.

When engaging in diminution training, a preliminary estimate of the "bigness" of a threat is taken. Then any one of the below techniques is utilized. Afterward, another estimate of the magnitude of the threat is taken, to assess how much the patient is able to lower the danger mentally.

To challenge extreme negative values placed upon something (e.g., disapproval, nonachievement), patients are instructed in anti-awfulizing training. They are to routinely dispute the "bigness" of irrational, unrealistic evaluations (something is not just bad, it is BAD!!!) by challenging beliefs vigorously. For example, for disapproval, sample self-questions include: "So what if s/he does not like me or disapproves of my behavior? Why does his/her estimate have so much worth? Why is s/he so important or more important than me?" The "so what" question is particularly helpful, critically looking at conclusions realistically to examine what something means in actuality. This is a favorite approach of REBT (Ellis & Harper, 1975; Ellis & MacLaren, 1998).

Exaggeration and overstatement can be helpful for challenging beliefs. For disapproval, the patient can say, "That person's disapproval means that I am a total scumbag, utterly worthless. That person is infinitely better than me. S/he knows all, sees all." For nonachievement, the patient can say, "I am a lowly ant because I did not achieve. I don't deserve anything." If need be, ridiculous punishments can be arranged to emphasize a point (e.g., therapist to patient: "You believe disapproval is so terrible. Therefore you ought to be punished for it. You can only sleep on a hard floor for a week.")

If a danger is exaggerated, then self-questioning is arranged to dispute it. Key self-questions include: "How likely is it that this danger will occur? Has this danger materialized in the past? What have I or others done to avoid or circumvent that danger in the past?" Self-ridicule and sarcasm are also helpful. For example, "Am I all-knowing so I can predict what will happen? Do I have a crystal ball? Who made me God?"

Imagery is also used extensively in diminution training. Once the patient agrees that his/her thinking is incorrect or that someone has acquired a bloated, unrealistic significance or worth, then imagery can interrupt inaccurate thinking and reduce the incorrect estimate of another person. For instance, Roger admits that he has exaggerated the degree of danger his boss poses for him, but cannot stop feeling frightened and anxious around him. The following imagery is assigned to him for this problem:

> Roger's boss is imagined to be a blown-up figure similar to a towering balloon. The boss/balloon dwarfs Roger. When the boss speaks, his voice echoes with a loud blast. Roger sees himself shaking and quaking in his presence. Then Roger gives himself a self-instruction: "Don't see him as different from me; just another person doing a job." Saying this, the boss/balloon loses air and shrinks down to the size of a real human being.

Another way to diminish the badness of a threat is to see its beneficial side or usefulness. To do this, *bright-side thinking* is introduced. Roger is asked to find the bright side to a negative occurrence such as being fired or having a coworker promoted over him. He learns how a situation is not all bad, which changes his black-and-white thinking.

☐ Strategy Four: Tolerance Training

When a danger is first identified and a determination is made that it is a real danger requiring immediate intervention, two options emerge. One, the individual can assume a nonsurrender strategy and confront the danger. Doing so, anxiety arises that will have to be tolerated. The second option is to assume a surrender strategy. This means agreeing to live with a danger or challenge. This too entails anxiety tolerance. Hence, knowing how to tolerate anxiety is a crucial skill in life in general and is most important for the treatment of GAD. Problematic situations are not desirable but can become livable by virtue of tolerance. Let us now discuss the interaction between self-efficacy, self-assurance, tolerance, and anxiety.

Self-assurance, Tolerance, and Anxiety

Barlow (1988) makes the important point that anxiety and panic can be reduced or eliminated by developing self-efficacy. A primary way to acquire it is by learning skills or securing information necessary to achieve the desired outcome. Theoretically, possessing the required skills necessary to achieve the desired outcome should diminish anxiety: someone has a goal and the means to achieve it so worry supposedly eases. Skill development is a primary concern of coping skills therapy. CCT examines where the patient is deficient in skill development and inculcates the needed ability.

However, even with skill acquisition, people may still be anxious if they do not believe that they are proficient in ability. The antidote for this is self-assurance that proficiency exists. *People not only have to be proficient but need to know that they are proficient. Only at that point does anxiety recede.* Hence, self-assurance makes self-efficacy possible.

Self-assurance helps in another way. *Even if people believe that they cannot control the outcome of a situation, if they are confident that they can tolerate the undesirable outcome, then anxiety decreases.*

Ironically, self-efficacy is obtained once someone is assured that not being able to control the outcome of a situation is tolerable. In that case, the undesired end result is not considered to be so bad. Hence, self-assurance is a very important factor in determining the level of anxiety. If present, there is less; if absent, there is more.

In the last chapter, self-assurance was cited as important for developing self-confidence that a goal can be obtained, which helps to avoid pessimism, self-doubt, and negative thinking—critical factors that cause depression and anxiety. In this chapter, self-assurance is cited as important for developing self-confidence that *even if a goal cannot be obtained, that too can be tolerated.* This is crucial. If symptomatology is believed to be intolerable or is rated as awful or terrible, then anxiety will arise when distress persists. However, knowing that a situation is tolerable automatically changes the extreme negative rating given to the situation. With tolerance, people no longer rate something as awful. (Only the absence of something that is deemed vital is intolerable, but something that is tolerable cannot be awful.) Further, absolutistic thinking changes as well once someone is assured that not obtaining a vital end goal is bearable. (If not obtaining it is bearable, then by definition the goal cannot be vital.)

Someone may have tolerance, though, but not know it. There may be lack of conscious knowledge that an undesirable state can be withstood, and has been withstood in the past. In that case, the person will still become anxious about being in a negative situation. Again, people have to be self-assured that they possess tolerance; they have to know that an undesirable condition can be withstood. At that point, anxiety recedes. Hence, therapists need to inquire how much the patient believes that s/he can tolerate undesirable conditions. An inventory has to be completed of past undesirable situations and how well they were tolerated.

In teaching tolerance, therapists have to be specific. There may be tolerance of one type of anxiety but not another. Rational emotive therapy (Dryden and Ellis, 1988) identifies two basic types of anxiety. One type is self-esteem anxiety, which deals with apprehension that a situation will assault or diminish self-esteem. A second type is discomfort anxiety, which deals with apprehension that frustration will be too uncomfortable or too painful to be endured. CCT proposes a third type of anxiety, helplessness anxiety, which is apprehension about a lack of personal control. We will first discuss self-esteem anxiety, which can be about two primary problems: anxiety about disapproval and anxiety about failure. Each requires tolerance to ease anxiety.

Disapproval Tolerance

Social-evaluative fear is one of the main causes of anxiety in GAD (Diffenbacher & Suinn, 1987) and one of Roger's main problems. Perceiving disapproval escalates Rogers' anxiety dramatically. Ellis (Ellis & Harper, 1975) has discussed one reason lack of approval or disapproval is so devastating. It is because of absolutistic thinking: the desire for approval is transformed into a must and is conceived of as vital or extremely important. Therefore, withdrawal of approval means withdrawal of a basic, vital need. Cognitive restructuring is needed in this case. One, it can challenge the meaning put on disapproval if it is inaccurate and unrealistic. Two, it can challenge imperative thinking ("Where is it written that you have to receive approval from others?").

In undergoing cognitive restructuring, there are many people such as Roger who intellectually agree that disapproval is not vital but yet continue to feel bad when they receive disapproval. This is due to positional slippage. To correct this problem, cognitive restructuring may try reiteration of disputation, rational emotive imagery, or an often repeated self-instruction dialogue. This is a "more of the same" strategy that assumes that further restructuring efforts will gradually overcome prior learning.

While this does have benefit with some patients, CCT offers an alternative—*approval-seeking training*. In this case, the therapist helps the patient become a *"better approval-seeker,"* which paradoxically can diminish the need for approval seeking. By working so hard to gain approval, a patient may realize that it is not worth all that is entailed in achieving it.

Approval-seeking Training

The first subskill in approval-seeking training is value clarification. The patient has to be clear that if approval seeking is chosen, s/he knows the consequences of that decision. An exertion of self-choice and freedom may not correspond to someone else's values and tastes, which in turn may cause disapproval. The will for freedom inevitably interferes with the gaining of approval. Because of that, personal autonomy will have to be surrendered situationally to avoid any chance of disapproval. Patients need to be confronted with the fact that they cannot have it both ways: they cannot be a free, independent adult who also covets approval from others. This is because the push for freedom will inevitably interfere with the gaining of approval. To be proficient in approval seeking, pleasing others must come first and remain the highest priority or value. Pleasing oneself must come second and be a lower value. Personal freedom can be enjoyed only when it does not upset others. Understanding this forces the patient to confront his/her own behavior and choices, to decide if this is what is wanted.

If approval seeking is still chosen, other skills are needed. First, the approval seeker needs *acceptance training.* S/he has to grasp the reality that approval is not always possible. The patient also has to accept what s/he can and cannot affect in his quest for approval. Second, the patient is taught *area thinking.* Roger is told to work only on his area, that is, what he can control. Within his area, he can make himself as pleasing to others as possible. This is a surrender strategy, to change his behavior and values if they upset other people. At the same time, he does have to surrender to what is outside of his area, namely, others' final evaluation of him. That can be influenced to some degree by his own behavior, but it is not totally under his control.

Third, a skill is needed to cope with negative evaluations when they occur, and that is *diminution training.* It lowers the meaning and significance of disapproval to a reasonable level. Self-questioning is used to reduce the magnitude of disapproval. Key self-questions include: "Is the other person's estimate of me a fact or an opinion? Is someone else the final authority on me?"

Another problem is the diminution of self. This occurs with reductionistic thinking (equating oneself to the negative rating received from another person). A fourth skill is needed in that case—*self-support training*—to inform the patient that s/he possesses positive qualities and to make those positive qualities salient or foreground. A list of positive qualities and achievements can be kept on cue cards and reviewed after receiving disapproval.

A self-instruction dialogue incorporates the above ideas to build tolerance of disapproval.

Self-talk to Tolerate Disapproval

I try to please others, but this may not always be possible.

I cannot always become what others want me to be.

Others have a mind of their own, and I cannot control their values and preferences. I may not meet their values, and this has to be accepted.

I have to tolerate disapproval because it is part of life.

Live with disapproval because it cannot be avoided. Accept it.

I don't like to receive disapproval, but I have to surrender to the fact that I cannot stop it from happening. That is outside of my area.

What is within my area of control is being the most likable person possible.

Disapproval does not make me a bad person. It only means I am not what someone else wants. I cannot be everything to all people.

Disapproval is not awful—it is just undesirable.

Disapproval feels bad, but I can tolerate it. It is not the worst.

Relax. Take a few deep breaths when receiving disapproval.

Get my mind on other things. Don't dwell on the disapproval.

Failure Tolerance

A second aspect of self-esteem anxiety concerns the issue of failure to succeed in an endeavor for whatever reason. Tolerance is needed when failure occurs, to live with the disappointment and sad feelings about not succeeding. To facilitate failure tolerance, *acceptance training* is again necessary, to realize that failure is unavoidable and part of life. *Diminution training* is then necessary to minimize the significance of failure, that it only means not meeting a goal or objective and is not a statement about the total goodness of the individual. Self-questioning is used to dispute the value placed on a failure (that it is not awful but undesirable or unfortunate). *Self-support training* is also included to refresh thinking about other victories and positive qualities to keep them in the foreground of the mind. A list of past victories can be kept on cue cards to balance the defeat in view. Once it is foreground, the victory competes for attention with the failure. These ideas are included in the self-instruction dialogue below.

Self-talk to Tolerate Failure

Everyone fails to meet their objectives—that is part of life.

That does not make me less of a person—just one who did not achieve what I wanted. That is not terrible, just undesirable.

The failure is not the worst thing in the whole world.

Look how I succeeded in other ventures.

I don't like to feel disappointed, but that does happen in life. Live with it.

Helplessness Tolerance

Another inevitable part of life is helplessness. What makes it so difficult to tolerate? There is the presumption that life is spiraling out of control and that forces within or outside of oneself are moving in an undesirable, unwanted direction. Cognitive restructuring can address the realism and accuracy of this judgment. Cognitive skill needs to be developed to question predictions about the future.

At the same time, helplessness is most difficult to tolerate when it is part of catastrophic thinking, a common cognitive pattern in GAD (Beck and Emery, 1985; Deffenbacher and Suinn, 1987). The patient with GAD erroneously predicts that s/he will become more and more helpless in the future. For this problem, *decatastrophizing training* is needed. This skill is acquired by disputing domino thinking (where a chain of events leads to an imagined, supposedly terrible conclusion). *Objectivity training* is first required to view the certaintistic thinking from the vantage point of another person. Self-questioning then occurs: "Does this event have to lead to this other event? What are alternative consequences besides the feared one? Can the feared event be tolerated? Has it been tolerated in the past? What are ways to resolve the consequences of the feared event?" These self-questions can be placed on a cue card that the patient can readily review when catastrophic thinking begins.

Another method for decatastrophizing is by *habituating to the "horrible" end result.* First, catastrophic thinking is prescribed, in which the patient deliberately engages in domino thinking. In fact, the patient is asked to take the most minor of situations, build it up to catastrophic proportions, and then vividly imagine and experience the worst-case scenario. Repeated visualization of the undesirable consequence produces exposure to it and in time habituation. This also makes the patient aware of how the act of catastrophizing is an ordeal that s/he creates and can suppress if desired (Haley, 1984). Finally, *problem solving* is used to resolve each problem in the chain of catastrophic events.

Acceptance training can also be used to overcome dislike about being helpless regarding a perceived danger. There needs to be acceptance that helplessness is part of life and cannot be avoided. The tendency of the GAD patient is to avoid situations in which s/he is helpless. When this is not possible there is consternation and anxiety. The patient wants to reject coexisting with a threat. To counter this desire, self-instructions need to be given to facilitate *threat coexistence* (see below). A historical review can be helpful at this point. The patient can recall situations from his/her past where s/he has had to tolerate a dangerous or unpleasant situation and did so successfully. This solidifies *self-assurance* that coping capacity exists.

The patient also has to know when a nonsurrender strategy in response to a threat is advisable. *Area thinking* is helpful for this. The patient is instructed to work his/her area and try to reduce or eliminate a danger.

At some point, though, a problem is determined to be beyond personal control or outside of one's area, and this needs to be accepted. The therapist needs to stress that helplessness does not mean the patient is inadequate; s/he just lacks means to affect the outcome of a situation. Surrender is appropriate at this point, and tolerance of helplessness is advisable. This reality is anathema to a GAD patient, who hates to surrender to a threat and live with it. This is why such an individual becomes preoccupied with danger—to find a way to eradicate it. Acceptance training teaches when this is not possible and the only answer is surrender and tolerance. Self-instruction training can facilitate a state of mind that accommodates helplessness.

Self-talk to Facilitate Acceptance of Helplessness

I cannot always be in control. There have been times where I didn't have control and things did not turn out badly.

I don't like having this problem in my life, but it cannot be resolved.

I can live with it or I can hate life being this way. It is my choice.

I am free to disapprove of this situation. I don't have to like it. But I do have to surrender to the fact that I am helpless to change this situation at this point in time.

Being helpless does not mean I am inadequate. It only means that I cannot affect the situation or what I dislike.

Surrender gracefully. Don't be a poor sport. This is what is.

I am tough enough to live with not getting my way.

Drop it. Don't dwell on things I cannot change.

Being upset only shows I am not accepting this situation I dislike.

I want to change what I cannot change. Don't be irrational.

Discomfort Tolerance

A GAD patient has to accept the fact that s/he will probably have more anxiety than the average person, even with the use of medication and the skills discussed in this chapter. This is because overlearned action tendencies and coping skills practiced for a lifetime will not simply disappear. This is not pessimism but realism. That is the anxious person's cross to bear. Also, if the patient boldly faces the dangers in his life/her (as recommended in "Threat management" below), then this too will produce greater anxiety. Further, therapy can alleviate anxiety and make life far more bearable or passable, but anxiety in general along with its unpleasant nature cannot be avoided. Presenting this fact to patients, the therapist has to be supportive and acknowledge the unpleasant, distressing, and uncomfortable life of a GAD patient. Because anxiety cannot be avoided, the *discomfort from anxiety has to be accommodated.* Hence, the treatment of GAD must include *discomfort tolerance training,* to learn how to cope with the unpleasant state of anxiety. This includes the following subskills.

First, a *self-monitoring skill* is needed to detect intolerance or rejection of discomfort. Indicators have to be identified that show intolerance of discomfort is occurring. Emotion indicators include frustration and irritability. Physical indicators include bodily tension and short, choppy breathing. A cognitive indicator is the belief, "I hate feeling this way."

Second, *self-assurance* is needed. A *GAD patient needs to reassure him/herself that unpleasant feelings can be tolerated.* A cognitive ability is needed to summon a feeling of self-assurance. One way to acquire it is by conducting a historical review. It supplies facts that anxiety and other unpleasant situations have been tolerated in the past. The patient can write a biographical sketch in which he lists difficult times that have been tolerated in his life.

A self-instruction dialogue is used to inculcate tolerance of discomfort. Notice how it cues coping responses while offering reassurance.

Self-talk to Tolerate Discomfort

I feel anxious. How much anxiety do I feel, from 0 to 5?

Face the fact that I will feel anxious in this situation. It cannot be avoided, but I can deal with it.

Feeling anxious is uncomfortable and unpleasant but not dreadful.

I have coped with discomfort in the past and I can cope with it now.

Don't reject being uncomfortable. It is part of being anxious and just comes with the territory.

I am an anxious person. Anxious people feel anxious.

CCT also uses a *paradoxical strategy* to show the patient that s/he can tolerate the discomfort from anxiety. This is a most helpful method for acquiring self-assurance. First, the patient is urged to stay with the anxiety and not try to diminish it by using anxiety reduction tactics (e.g., behavioral avoidance of the threat, distraction, relaxation). S/he is asked to fully notice and experience the symptoms. Next, s/he is told to allow the anxiety into his/her life and not hate it or reject it. Third, the patient is told to demand that each symptom (e.g., heart palpitations, sweating, hyperventilation) become worse. For instance, if there are heart palpitations, the patient demands that the heart pound furiously. If there is sweating, then the patient demands to become soaking wet from perspiration. If s/he feels dizzy, the patient demands that s/he faint immediately. In essence, *the worst fear is demanded, so the patient can realize and be reassured that it can be tolerated and is not so awful.* This procedure is influenced by Frankl's (1965) paradoxical intention technique and is used not only for anxiety but for panic disorder as well.

In part, this procedure is used to treat the anxiety about anxiety. The GAD patient has increased worry that his/her symptoms will worsen and become out of control. This is usually a false presumption, but the patient lives in fear that it will come to pass. The treatment requires testing the presumption by demanding that the worst-case scenario occur and then observing what will happen next. This allows the patient to realize that fears are not facts: fearing a symptom will occur does not mean that it will occur.

In addition, a new policy belief is introduced to replace the GAD policy of avoidance of situations that cause anxiety and discomfort. The new policy is *"Accept anxiety into my life—however it feels, whatever its effect."* This means accepting the fact that anxious people will often feel anxious, with affective and physiological concomitants. Once the anxious state is accepted as a given at that moment in time, ironically, it will drift into the background and become less noticeable and unpleasant. This strategy parallels the strategy for chronic pain treatment. Once the chronic pain patient accommodates to a life of pain and accepts the sensations of pain as part of normal bodily sensations, the pain drifts into the background and is not so dominant or focal. Hating pain, hating anxiety keeps it in the foreground. Acceptance of anxiety (or chronic pain) reduces the rejection of one's existence. Life is no longer spent hating one's existence. This key policy belief is a missing from in vivo treatment, which lacks a philosophy for exposing patients to anxiety-provoking situations.

☐ Strategy Five: Threat Managment

The initial part of treatment focused on how to manage the symptoms of anxiety and how to relate to it when it occurs. Once the patient feels more secure within the self, the focus then shifts to operating in situations where anxiety is present. This section discusses how to manage events or people designated as a threat. A new policy belief is introduced for threat management.

Cautious Boldness

A patient with GAD has a policy of maintaining safety, reducing risk, and avoiding threat. This policy controls the response to danger, is highly entrenched, and cannot be turned aside casually. Respect must be paid to it, because the patient believes in it faithfully. Also, to give credit where credit is due, the policy belief does contain wisdom and practical benefit. The problem is that the anxious patient carries out this policy to an inordinate, excessive degree. In addition, it is inappropriate for many situations where a threat has to be tolerated and coexistence with it is required.

CCT will conserve the GAD policy and find a way to satisfy it. This is done by inculcating a new policy belief, *cautious boldness,* that both preserves, supplements but also alters the old policy. While seeking to satisfy the dominant needs of a GAD patient, the new policy seeks a new direction and mission. It urges the patient to press forward, be more daring, take risks, suspend guardedness when not needed, be less inhibited, and "try on" new forms of being—to experience the self in different ways. For example, Roger is given the task to break out of old patterns and experiment, such as eating in new restaurants, vacationing in new areas, or wearing different types of clothes. Each task requires degrees of boldness and builds anxiety tolerance. At the same time, the call for boldness contains an admonishment to be ready to meet and manage anxiety while adopting new attitudes and behaviors. The policy calls for cautiousness intertwined with boldness. This way the GAD is able to test if being venturesome compromises safety.

Executive Beliefs for a GAD Patient

The next task is to literally write new executive beliefs for the patient with GAD. An anxious person has inveterate coping responses that habitually structure and organize how to proceed in a situation. They are an integral part of the personality and are highly ingrained. They cannot be ignored, dismissed, suppressed, or avoided entirely. More important, they have benefit if used appropriately, so CCT preserves them but modifies and rehabilitates them so that they are not injurious.

Instead of suppressing action tendencies, as Barlow (1998) recommends, the treatment plan calls for using them in the service of the patient, in an appropriate context and sequence. Habitual coping skills are supplemented with new beliefs and skills that both curtail and augment their activity. Although CCT seeks to implant a new set of executive beliefs, it continues to address the thrust of the old executive beliefs—to ensure safety and security. The use of signal anxiety—the hallmark of GAD—continues and is given a central place in the new orientation to provide advance warning.

The need to scan for danger, stay on guard, and be wary is utilized but contextualized. The GAD patient is asked to do what s/he does already: be aware of potential harm, problem-solve, minimize danger, and stay alert, *but only when danger is present or imminent.* Below are the self-instructions that form Roger's new executive beliefs.

1. Before entering a new situation, engage in forethought.
2. Scan for danger or challenges (which preserves the action tendency).
3. If a threat is identified, collect evidence to substantiate the threat. Engage in risk determination. Question descriptive and evaluative judgments for accuracy.
   a. Use consequential thinking to assess short- and long-term problems.
   b. If a danger appears overwhelming, use diminution training to reduce its imposing size, so the danger appears less intimidating and daunting.
4. Self-monitor the anxiety level before entering the situation. If anxious, use anxiety-reduction skills, such as relaxation and self-talk.
5. Determine when a threat has to be attended to in the future. Use a timeline and problem-solve to assess how a plan will be put in place and when to execute parts of the plan. Form a strategy for dealing with the threat. Identify skills and develop them if need be. Form contingency plans.
6. Depending on the assessment of the threat, determine the risk readiness position (RRP).
   a. If a threat is in the future, remain inert and resist the call to become alert or fully activated.
   b. If a threat is a real problem but still not an immediate danger, stay on alert and watch for changes in threat status. Resist the call for full activation. Remember that a plan is in place and can be readily implemented if needed.
   c. If a threat is immediate and an actual danger to self, execute the plan and confront the danger. Be bold and move forward. Do not avoid if avoidance is counterproductive.
7. Use anxiety reduction skills if too activated to form appropriate risk readiness position.
8. If a threat is not immediate:
   a. Maintain a present orientation by staying in the here-and-now. Deal with a threat only when it is impending.
   b. Employ "no mind, no thing" skill to quiet the mind and to stop mental chatter.
   c. Schedule a worry session to table further worry about the problem. In the session, review the plan of action if it needs to be modified. Do not worry or change the plan until the worry session. If the plan is deemed appropriate, do not think about it until the next worry session, and then use reassurance to

ease anxiety that the plan may not be enough to diminish danger.

9. If a threat is immediate and impending, enter the situation and face what is feared. Tolerate the unpleasant feelings of anxiety.
   a. Self-monitor throughout the encounter with the threat.
   b. Use anxiety reduction skills if feeling overwhelmed.
   c. Be ready to employ impulse control to resist exiting the situation to avoid experiencing the anxiety.
   d. Experience and embrace the danger. Get to know the threat. Discover what is truly dangerous about it, if anything.
   e. To determine further behavior, act on the experience of being with the threat and not preconceptions about it.
   f. Get involved with all facets of the experience. Do not stay focused on the threat alone. Use attention narrowing on the threat only when it is actually being menacing and potentially harmful.
10. When facing the threat, take risks and allow yourself to be influenced by the situation. Be influenced by the actual contact with the perceived threat. This may lead to behavioral avoidance or further engagement. Let the contact boundary between the threat and yourself form goals and objectives about how to act and think.
11. Based on the new evidence about the threat, redefine the danger. Determine how menacing it actually is, based on contact with it.
12. If the threat becomes menacing at any time:
    a. Employ quick activation and mobilization ability.
    b. Enact plan of action.
    c. Tolerate anxiety when confronted with danger
    d. Think of the goal state and become intrepid, a person not willing to be overcome by anxiety.
13. If anxiety becomes worse while encountering the threat:
    a. Demand that the anxiety become worse to test out the ability to tolerate it.
    b. Reassure oneself that the self can tolerate the discomfort of anxiety.
    c. Tolerate the helplessness of being anxious and not being able to remove the threat. Accept the reality that helplessness is part of life.
    d. Once reassured that the self can tolerate the anxious state, use anxiety reduction techniques to lower discomfort. Do not first turn to anxiety reduction out of panic and anxiety about being anxious.

CCT uses the Gestalt concepts of experiencing and the contact boundary to form behavioral plans (Polster & Polster, 1973). CCT wants the GAD patient not to use prescribed and outdated ideas about a threat or challenge to shape attitude and action. Rather, actual contact with the threat and knowledge gained from that experience guides behavior and affective response. CCT encourages the use of action tendencies and the coping skills of a patient to satisfy the policy belief of safety and low risk, but *only when* a danger has been appropriately appraised. When danger is not present, the new executive beliefs call for suppressing the action tendency and habitual coping responses. Instead, the patient is asked to become engaged in the situation, experience it, and let the situation move the individual in new, unforeseen directions. This entails willingness to be bold and uninhibited. The patient may be hesitant to suspend hypervigilant scanning for danger, so s/he has to be reassured that s/he already possesses a quick mobilization ability—from years of practice—to immediately problem-solve and implement a plan when necessary. Years of becoming prematurely ready for danger have developed the ability to immediately face danger. The patient has to be reassured that s/he has previously developed crisis management skills. The redundancy strategy is discouraged in general but facilitated in part by worry scheduling, which reviews plans at preset times.

The therapeutic intent is to *contextualize self-instructions regarding when to practice safety, risk reduction, and threat avoidance.* In some situations traditional GAD coping skills are utilized, while in other situations they are suppressed. In regard to the latter, *the patient commits a contextualization error regarding threat management* and uses inveterate coping strategies that are inappropriate. The GAD strategy calls for avoiding or reducing danger, but there are many contexts calling for coexistence with a threat, experimentation, experiential learning, risk taking, and assertiveness. In those situations, effort needs to be taken to tolerate a threat while getting to know it. Boldness to try new forms of thinking and acting need to be undertaken.

Following are two examples of contextualization errors. Roger has a roommate who seeks to move him in new directions. Instead of getting to know those directions, Roger feels anxious around him, avoids his initiatives to be different, and wants him to move out (an avoidance strategy). A better solution is learning by doing: trying on some of the actions that the roommate suggests, tolerating the anxiety increase from venturing into new ways of being, and then assessing their worth (experiential learning). In Roger's new job he is quite anxious around his boss. He stays guarded and busily scans for any and all dangers that can arise while his boss is there. He continues to problem-solve over and over to manage dangers that his boss may pose. He stays activated, aroused, and ready, due to preconceptions and prior characterizations of his employer. Instead, a better strategy is to suspend these activities using the "no mind, no thing" technique and respond to his boss spontaneously, based on what the latter brings to the contact boundary. Until a threat is immediate and known, Roger should shift to an inert risk readiness position, relax, suspend guardedness and problem solving, and focus on tolerating an uncertain situation with his employer.

Dating and Threat Management

To provide the reader with an example of how Roger's new policy and executive beliefs would operate, let us examine how they were applied to one of the major causes of anxiety in his life—his dating relationships. The new executive beliefs continue to call for Roger to scan for danger as he entered a new situation—in this case, his relationship with his newest girlfriend, Cindy. Threat appraisal determined that Cindy did not constitute an immediate danger at that time. Hence, the risk readiness position needed to be inert. When he became anxious around Cindy he practiced relaxation and self-talk to maintain a calm state.

Yet he worried about the relationship extensively, which was diagnosed as a contextualization error. With no immediate threat on the horizon, the appropriate coping response would be to experience the relationship, tolerate the discomfort from feeling anxious, and wait to problem-solve about threats until one actually arose. Hypervigilance is the wrong skill for that occasion.

To contain his worrying, worry scheduling was initiated. Each time Roger felt anxious about dating Cindy, he was to table that thought until a worry session, thus preempting the action tendency of hypervigilance. This halted the unneeded redundancy strategy of endlessly attending to a threat. During the worry session he reviewed his plan to continue dating Cindy. The plan would change only if definite signs were detected that she constituted a real danger. Following worry protocol, Roger worried intensely about the worst-case scenario: enduring a separation following a rocky, horrible marriage. He vividly imagined how both would proceed. Visualizing this repeatedly produced habituation. The fear produced by catastrophic thinking eased. He also time-projected six months into the future and visualized himself over his sadness about the imagined breakup. Diminution training was also used to diminish the magnitude of a separation (e.g., "So what if we separate? I have separated from women many times and I handled it, so why not now?").

One way Roger has coped in the past with his anxiety about dating was to find fault with the women he was seeing, to encourage his early exit from the relationship. But with his new policy of cautious boldness, Roger was encouraged to stay in the relationship. The objective was to develop discomfort tolerance, to learn that he can cope with anxiety. While in the relationship, Roger was to experience Cindy and the pleasures of a close relationship, and not prejudge her before collecting data on her.

Gradually Roger relaxed and continued to date Cindy. Therapy lasted six months longer on a staggered basis to focus on sustaining the relationship. During this period Roger was told to scan for danger periodically to spot any new threats in the relationship (the action tendency was again prescribed). If no threats were identified, guardedness and the action tendency of scanning for danger and guardedness were again suppressed. Any worries about the relationship were tabled until the next threat check.

In summary, *the executive beliefs for threat management used a combination of old and new coping skills, old and new executive beliefs.* Efforts were made to make him feel safe and to reduce risk, which satisfied his old policy belief. At the same time, the policy of boldness encouraged him to try on closeness, experience it, and then make a decision based on that data if he wanted more of it.

□ Conclusion to Treatment

Over the course of treatment, Roger learned new skills that indirectly changed his schemas that he will be inevitably vulnerable to harm and that he is lacking in many key regards. The anxiety reduction and worry management strategy gave him confidence that when anxiety occurs he can manage it effectively. This reduced his anxiety about becoming anxious. He spent far less time worrying. The threat reduction strategy reduced his number of perceived threats so he no longer believed that danger lurked everywhere. He felt more self-assured that he can cope with threats. His fear of life lessened greatly. He no longer felt unsafe. If he believed that he was unsafe, he felt assured that he can cope with that condition. Activation management training gave him practice in adjusting his anxiety level to be congruent to the actual degree of threat present. His risk readiness improved and he was better able to determine when there was an actual threat. In summary, he no longer felt vulnerable to perceived threat, and if he believed that there was a threat present he was able to bear it and experience it to learn more about it.

However, because he has the problem with generalized anxiety, he continued to find threats to his well-being. But with the use of his skills package, he was able to gain a realistic understanding of them so they did not dominate his consciousness. Not feeling dominated by anxiety, he felt better about himself and this challenged his self-lacking schema.

In regard to dating, Roger experimented with new situations and behaviors in his relationship with Cindy. By not avoiding anxiety-provoking situations and experiencing them, he learnd to tolerate the anxiety of a committed relationship. He continued to date Cindy and not find ways to prematurely end the relationship. He changed his schema that closeness is dangerous by learning how to manage in close relationships.

By changing his executive beliefs about how to cope with threatening situations, he subsequently changed his policy belief that he must stay safe from danger. He adopted the new policy belief of coping with danger. This allowed him to move into situations and be bold and adventuresome. His new executive beliefs still preserved his basic mission of being safe by learning how to be cautiously bold. He liked utilizing his old coping skills but with a new mission to take risks but minimize danger while doing so. Eventually, he took a new job in the company from a safe job in accounting to a bolder move into sales.

☐ Summary

The chapter discussed the treatment for generalized anxiety disorder. GAD is considered a coping skills excess, where valuable skills are used to excess and that is the reason for symptomatology. Five treatment strategies are proposed. One teaches the GAD patient how to lower anxiety, which in part is practiced to develop the self-assurance of being able to control arousal levels. Self-assurance is considered essential to develop self-efficacy. Anxiety reduction consists of self-monitoring, self-talk, relaxation, and perceptual shifting. To control worrying, the basic problem of GAD, worry management training is utilized, with worry sessions scheduled. To help quiet the busy mind of the GAD patient, a Zen technique is utilized—"no mind, no thing."

Because the patient sees more threats to well-being that actually exist, threat reduction is needed. In part it includes threat identification and threat appraisal. With a realistic assessment of the threat, the patient can then form a realistic risk readiness position. If the threats continue to be inflated, diminution training is employed to lower the threat's overall significance.

Tolerance of anxiety is considered very important in the treatment of GAD. Several types of tolerance skills are discussed: disapproval tolerance, helplessness tolerance, failure tolerance, and discomfort tolerance.

Finally, when an actual threat is identified, a new policy belief of cautious boldness is installed and new executive beliefs are formed to cope with it. The latter utilize the skills of an anxious person, but they are put in the proper sequence and practiced only when appropriate. Matching skill and context is important because a GAD patient commits a contextualization error. S/he uses scanning and the redundancy strategy when s/he should be tolerating, experiencing, and coexisting with the threat.

10
CHAPTER

Treatment of Borderline Personality Disorder

This chapter discusses the treatment of perhaps the most vexing patient seen in therapy—the person with borderline personality disorder (BPD). BPD is marked by broader and more severe disturbance than other personality disorders, with dysfunction on cognitive, affective, and behavioral levels. While it has unique features, it overlaps with several other personality subtypes (Millon, 1969). It shares many features with the three other cases presented in this book: dependency, affective disturbance, and anxiety.

The chapter illustrates how CCT works with contextual and time-fit errors. It shows the reader how CCT addresses patient resistance, noncompliance, and mistrust of the therapist. The cognitive set of a borderline personality is discussed. Four general coping skills are presented: anger management, relationship maintenance, consistency, and dependency training.

Millon (1996) describes four subtypes of BPD: discouraged, self-destructive, impulsive, and petulant. The case study in this chapter represents the petulant subtype.

Case Study: Darlene

Darlene is coming to treatment due to numerous complaints from subordinates and coworkers at her company. She has a position as a salesperson but also supervises a group of employees who are the support staff for her division. She is required to attend therapy as a condition of employment. She protests this, though, and stresses, "I would not be here otherwise." She dismisses the complaints of co-workers as "sheer foolishness."

Yet her boss corrects her conduct often and has told her that she would have been fired long ago if she were not so successful as head of sales for her company. On the job, she is described as intense, irritable, impatient, overly demanding, and negative. She vents anger quickly and vociferously, and subordinates are afraid of her. Irritation quickly escalates into outbursts without hesitation, disturbing everyone in the office. Fast to complain about other's work, she is difficult to please.

Her behavior is extremely inconsistent, unpredictable, irregular, and erratic—one moment friendly, pleasant, loving, kind, and supportive, the next moment petulant, rude, snarly, contrary, and rageful. This instability is manifested in multiple ways. There are days when she is upbeat and enthusiastic at work and other days where she is downcast, inward-focused, withdrawn, and noncommunicative. Her appearance varies from immaculate and fashionable to disheveled and sloppy. Her thoughts and attitudes fluctuate and change quickly. At one moment she is positive about and even idealizes a person, and at another moment she can denigrate that same individual. Likewise with herself, she can extol her accomplishments and feel overly confident, but then she can reverse herself and be self-doubting, self-critical, and self-demeaning, especially after a setback. While she never gets close to anyone on the job, she can be superficially friendly. However, this too quickly changes as she becomes distant, cold, and disengaged. Overall, she is unable to sustain a consistent level of energy, mood, and inhibitory control. Though not manic, when happy she is quite energetic, ebullient, and efficient, but this mood can easily shift to depression or anger when conflict arises.

She has similar inconsistent behavior at home with her husband and two teenage children. She is affectively unstable, one moment petulant and short-tempered and the next inordinately warm, supportive, and caring. Short periods of anxious involvement with her husband are followed by intense, bitter arguments that have gotten out of control, at times becoming violent. While she puts her husband on a pedestal and describes him as highly loyal to her, she admits that she has had several impulsive affairs in the past with bosses and customers. She has had a problem with all males with whom she has been intimate: lonely and insecure when independent of them, hostile and mistrustful when dependent on them. She likes momentary closeness but cannot sustain it due to fear that she will have to submit and acquiesce to the man's control.

She is most paradoxical. While she seeks approval and yearns to be liked, she is often difficult and unpleasant. Her outbursts of temper cause others to fear and reject her. This stirs intense separation anxiety and guilt. Feeling distant from others, she suddenly changes and strenuously courts their approval, becoming charming, servile, and overly contrite, which gradually wins them over. Equanimity cannot be sustained too long, though. As soon as others disappoint her, she makes an abrupt turnaround and again becomes irascible and critical. Each time others pull away she either moves forward to win back their affection and support or pulls away herself and becomes depressed or anxious. While she apologizes profusely for her eruptions and is her own worst critic regarding her errant behavior, she soon returns to being negative and prickly.

Darlene has difficulty maintaining relationships in an open, authentic, genuine way. She relates by donning a role like an actress. With pride, she emphasizes that she is very good at manipulating others to get what she wants. With her husband, customers, and superiors at work she can be a coquette, a flatterer, and quite charming. However, staying friendly when she does not feel like it and suppressing her anger result in a buildup of tension. Outbursts only offer her temporary relief, and then she is flooded with guilt and regret afterward. She has few relationships that can be described as close. When others try to get involved with her she feels anxious, but when they are distant or cold she also feels anxious.

The pattern of inconsistency and impulsivity began in her preteen years. Throughout school Darlene rotated between academic success and academic failure. At that time she became quite rebellious, engaged in self-mutilation, and tried halfheartedly to commit suicide on two occasions.

Darlene's parents are described similarly to herself. They are inconsistent and unpredictable: proud, nurturing, and doting parents one moment, harsh, denigrating, and depriving the next. They would hold high, almost unreachable standards for her one moment and then be overly permissive and indulgent the next. When angry with her as a child, they could be quite irrational, unreasonable, and frightening. In particular, she fought with her mother, who manipulated her with guilt and withdrawal of love and affection when Darlene would not obey. Today, she is close to her mother, but they continue to have a stormy relationship because of her mother's controlling ways. From age eleven to fourteen her father sexually abused her until she overcame her fear of being found out and threatened him with disclosure. He then stopped approaching her sexually and became the "best dad any child could want." He was an alcoholic who also had several sexual affairs. On some occasions he took her with him to meet girlfriends. Darlene felt guilty about this but could not betray him and tell her mother.

Diagnostic Considerations

Darlene presents with a variety of emotional and behavioral problems that overlap with Axis I and Axis II disorders. She can suffer from severe periods of anxiety. She can present as bipolar due to her mood instability. Throughout her teenage and adult life she has had short periods of recurring depression that runs the gamut from mild to severe. Her response is not always the result of cue conditions. Even when the precipitating event for a negative feeling is resolved, she can continue to feel upset regardless of the external condition. She has strong needs for dependence, can act dramatic like a histrionic, can be self-preoccupied and feel entitled to act the way she wants like a narcissist, or be cold, cunning, and manipulative like a sociopath. No one presentation of self lasts for long, as she vacillates between different ways of being.

Overall, there is a pervasive pattern of impulsiveness and instability since childhood. This instability has been damaging to her career and has undermined her intimate relationships. Along with this is an unstable self-image. She sees herself as bad and evil one moment, competent and virtuous the next. At times she views herself as either the innocent victim of others' deprivation and abandonment or the evil persecutor who forces others to withdraw.

Her affect is quite often intense and inappropriate. She makes a frantic effort to avoid abandonment and has rampant separation anxiety when others reject her. Anger or guilt is inappropriate and excessive. She exhibits transient paranoia and suspiciousness.

The instability is also pronounced on a cognitive level. She is a black-and-white or dichotomous thinker. At one moment she thinks of herself or others in an idealized way; then she switches to a totally negative perspective. Goals and objectives to achieve them also shift rapidly.

On an emotional level, her mood shifts are sudden, and she is highly reactive to events around her. The depression she shows is varied, from downcast and sad to agitated. At times she feels empty and at other times she is filled with joy from personal triumphs at work.

In conclusion, the severity and variety of her problems are typical of a borderline personality disorder (BPD). While she can receive several

Axis I diagnoses, they are secondary to the personality disorder that leads to persistent dysfunction in all areas of her life.

Cognitive Assessment

Discussions with Darlene reveal the following schemas, which are typical of a petulant BPD:

Emotional deprivation schema. The inconsistent parenting and conditional love of her parents has resulted in an emotional deprivation schema. Young (1999) describes this schema as an expectation that the normal amount of emotional support will not be adequately met by significant others, causing her to feel short-changed in relationships. At work, Darlene expects that she will be deprived of respect and empathy by her supervisors and employees, that they will not understand her needs and feelings. In her marriage, she expects her husband will deprive her of his attention, affection, nurturance, and support, resulting in a lack of safety, security, and stability.

Mistrust/abuse schema. The emotional deprivation from her mother and the sexual abuse by her father have led her to form a mistrust/abuse schema. This is a belief that others will intentionally hurt, abuse, humiliate, cheat, and take advantage of her. In addition, there is a belief that this is a permanent problem, that the self will always be cheated by others (Young, 1999). This has led Darlene to form two basic assumptions. One is that it is best not to trust others because they will not meet her needs or do what she desires of them. Two, close personal relationships will always cause pain and suffering. They lead to a secondary assumption that it is best to be suspicious of other people to avoid being hurt and disappointed.

Flawed autonomy schema. This is a belief that the self is incapable of being independent, self-contained, and self-governing. There is a belief that the self cannot survive or be happy if alone and independent. From this follows a basic assumption that the self must be dependent on others for security, satisfaction, and nurturance. There is a secondary assumption that without others' caring, the self will flounder. This results in severe separation anxiety following a disturbance or conflict with a significant other.

Following are two contradictory schemas that exert an influence at different times. They contribute to the unpredictability, erratic behavior, inconsistency, vacillation, and affective instability she exhibits in her relationships.

Insufficient self-control entitlement. This schema becomes activated during moments of anger and immediate disruption in a relationship. This is a derivative of the deprivation and abuse schemas and is a modification of Young's insufficient self-control schema (1999). Insufficient self-control entitlement is a belief that the self is entitled to not control or restrain oneself. Permission is given to express emotion and impulses. The self is also entitled to skip the struggle to tolerate life's frustration. License is given to not exercise self-discipline whenever one is feeling upset. Others' poor behavior provide an exemption from working on self-control. The schema allows Darlene to ignore others' negative feelings when she feels hurt or hurts others. At those times the schema permits her to be tactless or insensitive. The schema leads to a basic assumption—triggered at the moment of feeling upset—that others deserve the negative treatment they receive at her hands.

Evil self schema. Later, after an outburst and after others have withdrawn from the relationship, another schema may be activated that is contrary to the one above. This is a belief that the self is basically wicked, morally bad, malevolent, and blameworthy. Further, the self is believed to be the cause of the undesirable conditions that befall her. This results in self-denigration, self-blame, and self-castigation. Once she considers herself "bad," other people are entitled to deprive or abuse her. The belief led her to blame herself for her parents' inconsistent behavior and her father's sexual abuse. The schema causes Darlene to feel excessive guilt and shame after a conflict with another person.

How do these schemas affect Darlene's basic functioning? Because she believes that significant others (husband, boss, and colleagues) will eventually deprive and abuse her, she mistrusts them and remains somewhat paranoid when giving others assignments at work. While she desperately wants to succeed in her career, the insufficient self-control entitlement schema frees her to have outbursts of anger that are self-injurious and embarrassing. Because of the deprivation and abuse schemas, she feels scared to commit herself fully to her marriage and feels irritated and impatient with other people, waiting for the time when they will eventually disappoint her.

The insufficient self-control entitlement schema and the evil self schema exist side by side, and either can be triggered following a conflict or argument. During a conflict she may give herself permission to allow an outburst and ignore others' feelings, or condemn and punish herself with self-denigration if they reject her. After the conflict eases, the evil self schema can be triggered, and then she feels inordinate guilt and acts overly contrite. Oppositely, she can hold a grudge against others for not forgiving her and then rage against them for some other matter. The evil self schema may control her temper for a while, and she will try not to disappoint other people. However, because the emotional deprivation and abuse schemas are so entrenched, her anger returns shortly to cause her to feel contempt and short-tempered.

However, Darlene, like other people with BPD, cannot detach and act autonomously due to the flawed autonomy schema, which maintains that the self cannot function independently. Because of this belief she is driven to secure others' involvement and support and is flooded with anxiety that they will withdraw from her. At the same time, she has anger with the significant others she so desperately needs because they are viewed as depriving and abusive. If they stay withdrawn or are critical, the insufficient self-control entitlement schema may be triggered, and then she will rage at them for being depriving.

The schemas lead to contradictory policy beliefs. First, Darlene has a policy of *"license to act as I want"* and *"freedom to express whatever I feel."* The executive beliefs give her permission and encouragement to blast other people, ignore their feelings, and only focus on her own needs. They permit her to unleash sharp, critical, vociferous comments to others to compel others to act as she wants. They allow acting on whim when upset and engaging in excessive forcefulness or hostility. Concomitantly, she has another policy belief of *preserving her relationships no matter what.* This policy leads to executive beliefs that form a preservation coping skill. Self-instructions guide her to mend the conflict with other people and do whatever is necessary to win back their approval. They direct her to use tactics such as looking and acting pitiful and miserable to appeal to others' guilt about rejecting her.

Treatment Plan

Darlene enters adult life with major gaps in her functioning. She is ill prepared to manage as an independent person. No wonder individuals with BPD fear being alone—they are not equipped for it! The therapist decides that he can change her schemas by developing coping skills that will automatically dispute them.

Individual therapy is initiated to arm her with the skills she needs to possess. The focus is on changing her personality functioning. Conjoint therapy is also initiated to address her problems relating to others.

Treating Patient Resistance

As treatment begins, the therapist is confronted with resistance to being in therapy. This section is included to show how CCT deals with rejection of treatment. This is a common problem among borderlines who have problems with trust and involvement. Because of this, the first order of business is to establish a therapeutic relationship, to turn the resistant patient into a ready-to-work client. The following dialogue is included to show how CCT deals with resistence:

Therapist (T): So what brings you to therapy?

Darlene (D): I am told I have to be here. I do not want to be here. If I don't come, I will be fired.

T: So your employer thinks you lack some key skills necessary to make you as successful as you can be.

D: He thinks I have problems getting along with the people I supervise and others at work.

T: So your boss requires you to come to acquire the skills that you need. We can certainly work on that. [The therapist moves quickly to establish the basic assumptions of CCT that pathology is a result of a coping skills problem.]

D: If you want to put it that way. I think I can handle my problems on my own, but my boss doesn't believe me.

T: So you think you possess the skills needed to resolve your problems, at least at work?

D: I can get along with others if I want to. I will just try harder.

T: Are you not using the skills you have, then? What's keeping you from using your skills? [Darlene is silent and looks frustrated. She does not want to get involved in examining how she operates.] You don't want to talk?

D: As I said, I don't want to be here.

T: I can understand, it's frustrating being forced to see someone to help you when you can resolve the problem on your own. [Darlene nods in agreement.] So you think you have awareness of your feelings and what skills you need to possess and you know how to use those skills. Right?

D: That's right.

T: That's great. I am pleased for you. I am curious, though, about what makes you not use those skills. If you would, you would not have to be here at all.

D: I just get mad, and when I am that way I am not the most pleasant person to be around.

T: I see. Do you need help managing your temper and moods?

D: I don't need your help [said emphatically].

T: That's fine. I am pleased for you that you can manage well on your own. I can only assume, then, that the reason you are not using your skills is because you don't want to. Is that correct?

D: I want to use them. I want to get along with others.

T: So do it. Use what you have going for you. Set your mind to do it and use your willpower to control your temper and anger. Is that all that is necessary?

D: No [said with sadness].

T: My guess is that willpower alone is not enough to resolve this problem. My guess is that you have tried to use your skills, but that hasn't worked. You apparently lack some key skills. You can try on your own, but how will this effort be any different from any other time you have tried to control your anger?

D: I don't know.

T: My job is to give you the skills you need to succeed. You mean well, but you have not been able to put it all together on your own. My job is to take what skills you have and teach you some new skills, and together you will be able to operate better. You can be much more successful when this happens. That's what I am offering. Do you want to give that a try?

D: I will see how it goes [a hesitant commitment is made].

In this dialogue, the therapist uses the basic premise of CCT to induct the patient into treatment and to overcome resistance. He presents the role of the cognitive coping therapist—an expert in developing coping skills. He reassures the patient that she already has skills that can be used in this effort. He knows this because the basic assumption of CCT is that all pathology and dysfunction contain useful skills that just have to be readapted or recontextualized. The therapist does not have to threaten the patient with job loss because he can utilize what the patient wants—success and realization of goals, whatever they may be.

By offering tangible, useful, immediate benefits, the therapist demonstrates that therapy can be rewarding. This cements the bond between them. In general, cognitive-behavioral therapy (CBT) avoids relationship problems such as transference neurosis because it is more of a technical, consultative approach. The orientation to CCT can also reduce resistance. The therapist explains that the therapist is more of a teacher and guide and not an analyst of past business.

However, if mistrust of the therapist persists, one approach is to use cognitive restructuring and convert the mistrust into a hypothesis (e.g, "Therapy will be harmful") and test that hypothesis by collecting data to refute the unrealistic assumption.

CCT offers an alternative. It converts mistrust into a coping skill and then discusses the pros and cons of the skill of mistrust, identifying how mistrust helps and hurts patient safety. Further, CCT suggests prescribing the coping skill to assess its applicability, saying, "By all means continue to mistrust me. Collect data to learn if I or therapy can hurt you, and then decide if the data support your mistrust." When the therapist suggests to the patient to take risks and practice the coping skills modules recommended in this chapter, he can again prescribe mistrust. He asks the patient to think of ways that the prescribed skills can harm her. If any harm is found, then *problem solving* can be used to address the danger. If the therapist asks the patient to discuss a subject and she refuses or gives vague answers, again he compliments her for using mistrust as a self-protective measure. Then the same procedure is followed: assess risk in disclosing, collect data, and appraise the threat.

□ Strategy One: Anger Management

Darlene has now agreed to work on the problem that has brought her to therapy—her temper and difficulty controlling outbursts of anger. Mood management dysfunction is at the heart of her problem. "Petulant borderlines may be best characterized by their extreme unpredictability and by their restless, irritable, impatient, and complaining behaviors" (Millon, 1996, p. 669). In part, each of these emotions and behaviors, including the unpredictability, is a result of difficulty managing anger.

Following CCT practice theory, *the therapist reconceptualizes the presenting disorder* (Darlene's moods and angry responses) *as a type of coping skill* for handling problems, setting limits, motivating others, and releasing tension. Her coping skill, though, is then defined as the cause of her problems because it is used to excess, similar to generalized anxiety disorder.

The treatment strategy for this is threefold: (1) response control (anger reduction), (2) stimulus reduction (decreasing the number of threats promoting the anger response), and (3) response substitution (implanting a new and positive response to replace the anger response). These three strategies follow the same course used for generalized anxiety disorder (GAD). This is because petulant BPD patients and GAD patients are similar in the following regards: both groups have a problem with chronic, recurring autonomic arousal; both manufacture too many reasons to become aroused; and both use inappropriate, dysfunctional management strategies for dealing with troublesome stimuli. The primary difference between them is that GAD patients respond to threats to well-being with apprehension while petulant BPD patients respond with anger. Anger management is pursued to demonstrate to the patient that she can control herself. It is also pursued to help her manage in relationships, which can indirectly refute the flawed autonomy schema.

Anger Reduction Training

Anger reduction addresses one of the most striking features of BPD patients—their *intensity of mood.* Skill in knowing how to attenuate the intensity level is needed. Indirectly, this affects another dominant feature of BPD, the changeability of behavior. With less intensity there is less emotional reactivity, thus allowing the patient to gain cognitive control over decision making.

The initial focus is on assessing the patients' idiosyncratic methods of managing their angry feelings, the process of mood expression, when they have self-control and when they lose it, and contexts for feeling angry (cue determination). The patient is then informed about the physiology of anger and the need to address the anger response on multiple levels.

Next, the patients are *assessed regarding the degree of self-awareness* and ability to engage in *self-monitoring*. Linehan (1993) refers to this skill as "mindfulness." She maintains that patients with impulsive and mood-dependent disorders are really participating in a situation without awareness, which accounts for the mindless, emotionally driven responses. Mindfulness involves observing and describing the activating event and the responses to it. To acquire mindfulness, Linehan recommends the following components: a nonjudgmental attitude, a narrowing of attention, and a lack of concern about performing a response the "right" way.

CCT agrees with Linehan regarding the need for nonjudgmental observation. To acquire this ability, patients are taught how to *operate as phenomenologists:* to view and describe data sensorily without evaluating it. To accomplish this, patients are trained in *processing* (see chapter 8) to increase their capacity to observe and describe behavior unemotionally and noncritically. They are also lectured on the need for *evaluative restraint,* to experience oneself and others without making judgments.

Self-monitoring is taught to identify and label affect. Written records are most important for developing self-monitoring. Following basic CBT practice (Beck et al., 1979), a two-column table is kept initially, to identify the negative feeling (along with a rating of the intensity level) and the context for that feeling. A third column for the belief about the stimulus and response is added after a few sessions. Petulant BPD patients need to understand that their irritability is a ubiquitous and predominant emotion. To realize this, a continuous interval schedule can also be kept and filled out hourly, noting the highest level of anger experienced during that time period, from high to none. When anger is detected, patients are asked to be aware of bodily responses, which can serve as indicators of anger intensity levels.

With greater awareness of the effect of anger on the body, the next task is *emotion regulation,* especially to lower affective and physical arousal. Before embarking on this, though, there needs to be a discussion about why a patient may not be compliant with treatment recommendations for managing anger. This is because people with anger management problems in general have an approach-avoidance conflict regarding anger and arousal. They want to avoid the penalties from being angry but also want to preserve the rewards from acting angry (e.g., the reward from hurting someone who has hurt them, the catharsis of explosion, the energized feeling afterward). Many angry people like the feeling of anger, when they are revved up and feel powerful. Therefore, therapists need to discuss the incentives and disincentives in surrendering anger expression as a coping skill.

Anger is presented as an activation management problem, similar to anxiety disorders. There is too much anger or activation in proportion to the degree of threat or challenge in the situation. Hence the need for emotion regulation. One technique to lower sympathetic activity is *relaxation training*. First, the therapist assesses how the patient presently calms and soothes him/herself when angry. If any methods are useful, then they are retained in the treatment plan. The therapist then teaches methods of relaxation if needed. The ones that are selected need to be able to lower arousal and tension quickly. Deep breathing and progressive muscle relaxation are most helpful in this regard. Imagery is another possibility if combined with distraction. For example, Darlene is told to visually divert herself from the activating event (e.g., by tracing lines around objects in the room) and mentally focus on her right hand, which she pretends is submerged in a pool of cool water. A discussion has to be held about which relaxation techniques are most advisable for various situations in the patient's life.

A second technique for containing and directing anger is *stress inoculation training,* which features self-instructions (Meichenbaum,1977). The goal is to prepare for the anger-engendering situation with a prepared script, self-instructions when challenged, and reinforcement for adaptive responses. There is first a rehearsal phase, in which an inventory of anger-provoking cues are identified. Self-talk and relaxation are employed to lower stress and anger in fantasized situations. This is followed by a practice phase, in which skills are actively employed with the actual stressors.

A third technique includes *perceptual shifting methods* to erase or preempt anger-generating images and self-instructions. *Psychological distanc-*

ing is a most helpful way to do this. Visual or kinesthetic diversion can be employed, as the angry person refocuses on the edges of objects, the lines around objects, or internal sensations. This diversion technique keeps the angry person from feeling immediately involved with the object of anger, thus creating distance from it. Switching the foreground image to a value-neutral stimulus immediately decreases anger.

Threat Reduction

Anger reduction training is only a palliative, though. It does not address the BPD patient's tendency for threat proliferation. Petulant BPD patients typical response to a threat or challenge to well-being is anger. In part this is due to the common defense of splitting, where others suddenly become all bad when they are perceived as a source of threat, harm, or trouble. Fueling this are schemas that activate mistrust of others, so they are seen as more menacing than they are in actuality. Others are assumed to be challenging when they are not, or causing difficulties when this is not their intention. In essence, BPD patients perceive too many threats in their life, similar to GAD patient. To treat this problem, *the therapeutic strategy is to gain skill in reducing the number of threats that provoke anger and achieving an appropriate level of response to the threat itself.*

First, the patient has to be educated about personal indicators of anger once someone or something has been labeled a threat. There are emotional indicators such as irritation or impatience. There are physical indicators, such as tightness in particular body parts or short, choppy breathing. There are behavioral indicators, such as a prickly or peevish manner or complaining about others. Second, there needs to be an *affect analysis,* to reveal to the patient the other feelings present when a threat has been identified. Petulant borderlines need to be aware that the anger covers up other emotions such as anxiety, fear, guilt, shame, and sadness. Once the patient is aware that an object has been labeled as a threat, the third step is *risk determination*. This is a two-part skill. First, conscious understanding is required about who or what has been labeled a threat to well-being or a challenge to one's position. This is the skill of *risk identification*. This then proceeds on to the skill of *threat appraisal.*

Risk Determination Training

Risk identification focuses on the cognitive response to a threat. To increase awareness of the meaning placed on a threat, a four-column table can be used. Whenever anger is detected, a notation is made. In the first column the negative feeling is recorded, along with an intensity rating for that feeling (from 0 to 5). The second column is for providing a description of what is troublesome about the object (the cue), which is the perceived threat. The third column is the estimate of the perceived severity of the threat (a rating of how much of a problem or challenge someone or something is). The fourth column is an estimate of the perceived risk from that threat (a rating of the degree of susceptibility to danger). Together, the table's columns reveal the direct relationship between thought and emotion: the more severe the threat or the higher the perceived susceptibility, the more anxiety or anger is felt. This exercise will increase knowledge about how an activating event is rated and appraised. It will reveal what events are labeled as a threat. Discussion can then ensue about why an event is considered a threat.

Next, the severity and susceptibility ratings are examined for accuracy. Following cognitive restructuring protocol, the belief about the threat is converted into a hypothesis and data is collected to support or refute the contention. To turn cognitive restructuring into a skill, *patients need to be taught the steps for performing hypotheses testing.* In addition, patients need *threat appraisal training* to change their thinking once away from therapy. This includes several components. To treat severe, extreme ratings of a threat, there is a need for *anti-awfulizing and diminution training*. Patients have to be given self-questions to reflexively refute their value judgments (e.g., "Why is this challenge considered so bad? How can this threat hurt me?"). Because BPD patients have a tendency to identify threats when there is none, *descriptive judgment training* is necessary to gain proficiency in clarifying the basis for a belief. Patients are trained in how to observe phenomena, collect data, and then use the data as the basis for a judgment.

If a threat is identified as real, the next task is *problem solving* to lower the perceived vulnerability to a threat. The premise is that if patients know how to resolve a problem, then they will not feel so endangered. Training in problem-solving procedure is given, and in particular *alternative solution thinking* is stressed to find options for how to cope with a threat. Following problem solving, and once the patient knows how to overcome danger, the patient is asked to review the threat severity and susceptibility estimates and assess whether the intensity rating in column one has diminished.

Risk Readiness Training

After risk determination has determined the level of threat, the next step is *arriving at an appropriate risk readiness position* (RRP). If no threat or challenge to well-being is identified or is imminent, then the RRP should be set at an inert stage: an irritation-free state, with a calm, affable, and amiable manner and little complaining or impatience with others. If a risk is deemed to be moderate, irritation should be held to a minimum as the person moves into an alert stage. Energy is centered not in the emotions but in the intellect, to include problem solving, skill identification, and planning for deployment of skills in case they are needed. Once this is done, cognitive activity shifts to observing the threat for changes in status. If no threat appears imminent, then an inert RRP is appropriate. If a risk or challenge is imminent or real, then the patient moves into an alarm mobilization phase, ready to meet the challenge.

Petulant borderlines have several tasks in this phase, which is discussed with the patient. The patient needs to assess the following: What about the situation can provoke a response of anger? What are internal triggering factors, such as unfinished business from the past, fatigue, or feelings carried over from elsewhere? What self-talk and cognition contribute to anger? What are the coping skills chosen for the situation? (See Navaco, 1975.) A log can be kept of situations where anger is felt to enable the patient to identify these four factors. Especially, the therapist wants to learn what the prevailing executive beliefs are for handling high-risk circumstances promoting anger.

There needs to be a discussion about when anger is appropriate as a coping response in the alarm-mobilization phase. Anger is to be used only as a *secondary, tactical* option when relationship maintenance skills (e.g., *assertiveness training, conflict resolution skills*) have failed. The patient is cautioned that anger should then be used only in a judicious, measured amount to emphasize a point, motivate others, or set limits on another person—not for tension relief via cathartic explosions. Further discussion needs to be about goals when using anger, so that the patient has an objective when anger is employed. When anger is expressed, it needs to be combined with other skills such as assertiveness, problem solving, and forethought.

This approach differs from Langham (1993), who calls for suppressing the action tendency of anger. CCT calls for implementing it but only in an appropriate context and manner. The contextual sorting technique can be employed to rank-order which skills are best for the alarm stage.

The next step is training patients in how to adjust the level of activation (the RRP) to be appropriate to the level of risk or severity of threat. Tactics to lower the RRP include *self-monitoring, relaxation, self-instruction training, diminution training, perceptual shifting techniques, and psychological distancing.* Along with this, *restraint training* is employed (see "Strategy Three: Consistency Training," below).

Usually petulant BPD patients are too intense and too angry in all three risk readiness positions. For instance, others may be causing Darlene a low-level challenge (e.g., an assistant to Darlene is not getting materials ready on time for a sales presentation), but her response is rage. While Darlene is in the alarm stage, fully mobilized to meet a giant threat to well-being, the appropriate RRP should be an alert stage. Life situations such as this are examined to help patients select the appropriate RRP following risk determination, and then to choose tactics to adjust the RRP.

Threat Management Training

Once a threat has been identified and needs to be dealt with, attention shifts to threat management. The therapist stipulates that the patient has many useful skills but needs other ones to increase potency. Thinking is stimulated about *what type of person can be a role model* to the patient in regard to threat management. The therapist suggests one type of model—the patient with generalized anxiety disorder (GAD). *The intention is to teach the BPD patient how to approach life as a GAD patient, without the excess of GAD.* Making GAD into a role model for BPD offers several advantages. One is that impulsive, petulant, self-destructive BPD patients need the action tendency of vigilant scanning for danger. They need *forethought, consequential thinking, review of plans, attention to risk and danger, attention narrowing* on danger, and most important, the GAD patients's *ability to inhibit rash behavior.* The goal is to teach the BPD patients how to use signal anxiety as a tool. The mechanics and utility of each of these skills are then discussed.

The same policy belief recommended for generalized anxiety disorder is also prescribed for borderline personality disorder: *cautious boldness.* Opposite to what happens in GAD, BPD patients have no problem with being bold. They need help with what anxiety patients are is most skilled at—cautiousness. The policy belief involved in GAD (seek safety, reduce risk, and avoid danger) is discussed, citing its merits and drawbacks. This is compared to the policy belief in petulant BPD (license to be bold, do as I please). Cautious boldness is then presented as a compromise between the two, preserving the basic orientation of BPD but also addressing the need for risk management and control over impulsiveness and self-expression.

Once the BPD patient understands the need for acquiring the skills of a GAD patient, the same executive beliefs prescribed in a GAD for threat management (detailed in chapter 9) are prescribed for BPD. There is one basic modification. Instead of self-monitoring for anxiety, petulant BPD patients monitor for irritation, agitation, and anger, the reactions they have when they feel threatened. Following is a summary of the new executive beliefs: (1) enter the situation and scan for danger; (2) appraise the danger; (3) if the threat is not imminent, adjust the RRP to an inert stage and shift the focus to anger reduction; (4) if a threat is imminent and real, then engage in problem solving to select the best response possible, and to assess if anger as a solution is appropriate and timely for that context; (5) learn about the threat and experience it instead of reacting angrily to it as a danger; and (6) base future behavior on that experience.

Other skills discussed in chapter 9 for the treatment of GAD are also useful for BPD. After splitting has demonized an individual, BPD patients engage in internal discussions with themselves about the evil of that person. The *no mind, no thing technique* is practiced to quiet negative mental chatter about other people. *Diminution training* is practiced to reduce the size of the danger or the "badness" of the other person. This involves *objectivity training* to self-question inflated negative appraisals of others (e.g., "So what if others do this—why is that so bad?" "Are they always so bad, and where are they not so bad?").

☐ Strategy Two: Relationship Maintenance

The inconsistency, vacillation, changeability, and erratic behavior that typify BPD are most marked in patients' relationship with others. Emotional equilibrium is frequently challenged, and mood shifts are common. The level of intensity swings from high to low at a moment's notice.

Hence, a most important need is *relationship maintenance training*. This *is an ability to sustain successful behavior* with others at work or at home. This is needed *to overcome the paradoxical interpersonal conduct* of BPD patients, who desperately yearn for a stable relationship and security with others but then turn around and achieve neither due to explosive, irregular behavior. They want others' love and then act in a way that alienates them (Millon, 1996).

This strategy is also used to indirectly refute the emotional deprecation and abuse schemas. By maintaining relationships they improve, which decreases the possibility of being hurt in a relationship.

First, similar to Benjamin (1993), the therapist makes the patient aware of his/her paradoxical behavior, to recognize maladaptive patterns. Also, this is done to increase motivation to practice the skills cited in this section. To make the patient more aware of paradoxical behavior, mental images can be created. The following images are recommended for Darlene to help her realize her self-defeating behavior:

- She drains the pool and then yearns to go swimming in it.
- She chops down a tree and then tries to lean on it.
- She burns down a forest and then seeks to go camping in it.

A visual image (e.g., a drawing) of the mental image (such as a pool with no water in it, a cut down tree) is then placed in several locations, to cue relationship maintenance skills.

Relationship maintenance offers several benefits. First, it is needed to develop a positive self-image. Due to rapidly changing presentations of self, the BPD patient has contradictory self-representations (Millon, 1996). By achieving consistent, successful behavior with others, self-image can stabilize and improve. Two, relationship maintenance skills can ease separation anxiety and build self-efficacy. Borderline patients live in fear that if a primary relationship should end, they will be left abandoned, alone, and lonely. This results in separation anxiety whenever a relationship is threatened. With *self-assurance training*, they are reassured about what skills they possess to function adequately in relationships. They learn that they have some of the equipment and knowledge to start and sustain another relationship and to repair the present relationship. Third, by knowing how to meet their needs in relationships, patients correct their assumption that they will inevitably be deprived, abused, and mistreated by others. Instead, they will have a feeling of safety and security, because they know that they can make relationships work. They will not be so concerned about others' behavior because of trust in themselves regarding their own ability to function successfully and correct other's improper conduct.

Because relationship maintenance is a dyadic problem, Darlene's husband joins her in treatment during this phase. Both are taught the skills presented in this section and practice using them in session. Once adept at using them with him, she can apply them at work with coworkers.

Identifying Present Coping Skills

In working with couples, CCT examines the interpersonal coping responses of both husband and wife. The positive functions contained in the responses are detailed. CCT wants to make use of both parties' skills if they can be used judiciously and in the appropriate context.

While Darlene has frequent eruptions of anger, contained in that response are several positive functions:

1. *A limit-setting function.* Anger tells others, "No, no more."
2. *An energy mobilization function.* Anger galvanizes a person to take action.
3. *Emotional immediacy.* Anger gives quick, immediate voice to her emotions.

4. *Forcefulness.* Anger is power and makes Darlene feel powerful, which bolsters her self-esteem.

5. *Central positioning.* Anger positions her in the foreground of an interaction, because the angry person has to be dealt with.

What skills allow Darlene to explode and manipulate other people?

1. *Objectification.* This is a cognitive-perceptual ability. To accomplish this, perception ignores others' emotions, needs, problems, and personal history, so they have minimal impact. At the same time, thinking remains focused on how other people can be used as a means to an end goal. Others are turned into objects, a part of the production process.
2. *Desensitization.* This is an emotional ability to not feel others' emotions and remain unaffected by them.
3. *Interpersonal indifference.* This is an emotional ability to remain selectively apathetic to the needs of others.

Together, these skills allow the BPD patient to remain focused on personal priorities over the priorities of others. They allow the patient to manipulate without feeling guilty. When anger is felt, other people remain objects and their needs and feelings are ignored, thus allowing the borderline patient to speak and act without feeling inhibited.

Contextualizing Relationship Skills

Once the patient's skills are known, the next task is to assess whether they are used in an appropriate context. CCT refers to this as a *contextual search.* Petulant borderline patients have several negative, inappropriate, maladaptive coping responses that are dominant and basic features of their personality. CCT does not want to call for their total inhibition, in part because patients like those responses and rely on them. Because they are such a basic part of borderline functioning, discrediting them discredits the patient. Hence, the therapist confronts the use of these skills indirectly, through a contextual search. The skills are identified and the patient is asked in which context the skills are beneficial and have utility.

The first step in a contextual search is to *identify the positive and negative aspects of an irrational, maladaptive, or pathological response.* This separates the wheat from the chaff. The therapist then calls for preserving the good and inhibiting whatever is nonutilitarian. For example, the action tendency of irritation is a peevish, prickly demeanor. While this response in total is not helpful, it does contain valuable elements that need to be preserved, such as limit setting, review of other's behavior, declaration of a negative position, and a willingness to disagree. All these actions are conducive to independent action. The therapist identifies these positive parts of the peevish, prickly response but at the same time asks for the inhibition of the negative parts, such as querulous, fretful behavior. Further, the tendency to be querulous also contains positive aspects, such as an ability to be assertive, and that is separated from the negative aspects of that behavior, such as the focusing on negative issues.

The second step is to objectively discuss *where a skill has benefit*. For instance, the patient is asked where *desensitization, objectification,* and *indifference* have use. Darlene wants to preserve these skills for work when she delegates tasks. She needs to stick to her agenda, stay emotion-free, and use workers as objects at that time. For another example, the action tendency of anger is an approach-attack-fight response. Again, to *contextualize a skill,* the patient is asked where this response has value. Darlene believes it has use with her teenagers, who test her limits regularly. A measured response of anger can show her kids when enough is enough. The discussion does reveal a limited use for the attack-fight response, because it is inapplicable and harmful in most settings. In summary, the contextual search technique is able to confront her behavior—indirectly—while preserving rapport between therapist and patient.

Once a skill is placed in an appropriate context, there is a discussion about how to rehabilitate or convert a dysfunctional response into a desirable response. In order to do this, the *skill has to be linked or matched with other responses*. The sequence for using skills is then selected. *Indifference* can be rehabilitated as a part of a professional, businesslike attitude. This has appeal to Darlene because she is quite serious about her job and meeting sales quotas. She takes a no-nonsense approach to work when delegating assignments. At this time *objectification* is used, in which people become objects as part of a process to attain a goal. However, *indifference* is a sterile and cold response, so it is *matched with emotional support and* a selective use of *humor*. If subordinates show hesitation, anxiety, or consternation about an assignment, then emotional support and humor can be used to overcome their reluctance. Together, this package of skills acts to humanize the businesslike attitude and avoid a backlash from others when they are treated as objects.

The relationship skills that Darlene possesses that are positive are also encouraged. For example, she is most adept at being contrite and apologetic. She can quickly become warm and effusive when she seeks forgiveness. The therapist then inquires into *the mechanism of action* for these skills. For example, what is her method of producing warmth when she otherwise feels irritable? She learns from such question that she uses a perceptual skill of focusing on other people's positive qualities (trait salience) to generate warmth toward them. Once aware of her method for producing warmth, she can feel that way when desired, upon self-command.

Contextual sorting is an alternative to a contextual search, to identify the most appropriate and utilitarian beliefs and skills for a given context. This technique requires *alternative solution thinking.* A list of situations is presented to Darlene, and she then generates options for handling those situations. The options are rank-ordered regarding which are the best beliefs and coping responses for those contexts. For instance, when Darlene handles protests from a subordinate at work, what approach should be adopted first? If that does not work, what skill is used next? The discussion shows the patient how she habitually turns to anger first as her coping choice, when other responses are preferable.

Rapport Maintenance Training

Once the patient's present interpersonal skills are contextualized, the focus can shift to addressing coping skill deficits and skill building. To maintain rapport, rapport maintenance skills are taught. Rapport is confluence, being able to flow with another person. To do this, there is a need to first assess how the patient achieves rapport with others and how she copes when it has been broken. Borderline patients need awareness of this because they are frequently out of rapport with others. They have to be cognizant of indicators that reveal when rapport has been established (such as similar breathing patterns, a relaxed musculature, and calm, flowing speech) and when rapport has been broken (such as when there is muscle tension, agitation, restlessness, or labored, pressured speech).

The goal is to maintain rapport even when there is conflict. Several interpersonal skills are taught for this purpose:

1. *Assertiveness techniques* are taught to stand up to others, give instructions, and make a complaint. Alberti and Emmons (1978) and Sprafkin and colleagues (1993) provide a fuller discussion. There is a need for exploration of the difference between assertiveness, aggressiveness, and passivity. See Wine and Smye (1981) for a fuller discussion.
2. Basic *rapport maintenance skills* are given, including acknowledging another's approach or idea, matching the other person's nonverbal behavior (e.g., nodding or smiling at the same time the other person does), questioning to sustain a conversation, active listening, and giving compliments.

3. *Integrative negotiating skills* (Fisher, 1991) are taught to help both parties in a relationship realize their goals and satisfy both of their interests. Attending skills are taught in order to address the other person's concerns. The goal is maintaining rapport while negotiating differences in position.
4. *Conflict resolution skills* are taught to find the overriding, common value for both conflicting positions. There is training in interviewing skills, finding encompassing values between those in conflict, how to form probing questions to learn more about the other's opinions and values, and giving feedback without stifling the other.
5. *Expression modulation training* is initiated to help Darlene moderate the intensity of her responses to others. While petulant borderlines have no problem raising the intensity level, they need practice expressing the content of the message in mild to moderate ways, to show displeasure with less degree of consternation. This includes the following steps and skills: setting a goal regarding the outcome of the interaction using *end-means thinking* (see below), achieving a lower intensity level using relaxation, and communicating the message using the above four skills.

Together, these skills help to overcome a borderline's belief in emotional deprivation and abuse schemas. By becoming interpersonally potent, patients reduce the possibility that others can deprive or abuse them. The above interpersonal skills increase trust in self and raise self-assurance. The combined benefit of these skills indirectly challenges the flawed autonomy schema.

Empathy Training

One way to temper and avoid angry outbursts is to understand and feel the problems, needs, limitations, history, expectations, and internal conflicts of the object of anger. Anger is involvement in one's own world. Anger dissolves when a person becomes involved with the other person's world, experiences it, and gains an understanding of his/her life. This requires *empathy training.*

There are three basic subskills of empathy: *active listening, accurate interpretation of interpersonal cues,* and *responding empathically* (Sperry, 1999; Guerney, 1977). The therapist has to assess the patient's capacity regarding each of these skills. Active listening focuses on the verbal part of the interaction, while the interpretation of interpersonal cues focuses on the nonverbal component. Together, they can deliver a partial understanding of the other person's thoughts, feelings, and motives.

These two skills are especially important for borderline individuals because they "fail to accord their unstable mood levels with external reality" (Millon, 1996, p. 665). They do not respond to what is actually present in the environment. Rather, they respond to "inner structures that exist in sharply segmented and conflictful configurations" (Millon, 1996, p. 665). CCT would call those inner structures the executive beliefs, which interpret the activating event and then issues self-instructions about how to respond to it. Active listening and maximum attention to interpersonal cues obviates or circumvents the influence of inner structures or entrenched executive beliefs by first getting involved with the world of the object or external reality.

To accurately interpret interpersonal cues, patients need to be trained in the microskill of *external cue sensitivity*. This is an ability to first *narrow attention* onto the object's nonverbal behavior and then *observe* it, especially facial expression. At the same time the patient has to become nonresponsive to her own needs and goals while preventing emotional reactivity. Finally, using the data gained by observation, an *interpretation* can be made about nonverbal behavior.

While this is occurring, active listening is proceeding. This also requires *suppression of emotional reactivity* to the object's words and maximal focus on what the other person is saying. *Summarization* of the object's words is a helpful skill, and it is used before speaking. This simultaneously restrains emotions and allows an accurate understanding of the other person's ideas.

To become empathic, two steps are required. The patient has to understand what the situation looks like from the vantage point of the other person. This requires the microskill of *perspective taking*. To do this, the patient has to imagine what life is like for the other person, both in general and in that specific interaction. Next the patient has to experience herself after acquiring the information about how she is viewed by the object. This will facilitate an empathic response to the other person. If the patient continues to lack the feeling capacity required for empathy, then she will have to be trained to *mechanically give empathic responses* (e.g., the patient is told to say, "Oh, I see what you mean" while nodding, to show concurrence).

Adjudication Training

Not only do borderline patients have a problem with relationship maintenance with other people, they have a problem maintaining a relationship with themselves. They become furious with themselves, self-rejecting, self-hating, and self-denigrating. Excessive guilt for a misdeed is felt, which is often triggered when the patient is rejected by another person. At that time the patient may become overly contrite, unforgiving of herself, and cast total blame on herself for causing problems in the relationship.

To treat this problem, *forgiveness training* is first taught, to give a more objective view of the situation and to understand the role of both parties in the conflict. However, because of dichotomous thinking, the patient can turn against herself instantly and only conceive of herself as all negative, thus remaining self-critical and self-denigrating. In that case, there is unwillingness to forgive. Cognitive restructuring can dispute erroneous charges against the object of anger. However, the tendency to slip into hypercritical, one-sided thinking is highly ingrained in the BPD individual.

A cognitive skill is needed to overcome cognitive rigidity and reflexive dichotomous thinking, and that is *adjudication training*. It is a procedure inculcated to replace the intropunitive response pattern and to challenge the evil self schema. Adjudication training looks at the event in a legalistic, judicial way, to boost cognitive control over the emotions.

First, the patient assumes her habitual role of persecutor (the prosecutor role) and presents the actual charges against the object (who can be another person or oneself). The position of the persecutor and the evidence are presented to the jury—the objective side of oneself. Second, the patient, as the jury, must ignore hurt feelings generated by the persecutor's hypercritical comments and instead objectively and impartially hear the charges as presented by the persecutor. This is to prevent becoming confluent with the critical part-of-self and immediately becoming depressed about being criticized. Third, the borderline creates a new part of self, a defense attorney to defend herself against the charges. This is installed to force the patient to broaden her thinking and hear another point of view. Empowering the "defense attorney" is important. Finally, the mental jury weighs the evidence and declares the object of anger guilty or innocent.

If the patient is found guilty as charged, then a way needs to be developed to end run-on self-criticism and self-castigation. The internal jury has to decide if the self has suffered enough; it can grant a suspended sentence, order probation (where the self will be watched by an internal "probation officer" to avoid making the same mistake again), or give a real punishment chosen by the patient. Examples of a punishment include giving a sum of money to a charity, writing an essay about the misdeed and giving it to the hurt party, or doing something as silly as eating standing up on one leg for a week. The purpose is to make the patient pay for the crime in a reasonable way, but also to give her what she wants—a measure of self-castigation. There is a need to put parameters on the punishment so it lasts for only a specific time period and is not excessive.

If someone else has committed the crime against the patient, then the same procedure is followed. If the other party is found guilty and a punishment is desired, then types of punishments are discussed. The patient's typical ways of punishing others is explicated and the advisability of using that form of punishment is discussed. The intention is to make the patient take responsibility for how she punishes another person, to decide if it is productive, moral, prudent, and useful for a relationship. Criteria for a punishment has to be discussed: (1) it must not harm the relationship, (2) it must not prolong a struggle or conflict, and (3) it must not accrue a secondary gain.

The primary rational for adjudication training is to facilitate reconciliation with oneself or another person. It provides a vehicle to challenge self-denigration, which reduces or neutralizes the effect of the evil self schema. The adjudication process creates objectivity in reviewing the supposed crime and provides a noninjurious outlet for intropunitive, self-rejecting behavior. This occurs by finding rational punishment (e.g., verbal disapproval) instead of irrational punishment (e.g., self-mutilation or self-denigration). By making punishment an overt, self-chosen action, it brings to consciousness what is occurring unconsciously. At that point, the borderline can decide if she or others have suffered enough and can be "paroled."

☐ Strategy Three: Consistency Training

The problem of inconsistency and erratic behavior is a hallmark of BPD. Such patients are noted for their capricious, flighty, impulsive behavior. Because of this, borderlines feel scattered and unintegrated, "responding as a child to every passing interest or whim and shifting from one momentary course to another" (Millon, 1996, p. 664). This section first presents skills to overcome behavioral inconsistency.

End-Means Training

Borderline patients lack an ability to set goals (Beck and colleagues, 1990). The lack of a clear, stable identity harms effort to set and sustain priorities. The impulsive, spasmodic, desultory nature of BPD patients causes frequent disruptions in the link between action and long-term goal attainment. In the rush to express negative feelings, long-term goals are shoved aside.

To treat this problem, *end-means thinking* is inculcated. It develops a cognitive ability to focus on long-term goals first and foremost, and then identify the in-between steps that will lead to that goal. This is an ability to engage in prospective processing, where steps are plotted into the future that eventuates in a chosen end goal. The overriding principle is to organize behavior so there is a relationship between actions and goals. This way, one behavior complements and builds on another in a linear sequence, thus creating *distal-proximal consistency:* short-term behavior leading to long-term desired outcomes. This trains the BPD patient not only in being goal-oriented but also in goal maintenance.

The first step in end-means training is to assess what type of goals to select (short- or long-term) and what internal or external factors prevent the patient from reaching those goals. Next, the therapist needs to implant a capacity in the patient (via self-instructions) to interrupt impetuous, nonreflective decision making (e.g., "Stop, halt. I'm upset. Don't make any snap decisions"). Third, an objective stance is called for to force reflection and deliberation before taking acting. Fourth, the patient is asked to select a long-term goal. Fifth, consequential thinking is exercised to assess any problems that can arise from working to achieve that goal. Sixth, the patient is asked to engage in alternative solution thinking to consider various means to accomplish the goal. Finally, the means to reach the end goal (by using *means-end thinking*) are plotted. This forges a consistent purpose for behavior and a clear focus for the future.

Once the long-term goal is selected, the next step is *goal maintenance.* This requires other subskills. Upon entering a situation, the patient is asked to engage in *goal-cueing,* to cue herself to remain focused on long-term goals throughout the interaction. Second, self-talk is implanted to maintain a constant, desired role while in the interaction. For example, Darlene is given the following self-talk to be said in the workplace: "Who do I want to be? How do I want to be seen? Become who I want to be. Focus on the goal and maintain it."

Third, actions inconsistent to long-term goals have to be examined. For this, a continuous predictive ability is needed, in which the patient asks herself, "What will happen if I do this?" This is the subskill of *prognostication,* which is needed to identify consequences for one's behavior. Two microskills can aid this effort. One is *psychological distancing,* the ability to psychologically disengage from the present situation and view it as an observer. In that role the patient views the situation as if it is happening on screen, positioning herself in the audience watching the event as a movie. Once distanced from the situation, the person makes a prediction about how the movie will turn out. A second microskill is *time projection,* to view present behavior from a future vantagepoint. The BPD patient looks at an action one week or six months from that moment in time and asks, "How will I feel about this action then? Will I still think this action is advisable?" (Lazarus, 1968). If present behavior is predicted to be antagonistic to long-term goals, then it is suppressed.

Restraint Training

Restraint training works in tandem with end-means thinking. Once a goal has been selected, any other pursuit inconsistent or in opposition to that goal (termed goal-deviant behavior) has to be restrained. The purpose of *restraint is to limit freedom and surrender options that are incongruent to long-term goals and a desired presentation of self.*

To achieve restraint, *self-awareness* is necessary to track impulses and identify drives that are goal-deviant. To maintain vigilance in self-awareness, visual cues (e.g., the image of eyeglasses) are placed around the office and house to serve as a reminder to observe one's behavior so it continues to lead to goal attainment. Self-awareness has a detaching, distancing function as the patient watches herself function, which inadvertently restrains impulsivity. Self-awareness also cues the need for *relaxation* to curtail emotional reactivity that can side-track goal maintenance.

Role assumption is often used in CCT to restrain goal deviance. The patient is asked to *adopt the "as if" role,* where she acts as if she is another person capable of attaining the desired end goal. Darlene admires Katherine Hepburn for the poise and self-control she exhibits in her films. She then pretends to be her at work when she handles conflicts with subordinates. An alternative is to develop a desirable part-of-self that can become a consistent presentation of self. Inadvertently, this inhibits responses contrary to that part-of-self. Darlene wants to develop a friendly, affable presentation. She places cues around the work environment to sustain that role (a stimulus control technique). She adjusts behavior appropriately to operate only in that part-of-self.

Restraint training is also needed to check undesirable emotional influence on behavior and to install cognitive control. Borderlines are more influenced by their emotions rather than their intellect in selecting their goals and the next course of action. This often results in a disconnect between present behavior and long-term goals, situational obligations, and role expectations.

One important method to restrain emotion is self-instruction training (see Navaco, 1975). A physical stimulus control technique can also restrain dysfunctional emotional responses. Upon entering a situation, a bodily cue is activated to maintain role appropriate behavior. For example, Darlene selects a bodily cue where she drops her jaw slightly to the left, adopts a half smile, and opens her eyes fully. She calls this her friendly face, and she holds it throughout the encounter with co-workers. It acts to limit responses counter to that desired part-of-self. A *counterresponse* can also inhibit emotional reactivity. Anger often has an individualized physical action tendency. For example, Darlene tightens her jaw, holds her breath momentarily, and puffs out her chest when she feels angry. To inhibit her anger she practices a "sag response," where she deflates her lungs and lets her jaw drop in a flaccid manner. This derails the physical action tendency that simultaneously interrupts the chained, automatic, stimulus-response sequence leading to anger.

Spontaneity Training

A hallmark of borderline functioning is impulsive behavior, which in turn results in inconsistent, rash behavior and abandonment of goals. The BPD patient allows sudden urges that are not governed by reason and in many cases are contrary to reason. Therapists such as Sperry (1999) and Linehan (1993) try to suppress impulsiveness. Yet, acting on impulse can be a highly desirable way of responding—when it includes a cognitive component that prevents the individual from engaging in self-injurious behavior. CCT recognizes this and does not want to suppress spontaneous behavior that is a dominant component of borderline functioning. Instead, it seeks to make the impulsive borderline into a "better" impulsive person. To do this, *spontaneity training* is taught. To create a semantic differential from previous, dysfunctional behavior, the therapist gives a new name to impulsiveness—spontaneity. It is defined as acting on whim with the assistance of reason. Essentially, impulsiveness is prescribed, but new skills are added to the knee-jerk response, which can decrease the chance of self-harm.

The treatment of impulsiveness proceeds in the following fashion:

1. The therapist assesses where and how the person is impulsive.
2. An incentive analysis is conducted, listing the pros and cons of impulsiveness. Benefits of being this way are acknowledged, such as quick mobilization of behavior, an immediate expression for emotion, seizing the moment unencumbered by forethought, and breaking through inhibitions to express native tendencies.
3. The therapist labels impulsiveness a coping response, a positive behavior that requires the addition of other skills to function productively. At this point, impulsiveness is relabeled as spontaneity.
4. The patient is trained to use *forethought* to scan for danger before taking action—the "look before leaping" response.
5. The patient is instructed to check if the spontaneous behavior is

consistent to long-term goals. If no danger is noted, then the spontaneous urge is permitted.

6. As it is exercised, checkpoints are arranged to engage in forethought again. At this time, two problem-solving skills are utilized. One is *consequential thinking* ("Will this action cause me a problem?") and the other is *alternative solution thinking* ("Are there other ways to act besides this way?"). Again, if no problems are noted, spontaneous expression proceeds forward.
7. If dangers are noted, restraint is used to curtail the impulse. Methods to restrain oneself include *self-instruction training, relaxation,* and *distraction* to delay the urge to take action.

Working together, end-means thinking, restraint, and spontaneity training challenge the insufficient self-control schema. They demonstrate to the patient that she can maintain self-management.

Treating Dichotomous Thinking

Having discussed methods to manage behavioral inconsistency, we will now shift the discussion to skills for treating cognitive inconsistency. A chief reason for the latter in BPD is dichotomous thinking (Beck and colleagues, 1990). It categorizes people or events as all one way, all-good or all-bad. Someone is either idealized and venerated or denigrated and disrespected. It is a faulty information processing structure because important data are either ignored or given inordinate weight. It contributes to pathology in several ways. It results in splitting, which in turn proliferates the number of threats to well-being and in so doing increases the overall level of anxiety. It triggers schemas that others will deprive the patient or be abusive, which further increases anger toward the object. Labeling people (including the self) as all bad one moment and all good the next results in incompatible object representations and contradictory presentations of self. Labeling the object as all-bad results in rejection of the object or, at a minimum, ambivalence and vacillation about how to treat the object. Dichotomous thinking, when others are labeled as all-bad, lends supports to the mistrust/abuse schema.

Cognitive restructuring treats dichotomous thinking as an inaccurate belief. It converts the contention about the object into a hypotheses and collects data to disprove the thought. Beck and colleagues (1990) have the patient reflect if people are always a certain way, such as always mean or always cheap. CCT views dichotomous thinking as extreme evaluative thinking. To correct this problem, *evaluative restraint* is first emphasized. Next, the BPD patient receives *sensory-based descriptive judgment training and training in retrospective processing training,* to review the behavior of oneself and others. This is done to forge a more realistic view of the object. This is a response substitution strategy, where the patient trains herself to describe rather than evaluate. Once more adept at collecting data by making sensory-based descriptive judgments, borderline patients can better assess their thinking for accuracy using hypotheses testing protocol.

Another approach is to help the patient become a "better" evaluative thinker. To accomplish this, the BPD is trained to engage in *continuum thinking* instead of dichotomous thinking, which is encouraged by Beck and Freeman (1990). The former is an ability to rate or evaluate others' behaviors on a continuous measure. Below are the steps for developing this ability:

1. Identify the extreme rating being used (e.g., "jerk," "loser").
2. Form a continuum from high to low for the quality being considered (high to low "jerkiness"). Mark several points on that continuum (e.g., mild or medium jerk).
3. Identify criteria for giving someone a label for each point on the continuum. For example, the patient describes how someone would have to act to be considered a mild or severe jerk.
4. Decide where the object lies on that continuum, taking into consideration the criteria. This entails descriptive judgment training to assess and describe the object's behavior and then compare it to the criterion.
5. The patient then decides if the label is warranted. If so, the description of the object has to match the criteria for the label.

Finally, the patient is asked to make a comparison between dichotomous and continuum thinking, regarding which yields more precise evaluations of another person.

Dichotomous thinking contains a rating. Another way to treat this way of thinking is to *contextualize the rating.* In this method, the therapist does not disagree with the rating but inquires where the rating is applicable. Is someone generally a certain way or only in certain contexts? For example, Darlene evaluates her staff as "a bunch of total losers." The context for such an evaluation is described (e.g., they put out poor work, whine, and procrastinate when she reacts to them with hostility). Learning this changes her feeling toward them, because she then understands her role in influencing their behavior.

An alternative way to treat dichotomous thinking is to learn skills that lessen its injurious effect. For the moment, the evaluation of the object is taken as accurate, that someone or something is all bad, a complete jerk, and so on. The BPD patient then learns *optimism training* (see chapter 8), where bright-side thinking is used to perceive the overlooked benefits to a uniformly perceived, all-negative event. *Forgiveness training* (see chapter 7) is taught to forgive someone easily when s/he is viewed as all-bad. This skill reveals the complexity of human behavior, teaching the BPD patient to consider the many reasons why people act as they do (e.g., personal history, the influence of others). Once the complex reasons for actions are understood, this simultaneously tempers extreme labeling. *Adjudication training* is installed to collect data for the purpose of exonerating the patient or others when either is incorrectly charged with a "crime." Because of these three skills, an object may still be labeled as bad but there is less of a negative feeling toward that person. Each of these three skills challenges dichotomous thinking and discredits it, indirectly producing a fuller, more comprehensive way to evaluate and understand human behavior.

If the patient persists in thinking dichotomously, this pattern of thinking along with its consequences is described to the patient. The patient is then asked to foretell what will happen to relationships if she continues to think that way. This reveals the nonutilitarian nature of this thought pattern.

Overcoming dichotomous thinking helps to challenge the emotional deprivation and abuse schemas. The patient is less prone to make generalizations about other people. Not seeing the self as all-bad reduces the influence of the evil self schema.

☐ Strategy Four: Dependency Training

Darlene typifies the struggle of borderlines regarding dependency needs. Exceedingly dependent, she requires substantial reassurance, admiration, encouragement, and love from others in order to feel stable, calm, and motivated to do her best. She feels angry when others disappoint her and do not satisfy her needs. She also feels angry with herself for being needy and not being more independent. Her dependency lowers her self-esteem and is a blow to her pride. Due to her schemas, she fears and resents being dependent on people because she assumes that they will eventually deprive, abuse, or neglect her. Her dependency results in constant interpersonal tension that ultimately results in outbursts that drives others away, proving her contention that others will harm her in the end. Feeling all alone and rejected, she experiences intense separation anxiety that drives her to seek reunion with the same people she resents. In summary, she cannot enjoy or take comfort in her dependency.

In treating this problem, the therapist asks the patient the general question: what allows someone to function in a dependency relationship, and what skills or what mind-set is necessary to have a successful experience when depending on another person? Skills are then taught to help the patient adjust to the dependent role; to be a "better" dependent person.

First, though, the therapist assesses how the patient functions when in a dependency role. What does she do when others do not meet her dependency needs, or what is her means of coping at that time? How does the patient get others to meet her needs? What is the patient's ability to tolerate unmet needs?

Self-Assurance Training

With self-assurance, people believe that they can manage both in and out of a relationship. With it, separation anxiety eases, and there is less catastrophic thinking following an argument. One way to gain self-assurance is by gaining awareness of personal qualities. However, borderline patients have a problem in this regard because they "lack an inherent sense of self" (Millon, 1999, p. 646). *Self-support training* (see chapter seven) is necessary to identify their positive qualities and behaviors useful to relationships. Borderline patients also need to review past relationships to become aware of what they did to make those relationships successful. Third, times when they successfully operated as an independent, single person also have to be noted, along with what they specifically did to make that happen. With this review, patients are reassured that they possess solutions for relationship problems or for a single's life. This approach disputes the flawed autonomy schema.

Millon states that borderline patients "lack the wherewithal, know-how, and equipment for . . . independent action" (Millon, 1999, p. 646). Learning the rapport maintenance skills (discussed above) and increasing self-assurance increases self-confidence that the self can operate as an independent person. There is greater confidence that they can start and maintain another relationship if the present one fails.

However, borderline patients are often not aware of their capacities and abilities because they are embedded within problematic, pathological behavior. To address this problem, CCT recommends a *skills analysis*:

1. A problem behavior is identified.
2. The therapist identifies the positive aspects and skills contained in that problematic behavior.
3. The therapist discusses where that problematic behavior can be

useful. Negative actions are placed in an appropriate context where they have utility.

4. The therapist discusses how present negative behavior can be beneficial if combined with other coping skills. Within the right combination, the negative response has benefit for a relationship.
5. The therapist shows how negative outcomes can be avoided when present skills are put in the proper sequence.

The overall effect of this approach is to impart a message that past dysfunction was due not to basic inadequacy but a skills dysfunction.

Borderline patients react intensely to rejection, which feels devastating to them. They need *disapproval tolerance training* to cope with it. This will increase self-assurance that they can function successfully if approval is withdrawn. At the same time, they need to know how to garner approval, so *approval training* is prescribed (see chapter 9 regarding both skills). This too increases self-assurance that they know what it takes to gain approval from others.

Further, borderlines assume that they will be devastated if left to function alone. They need to know that a single life can be tolerated. They need self-assurance that if the worst-case scenario does occur—there is a permanent breach in the relationship—the self can still survive and may even prosper. To make this point, *problem solving* needs to be initiated to identify what can be done if they had to function alone. To increase habituation to separation, patients can fantasize being alone and in time it will not appear devastating. This is the skill of *time projection*, where patients project into the future—six months or a year following separation—to realize that they will be more accustomed to this condition. They can also engage in *bright-side thinking* to find the benefits in being alone or having a relationship end.

Finally, borderline patients assume that the people in their lives will eventually deprive or abuse them. They need to perform a *reality check* on their present relationships. Data are collected to assess if it supports a conclusion. Darlene concludes that her work and personal life relationships will eventually be depriving. She has to assess past history to determine if that has been the case. Have significant others been trustworthy and reliable or depriving? Further, Darlene needs to distinguish the present people in her life from ones in her past who did deprive and abuse her (e.g., her father). *Comparison thinking* is needed for this effort to assess if she is relating to others through transference. Gaining this knowledge, she is reassured that she is in relationships that will meet her needs, which simultaneously disputes her emotional deprivation schema.

Neediness Tolerance

Relationships stimulate and expose people's needs. They create needs that were not present previously or were suppressed. Hence, neediness is a fact of life whenever anyone enters into a relationship. Everyone feels needy routinely in relationships. Borderline patients, though, have a particular problem with neediness and find it difficult to tolerate. This is because so many of them have experienced substantial neediness as a child, due to inconsistent or depriving parents. When neediness is then experienced, they react intensely with severe anxiety and/or anger. In addition, due to paradoxical conduct, such patients drive others away, so their needs continue to be unmet, which in turn increases neediness.

Hence, treatment needs to help the BPD patient learn to tolerate neediness. Dependence on others will not be so frustrating if neediness can be withstood. To develop neediness tolerance, the patient first needs to be aware of her pattern of responding when needs are not met. Next, *acceptance training* is initiated to help the patient accept basic realities about relationships—that the feeling of neediness is a part of all relationships to some degree. Another reason neediness is hard to tolerate is because patients commonly equate themselves to their needy state ("I am needy, so I must be inadequate"). Cognitive restructuring can be used to correct this example of reductionistic thinking.

Neediness tolerance inevitably involves two other subskills. One is *frustration tolerance*: learning to bear the discomfort from not having a need met. The second skill is *helplessness tolerance*: learning to bear not being in control and having to rely on someone else (see chapter 9 regarding both skills). To borderline patients, helplessness equates to subjugation and subordination, even if they have greater power than the person satisfying the need. To develop tolerance in each of these two areas, self-instruction training is helpful.

Self-talk to Tolerate Feeling Needy

Not having a need met does not feel good, but it is not the worst situation possible.

Satisfying my needs is not vital—just preferable.

Not having a need met is not awful. It is just unpleasant but I can tolerate it. I have had to tolerate other needs not being met, and this is no exception.

Live with the frustration. It is bearable. Don't make it a must that someone satisfies me. That will only make it worse.

I have to rely on others because I choose to. Tolerate not being in control. I am not helpless generally.

Disappointment Tolerance

When others do not meet the needs of the borderline or dependent person, disappointment is intense and anger or rages often result. To treat this problem, *disappointment tolerance* is reqired. To acquire it, the subskill of *acceptance* is again required, to learn to live with the reality that inevitably others will not meet all expectations and that a measure of disappointment is a given in all relationships. In addition, imagery sessions are useful for developing tolerance to disappointment. Scenes are solicited where disappointment has occurred in the past. Self-talk and relaxation are then used to develop tolerance of this feeling.

However, at the moment of disappointment, absolutistic thinking ("Others must meet my needs") and the tendency for awfulizing ("If they don't meet my needs it is awful") may inflame negative feelings, turning irritation into anger. These absolutes and the severe, extreme rating placed upon others' behavior has to be identified and changed via cognitive restructuring. Often, though, after treatment ends, patients slip back into brooding when disappointed by others. Hence, they need *training in anti-imperative thinking* to supplement cognitive restructuring, to avoid slipping back into imperative thinking.

Self-instruction training is helpful for tolerating disappointment, inculcating acceptance of it, disputing absolutes, and overcoming imperative thinking.

Self-talk to Tolerate Disappointment

Preparing for possible disappointment:

This person has disappointed me in the past, and it may happen again.

Disappointment is a part of life that has to be accepted. I do not have to approve of being disappointed, but I do have to accept it.

If I choose to rely on him/her, I may not get what I want. I may not like what occurs, but I can tolerate it—if I choose to.

Disappointment feels bad, but it is tolerable. I can live with it.

When feeling disappointed in another person:

Don't get angry. That will only make him/her less willing to meet my needs. Don't make the situation worse.

Relax. Don't get tense and angry. Stay in control.

Disappointing me does not make him/her a bad person.

I am only disappointed. The situation is not catastrophic.

Treatment of Childhood Trauma

The treatment strategy up to this point has been to improve present functioning. As the relationship with the cognitive coping therapist continues to yield concrete help for Darlene, she has become much more willing to trust the therapist and reveal archaic conflicts, areas of shame, and trauma. Because the childhood of BPD patients is often so devastating, CCT maintains that there is a need to work with the past and its effect on the present. It does this in the latter stage of treatment, once the BPD is ready to address painful, past situations.

Many of Darlene's responses to present situations are a result of a *time-fit error*. This is a most common problem among the BPD. Due to inconsistent, abusive, and neglectful parenting, Darlene developed coping responses to meet her needs, that were useful in her childhood. For instance, she gave herself permission to have outbursts of anger to show her parents how hurt she was. She learned how to objectify them and desensitize herself so she would not feel their pain when she exploded at them. She learned to engage in dichotomous thinking to help her cope with disappointment and trauma. Seeing her father as all good blocked out negative feelings toward him for sexually abusing her and cheating on her mother. This helped her to suppress rage toward him that would have jeopardized the relationship. These methods of coping as a child helped her to survive and were useful at an earlier age, but they are no longer helpful when used in adulthood most of the time.

To treat time-fit errors, the following steps are practiced.

1. The therapist has the patient make a list of coping responses used as a child.
2. The benefits of those skills in childhood are detailed.
3. Past incidents in which those skills were deployed are then recalled and reexperienced, focusing on the patient's emotions at that time. This is important to understand and recognize—on an emotional level—why the patient employed those responses as a child. The therapist asks the patient to feel grateful to those past skills for helping her survive and be less vulnerable.
4. The patient's feelings toward those old skills are then discussed. The intention is to bring to the surface unwillingness to surrender those skills if not appropriate for present-day contexts.
5. Present people in her life are then discussed, to decide if old coping skills are helplful with them. The intention is to learn if past coping responses fit or are applicable for present life circumstances.

6. The focus then shifts to helping the patient surrender or say good-bye to old coping skills, at least how they were practiced from childhood.
7. The skills from childhood are then examined to assess how they would have to be readapted to be beneficial for adult life, and what skills have to be added to them to form a more potent ability.
8. The contexts for using childhood skills in adult life are assessed. A contextual search is conducted to deploy childhood skills in appropriate, present-day contexts.

Past Object Reconstruction

Building on the work with time-fit errors, the technique of *past object reconstruction* can be employed. This technique is most useful for healing the wounds from childhood trauma and for repairing a negative self-image. Below are the steps:

1. The skills the patient lacked as a child are identified.
2. The skills the patient has learned as an adult and in therapy are identified.
3. The patient then "reconstructs herself" as a child, incorporating the coping skills that she has learned. She is asked to experience herself as a child possessing and practicing those abilities, especially in situations where there was a negative outcome.
4. She is asked to feel the power and potency from employing her newly learned skills.
5. Past situations are recalled and replayed in the first person, as if they were presently happening, to make them feel immediate and real. The patient then discusses how they would turn out differently by using the skills learned in adulthood.

   For example, Darlene adds the skills of restraint, assertiveness, and self-support to boost her self-esteem regarding her past sexual abuse. Replaying a scene, she reports, "My father is coming into my room. I tell him to leave and to not touch me again. I speak to him strongly, emphatically. I do not back down when he ignores me and tries to touch me. I do not blow up. I like my power. I handle him well."
6. The patient's history is recalled, cataloging how momentous situations could have been different if particular skills had been known at that time.

Object reconstruction can be particularly useful for adult survivors of sexual abuse such as Darlene. It facilitates understanding of how the abuse continued for so long due to the absence of key skills in both her and the abuser.

Another option is to reconstruct other people. They can be given skills that could have resulted in different circumstances as a child. For instance, Darlene's father could be reconstructed to include skills he did not possess, such as empathy. This helps Darlene to realize that he acted as he did due to the absence of key capacities.

The empty chair technique from Gestalt (Polster & Polster, 1973) can also be used with the object reconstruction technique. Darlene can talk to her father in the empty chair in her newly constructed form and feel more potent than she did as a child. In this new form she can talk to herself as a child about how life could have been different if she'd had these newly learned abilities. Another option is to become the new, reconstructed parent. Darlene can become her father and talked to herself as a child, telling her how he would have treated her differently if he'd had different skills while she was growing up.

This technique is much more than wishful thinking. It illustrates the power and importance of coping skills, especially at key stages in a child's life. It merges the past person with all of her deficits and negative self-image with a powerful, adequate construction. This helps to overcome the sense of inadequacy by showing the patient that a lifelong negative self-image results from a lack of coping skills. By adding new skills at a particular life stage, a past, virulent self-image changes in the process. The different twists and turns a life can take are seen as a result of a coping skills excess or deficit.

Conclusion to Treatment

As a consequence of anger management training, Darlene has been much better able to control her temper and has curtailed her outbursts significantly. As a result of relationship maintenance training, her relationships with others has improved significantly. There have been fewer conflicts at work and at home. As a consequence of threat reduction training, she does not perceive so many situations as threatening to her well being, so she does not get as angry as often as a consequence. When she does feel threatened and feels angry, she is much more cautious about how to act. Threat management training has prepared her to vigilantly scan for danger, but to also experience the danger without her presumptions. This way a threat that formerly would have been immediately received with hostility and irritation is experienced on its own merits. This leads to different behavior regarding the supposed danger. Consistency training has prepared her to think about long-term goals and to work to achieve them, resulting in a more consistent presentation of self. Her self-image has been able to stabilize as a result. Overall, her mood and behavior have been much more stable.

Indirectly, a coping skills approach has altered her schemas. New coping skills have refuted her deprivation and abuse schemas. Because she is receiving better treatment from others, in large part due to a change in her own behavior, she no longer presumes that relationships will eventually be depriving and abusive. Also, by learning to trust that she can be capable in relationships, she has reduced her overall mistrust that relationships will disappoint and abuse her in the end. If they turn out that way, she believes that she can correct the problem with her new relationship maintenance skills. She realizes that she plays a large role in why she is deprived. By functioning better, she has also indirectly disputed her evil self schema. By learning how to control her anger and tolerate frustration, she no longer subscribers to the insufficient self-control entitlement schema. There is no reason to think this way any longer, because she realizes that self-control can be attained and will lead to desirable results. Finally, by learning relationship and anger management skills she realizes that she can be autonomous and succeed as a single person if need be. She is self-assured that she can function successfully in relationships. Hence, independence and rejection do not create the intense separation anxiety that they once did.

☐ Summary

As a petulant borderline personality, Darlene presents with four dominant problems: difficulty managing anger, paradoxical interpersonal conduct, inconsistency in mood, thinking, and behavior, and difficulty functioning in a dependency relationship. Four general skills are recommended for them respectively: anger management training, relationship maintenance training, consistency training, and dependency training. Anger management includes (1) training in anger reduction, involving self-monitoring, relaxation, self-instructions, and perceptual shifting, (2) threat reduction, involving risk determination and risk readiness, and (3) threat management. The patient is asked to incorporate some of the skills of a generalized anxiety disorder and their executive beliefs for managing threats. Relationship maintenance includes the readapting of present skills, rapport maintenance, external cue sensitivity, and adjudication training. Consistency training involves restraint training, end-means thinking, which involves prognostication and psychological distancing, and spontaneity training. Finally, dependency training includes self-assurance training, neediness and disappointment tolerance.

In addition, problems in her childhood are addressed using past object reconstruction. Many of her present-day problems are reconceptualized as a time-fit error. Her problem with anger is also considered a coping skill excess.

REFERENCES

Abraham, K. (1911). Notes on the psychoanalytic investigation and treatment of manic-depressive insanity and allied conditions. In: *Selected papers of Karl Abraham*. London: Hogarth.

Abramson, J., Seligman, M., & Teasdale, J. (1978). Learned helplessness in humans: Critique and reformulation. *J. of Abnormal Psychology, 87*, 49–74.

Adler, A. (1929). *Problems of neuroses: A book of case histories*. London: Kegan, Paul, Trench, Treubner.

Akiskal, H. (1983). Dysthymic disorder: Psychopathology of proposed chronic depressive subtypes. *American Journal of Psychiatry, 140*, 11–20.

Akiskal, H. (1997). Overview of chronic depressions and their clinical management. In H. Akiskal & G. Cassano, *Dysthymia and the spectrum of chronic depressions* (pp. 1–35). New York: Guilford.

Alberti, R., & Emmons, M. (1978). *Your perfect right: A guide to assertive behavior*. San Luis Obispo, CA: Impact.

Andrasik, F., & Matson, J. (1985). Social skills training for the mentally retarded. In L. L. Abate & M. Milan (Eds.), *Handbook of social skill training and research* (pp. 418–457). New York: Wiley.

Bandler, R., & Grinder, J. (1982). *Reframing*. Moag, Utah: Real People.

Bandura, A. (1969a). *Principles of behavior modification*. New York: Holt, Rinehart, and Winston.

Bandura, A. (1969). Social learning theory of identificatory processes. In R. Goslin (Ed.), *Handbook of socialization theory and research*. Chicago: Rand McNally.

Bandura, A. (1977). Self-efficacy: Toward a unifying theory of behavioral change. *Psychological Review, 84*, 191–215.

Bandura, A. (1980). Gauging the relationship between self-efficacy judgment and action. *Cognitive Therapy and Research, 4*, 263–268.

Bandura, A. (1982). Self-efficacy mechanism in human agency. *American Psychologist,37*, 122–147.

Bandura, A. (1984). Recycling misconceptions of perceived self-efficacy. *Cognitive Therapy and Research, 8*, 231–255.

Bandura, A. (1986). *Social foundations of thought and action: A social cognitive theory*. Englewood Cliffs, NJ: Prentice-Hall.

Bandura, A. (1997). *Self-efficacy: The exercise of control*. New York: Freeman.

Barkovec, T., Wilkinson, L., Folensbee, R., & Lerman, C. (1983). Stimulus control application to the treatment of worry. *Behavior, Research, and Therapy, 21*, 247–251.

Barlow, D. (1988). *Anxiety and its disorders: The nature and treatment of anxiety and panic*. New York: Guilford.

Barlow, D., Blanchard, E., Vermilyea, J., Vermilyea, B., & DiNardo, P. (1986). Generalized anxiety and generalized anxiety disorder: Description and reconceptualization. *American Journal of Psychiatry, 143,* 40–44.

Barlow, D., diNardo, P., Vermilyea, B., Vermilyea, J., & Blanchard, E. (1986). Co-morbidity and depression among the anxiety disorders: Issues in diagnosis and classification. *Journal of Nervous and Mental Disorders, 174,* 63–72.

Beck, A. (1976) *Cognitive therapy and the emotional disorders.* New York: International Universities Press.

Beck, A., & Emery, G. (1985). *Anxiety disorders and phobics: A cognitive perspective.* New York: Basic Books.

Beck, A., Freeman, A., & Associates (1990). *Cognitive therapy of personality disorders.* New York: Guilford.

Beck, A., Rush, A., Shaw, B., & Emery, G. (1979). *Cognitive therapy of depression.* New York: Guilford.

Belmont, J., & Butterfield, E. (1977). The instructional approach to developmental cognitive research. In R. Kail & J. Hagen (Eds.), *Perspectives on the development of memory and cognition.* Hillsdale, NJ: Lawrence Erlbaum.

Bem, D. (1965). An experimental analysis of self-persuasion. *Journal of Experimental Psychology, 1,* 199–218.

Benjamin, L. (1993). *Interpersonal diagnosis and treatment of personality disorders.* New York: Guilford.

Benson, H., Beary, J., & Carol, M. (1974). The relaxation response. *Psychiatry, 37,* 37–46.

Berne, E. (1961). *Transactional analysis in psychotherapy.* New York: Grove.

Berne, E. (1973). *What do you say after you say hello?* New York: Bantam Books.

Bowlby, J. (1982). *Attachment and loss,* vol. 1: *Attachment.* New York: Basic Books (original work published 1969).

Burns, D. (1980). *Feeling good: The new mood therapy.* New York: Signet Books.

Candland, D. (1977). The persistent problem of emotion. In D. Candland, J. Fell., E. Keen, A. Lesow, R. Platchik, & R. Tarpy (Eds.), *Emotion.* Monterey, CA: Brooks/Cole.

Cautela, J. (1967). Covert sensitization. *Psychological Reports, 20,* 459–468.

Christoff, K., & Kelly, J. (1985). A behavioral approach to social skills training with psychiatric patients. In L. L'Abate & M. Milan (Eds.), *Handbook of social skills training and research* (pp. 361–388). New York: Wiley.

Craske, M., Barlow, D., & O'Leary, T. (1992). *Mastery of your anxiety and worry.* Albany, NY: Graywind.

Deffenbacher, J. & Suinn, R. (1987). General anxiety syndrome. In L. Michelson & L. Ascher (Eds.), *Anxiety and stress disorder* (pp. 332–361). New York: Guilford.

deShazer, S. (1985). *Keys to solution in brief therapy.* New York: Norton.

deShazer, S. (1988). *Clues: Investigating solutions in brief therapy.* New York: Norton.

Dobson, K. (1988). *Handbook of cognitive-behavioral therapies.* New York: Guilford.

Dobson, K. (2001). Handbook of cognitive behavioral therapies (2nd ed.). New York: Guilford.

Dobson, K., & Block, L. (1988). Historical and philosophical bases of the cognitive behavioral therapies. In K. Dobson (Ed.), *Handbook of cognitive-behavioral therapies* (pp. 3–39). New York: Guilford.

Dollard, J., Doob, J., Miller, N., Mowrer, O., & Sears, R. (1939). *Frustration and aggression.* New Haven, CT: Yale University Press.

Dryden, W., & Ellis, A. (1988). In K. Dobson (Ed.), *Handbook of cognitive-behavioral therapies* (pp. 214–273). New York: Guilford.

D'Zurilla, T., & Goldfried, M. (1971). Problem solving and behavior modification. *Journal of Abnormal Psychology, 78,* 107–126.

D'Zurilla, T., & Nezu, A. (1982). Social problem solving in adults. In A. C. Kendal (Ed.), *Advances in cognitive-behavioral research and therapy* (vol.1). New York: Academic.

Edwards, W. (1954). The theory of decision-making. *Psychological Bulletin, 51,* 380–417.

Egan, G., & Cowan, M. (1979). *People in systems: A model for development in human service professions and education.* Monterey, CA: Brooks/Cole.

Ellis, A. (1957). *How to live with a "neurotic"* (rev. ed.). New York: Crown. North Hollywood, CA: Wilshire Books.

Ellis, A. (1962). *Reason and emotion in psychotherapy.* Secaucus, NJ: Lyle Stuart.

Ellis, A. (1970). *The essence of rational psychotherapy: A comprehensive approach to treatment.* New York: Institute for Rational Living.

Ellis, A. (1971). *Growth through reason.* North Hollywood, CA: Wilshire Books.

Ellis, A. (1973) *Humanistic psychotherapy: The rational-emotive approach.* New York: McGraw-Hill.

Ellis, A. (1979) *Reason and emotion in psychotherapy.* New York: Citadel.

Ellis, A., & Harper, R. (1975). *A new guide to rational living.* North Hollywood, CA: Wilshire Books.

Ellis, A., & MacLaren, C. (1998). *Rational emotive behavioral therapy.* San Luis Obispo, CA: Impact.

Ellis, A., McInerney, J. F., DiGiuseppe, R., & Yeager, R. J. (1988). *Rational-emotive therapy with alcoholics and substance abusers.* New York: Pergamon.

Festinger, L. (1957). *A theory of cognitive dissonance.* Stanford, CA: Stanford University Press.

Fisher, R. (1991). *Getting to yes: Negotiating agreement without giving in* (2nd ed.). New York: Viking.

Frankl, V. (1965). *The doctor and the soul: From psychotherapy to logotherapy.* New York: Beacon.

Frankl, V. (1975). Paradoxical intention and dereflection. *Psychotherapy: Theory, Research and Practice, 12,* 226–237.

Forman, S. (1995). *Coping skills interventions for children and adolescents.* San Francisco: Jossey-Bass.

Freud, S. (1925). Some character-types met with in psychoanalytic work. In *The standard edition of the works of Sigmund Freud* (vol. 14, pp. 310–333). London: Hogarth (original work published 1916).

Freud, S. (1964). The neuro-psychoses of defense. In *The standard edition of the complete psychological works of Sigmund Freud* (vol. 3, pp. 45–61). London: Hogarth (originally published in 1894).

Gagne, R., & Briggs, L. (1974). *Principles of instructional design.* New York: Holt, Rinehart & Winston.

Galassi, J., Galossi, M., & Vedder, M. (1981). Perspectives on assertion as a social skills model. In J. Wine & M. Smye (Eds.), *Social competence* (pp. 287–346). New York: Guilford.

Geer, J., Davison, G., & Gatchel, R. (1970). Reduction of stress in humans through nonverdical perceived control of aversive stimulation. *Journal of Personality and Social Psychology, 16,* 731–738.

Glasser, W. (1965). *Reality therapy.* New York: Harper and Row.

Goldfried, M. (1980). Psychotherapy as coping skills training. In M. Mahoney (Ed.), *Psychotherapy process: Current issues and future directions* (pp.89-121). New York: Plenum.

Goldfried, M., & Davidson, G. (1976). *Clinical behavior therapy.* New York: Holt, Rinehart, & Winston.

Goldfried, M. & Merbaum M. (1973). *Behavior change through self-control.* New York: Holt, Rinehart, & Winston.

Gordon, T. (1970). *P.E.T.: Parent effectiveness training.* New York: Wyden.

Gordon, T. (1976). *P.E.T. in action.* New York: Bantam Books.

Gorton, B. (1959). Autogenic training. *American Journal Clinical Hypnosis, 2,* 31–41.
Greenberg, L., & Safran, J. (1987). *Emotion in psychotherapy: Affect, cognition, and the process of change.* New York: Guilford.
Guerney, B. (1977). *Relationship enhancement: Skills program for therapy, problem prevention, and enrichment.* San Francisco: Jossey-Bass.
Guidano, V. (1987). *Complexity of the self: A develpmental approach to psychopathology and therapy.* New York: Guilford.
Guidano, V. (1988). A systems, process-oriented approach to cognitive therapy. In K. Dobson (Ed.), *Handbook of cognitive-behavioral therapies* (pp. 307–357). New York: Guilford.
Guidano, V., & Liotti, G. (1983). *Cognitive processes and emotional disorders.* New York: Guilford.
Haley, J. (1973). *Uncommon therapy.* New York: Norton.
Haley, J. (1976). *Problem solving therapy.* San Francisco: Jossey-Bass.
Haley, J. (1984). *Ordeal therapy.* San Francisco: Jossey-Bass.
Haley, J. (1987). *Problem solving therapy* (2nd ed.). San Francisco: Jossey-Bass.
Hamilton, V. (1982). Cognition and stress: An information processing model. In L. Goldberger & S. Brenitz (Eds.), *Handbook of stress: theoretical and clinical aspects.* New York: Free Press.
Heider, F. (1958). *The psychology of interpersonal relations.* New York: Wiley.
Hoberman, H., & Lewinsohn, P. (1985). Behavior treatment of depression. In E. Beckham & W. Leber (Eds.), *Handbook of depression* (pp. 39–82). Homewood, IL: Dorsey.
Homme, L. (1965). Perspectives in psyhchology: XXIV. Control of coverants, the operants of the mind. *Psychological Reports, 15,* 501–511.
Horney, K. (1973). *The neurotic personality of our time.* New York: Norton.
Izard, C. (1971). *The face of emotion.* New York: Appleton-Century-Crofts.
Izard, C. (Ed.) (1977). *Human emotion.* New York: Plenum.
Jacobson, E. (1938). *Progressive relaxation* (2nd ed.). Chicago: Chicago University Press.
Jacobson, E. (1972). *You must relax* (4th ed.). New York: McGraw-Hill.
Jacobson, Edith. (1971). *Depression.* New York: International Universities Press.
Jacobson, N., & Margolin, G. (1979). *Marital therapy: Strategies based on social learning and behavior exchange principles.* New York: Brunner/Mazel.
James, M., & Jongeward, D. (1973). *Born to win: Transactional analysis with Gestalt experiments.* Reading, MA: Addison-Wesley.
Kahn, E. (1931). *Psychopathic personalities.* New Haven, CT: Yale University Press.
Kanfer, F. (1970). Self-regulation: Research issues and speculations. In C. Neuringer & L. Michael (Eds.), *Behavior modification in clinical psychology.* New York: Appleton-Century-Crofts.
Kanfer, F. (1971). The maintenance of behavior by self-generated stimuli and reinforcement. In A. Jacobs & L. Sachs (Eds.), *The psychology of private events: Perspectives on covert response systems.* New York: Academic.
Kazdin, A. (1978). The application of operant techniques in treatment, rehabilitation, and education. In S. Garfield & A. Bergin (Eds.), *Handbook of psychology and behavior change* (pp. 549–591). New York: Wiley.
Kelly, G. (1955). *The psychology of personal constructs,* vol. 2. New York: Norton.
Kendall, P., & Hollon, S. (Eds.). (1979). *Cognitive-behavioral interventions.* New York: Academic.
Kernberg, O. (1984). *Severe personality disorders.* New Haven, CT: Yale University Press.
King, M., Novik, L., & Citrenbaum, C., (1983). *Irresistible communication.* Philadelphia: Saunders.
Klein, D., & Miller, G. (1997). Depressive personality: Relationship to dysthymia and major depression. In H. Akiskal & G. Cassano (Eds.), *Dysthymia and the spectrum of chronic depressions* (pp. 87–95). New York: Guilford.

Koffka, K. (1935). *Principles of gestalt psychology.* New York: Harcourt, Brace & World, 1935.
Kohler, W. (1947). *Gestalt psychology.* New York: Liveright.
Ladd, G., & Asher, S. (1985). Social skills training and children's peer relations. In L. L'Abate & M. Milan (Eds.), *Handbook of social skills training and research* (pp. 219–244). New York: Wiley.
Lazarus, A. (1968). Learning theory and the treatment of depression. *Behavior Research and Therapy, 6,* 83–89.
Lazarus, R. (1966). *Psychological stress and the coping process.* New York: McGraw-Hill.
Lazarus, R., & Folkman, C. (1984). *Stress, appraisal, and coping.* New York: Springer.
Leventhal, H. (1984). A perceptual-motor theory of emotion. In L. Berkowitz (Ed.), *Advances in experimental social psychology.* New York: Academic.
Libet, J., & Lewinsohn, P. (1973). Concept of social skill with special reference to the behavior of depressed persons. *Journal of Consulting and Clinical Psychology, 40,* 304–312.
Linehan, M. (1993). *Cognitive-behavioral treatment of borderline personality disorder.* New York: Guilford.
Luria, A. (1961). *The role of speech in the regulation of normal and abnormal behaviors.* New York: Liveright.
Mahoney, M. (1974). *Cognition and behavior modification.* Cambridge, MA: Ballinger.
Mahoney, M. (1977). Personal science: A cognitive learning therapy. In A. Ellis & R. Grieger (Eds.), *Handbook of rational psychotherapy.* New York: Springer.
Mahoney, M. (1988). The cognitive sciences and psychotherapy: Patterns in a developing relationship. In K. Dobson (Ed.), *Handbook of cognitive-behavioral therapies* (pp. 357–387). New York: Guilford.
Mahoney, M., & Arnkoff, D. (1978). Cognition and self-control therapies. In S. Garfield & A. Bergin (Eds.), *Handbook of psychotherapy and behavior change* (pp. 689–723). New York: Wiley.
Mahoney, M., & Thoreson. (1974). *Self-control: Power to the Person.* Monterey, CA: Brooks/Cole.
Marks, I. (1978). Behavioral psychotherapy of adult neuroses. In S. Garfield & A. Bergin (Eds.), *Handbook of psychotherapy and behavior change* (pp. 493–549). New York: Wiley.
Maslow, A. (1962). *Toward a psychology of being.* Princeton, NJ: Van Nostrand.
May, R. (Ed.). (1961). *Existential psychology.* New York: Random House.
Meichenbaum, D. (1971). Examination of model characteristics in reducing avoidance behavior. *Journal of Personality and Social Psychology, 17,* 298–307.
Meichenbaum, D. (1977). *Cognitive-behavior modification: An integrated approach.* New York: Plenum.
Meichenbaum, D. (1985). *Stress inoculation training.* New York: Pergamon.
Meichenbaum, D., & Asarnow, J. (1979). Cognitive-behavioral modification and metacognitive development: Implications for the classroom. In P. Kendall & S. Hollon (Eds.), *Cognitive-behavioral interventions* (pp. 11–32). New York: Academic.
Meichenbaum, D., & Cameron. R. (1973). Training schizophrenics to talk to themselves: A means of developing attentional controls. *Behavior therapy, 4,* 515–534.
Melzack, R., & Wall, P. (1965). Pain mechanisms: A new theory. *Science, 50,* 971–979.
Milan, M., & Kolko, D. (1985). Social skills training and complementary strategies in anger control and the treatment of aggressive behavior. In L. L'Abate & M. Milan (Eds.), *Handbook of social skills training and research* (pp. 101–136). New York: Wiley.
Millon, T. (1969). *Modern psychopathology: A biosocial approach to maladaptive learning and functioning.* Philadelphia: Saunders.
Millon, T. (1996). *Disorders of personality: DSM-IV and Beyond.* New York: Wiley.
Millon, T. (1999). *Personality guided therapy.* New York: Wiley.
Naranjo, C. (1980). *The techniques of Gestalt therapy.* Highland, NH: Gestalt Journal.

Navaco, R. (1975). *Anger control: The development and evaluation of experimental treatment*. Lexington, MA: Heath.
Neimeyer, R., & Raskin, J. (2001). Varieties of constructivism in psychotherapy. In K. Dobson (Ed.), *Handbook of cognitive behavioral therapies* (pp. 393–431). New York: Guilford.
O'Hanlon. W. (1987). *Taproots*. New York: Norton.
O'Hanlan, W.. & Weiner-Davis, M. (1989). *In search of solutions: A new direction in psychotherapy*. New York: Norton.
Osborn, A. (1963). *Applied imagination: Principles and procedures of creative problem solving* (3rd ed.). New York: Scribner.
Pelletier, K. (1977). *Mind as healer, mind as slayer*. New York: Dell.
Perls, F., Hefferline, R., & Goodman, P. (1951). *Gestalt therapy*. New York: Julian.
Phares, E. (1969). *Locus of control in personality*. Morristown, NJ: General Learning.
Piaget, J. (1970). *Psychology and epistemology: Towards a theory of knowledge*. New York: Viking.
Polster, E., & Polster, M. (1973). *Gestalt therapy integrated*. New York: Vintage Books.
Rachman, S. (1981). The primacy of affect: Some theoretical implications, *Behavioral Research and Therapy, 19*, 279–290.
Rehm, L. (1977). A self-control model of depression. *Behavior Therapy, 8*, 787–804.
Rosenberg, M. (1960). Cognitive reorganization in response to the hypnotic reversal of attitudinal affect. *Journal of Personality, 28*, 39–63.
Sacco, W., & Beck, A. (1985). Cognitive therapy of depression. In E. Beckham & W. Leber (Eds.), *Handbook of depression* (pp. 3–39). Homewood, IL: Dorsey.
Salter, A. (1949). *Conditional reflex therapy*. New York: Farrar, Straus, and Giroux.
Satir, V. (1967). *Conjoint family therapy*. Palo Alto, CA: Science and Behavior Books.
Schacter, S., & Singer, J. (1962). Cognitive, social and physiological determinants of emotional state. *Psychological Review, 69*, 379–399.
Schneider, K. (1950). *Psychopathic personalities* (9th ed.). London: Cassell (original work published 1923).
Selekman, M. (1999). *Pathways to change: Brief therapy solutions with difficult adolescents*. New York: Guilford.
Seligman, M. (1975). *Helplessness: On depression, development and death*. San Francisco: W. H. Freeman.
Smye, M., & Wine, J. (1981). *Social competence*. New York: Guilford.
Snyder, C., & Dinoff, B. (1999). Coping: Where have you been? In C. Snyder (Ed.), *Coping: The psychology of what works* (pp.3–20). New York: Oxford University Press.
Sperry, L. (1999). *Cognitive behavior therapy of DSM-IV Personality disorders*. New York: Brunner/Mazel.
Spivack, G.. Platt, J.. & Shure, M. (1976). *The problem-solving approach to adjustment*. San Francisco: Jossey-Bass.
Spivack, G., & Shure, M. (1974). *Social adjustment of young children: A cognitive approach to solving real-life problems*. San Francisco: Jossey-Bass.
Sprafkin, R., Gershaw, N., & Goldstein, A. (1993). *Social skills for mental health*. Boston: Allyn & Bacon.
Suinn, R. (1976). Anxiety management training to control general anxiety. In J. Krumbolta & C. Thoresen (Eds.), *Counseling methods*. New York: Holt, Rinehart, and Winston.
Turk, D., Meichenbaum, D., & Genest, M. (1983). *Pain and behavioral medicine: A cognitive behavioral perspective*. New York: Guilford.
Vygotsky, L. (1962). *Thought and language*. New York: Wiley.
Wackman, D., & Wampler, K. (1985). The couple communication program. In L. L'Abate & M. Milan (Eds.), *Handbook of social skills training and research* (pp. 457–476). New York: Wiley.

Watts, A. (1965). *The way of Zen*. New York: Random House.

Watzlawick, P., Weakland, J., & Fisch, R. (1974). *Change*. New York: Norton, 1974.

Weeks, G., & L'Abate, L. (1982). *Paradoxical psychotherapy: Theory and practice with individuals, couples, and families*. New York: Brunner/Mazel.

Wessler, R., & Wessler, R. (1980). *The principles and practice of rational-emotive therapy*. San Francisco: Jossey-Bass.

Wine, J. (1981). From defect to competence models. In J. Wine & M. Smye (Eds.), *Social competence* (pp. 3–36). New York: Guilford.

Wine, J., & Smye, M. (1981). *Social competence*. New York: Guilford.

Wolpe, J. (1958). *Psychotherapy by reciprocal inhibition*. Stanford, CA: Stanford University Press.

Wolpe, J. (1973). *The practice of behavior therapy* (2nd ed.). New York: Pergamon.

Young, J. (1999). *Cognitive therapy for personality disorders: A schema-focused approach*. Sarasota, FL: Professional Resource.

Zajonc, R. (1980). Feeling and thinking. *American Psychologist, 35,* 151–175.

Zinker, J. (1977). *Creative process in Gestalt therapy*. New York: Brunner/Mazel.

INDEX